THE COMING OIL STORM

RON RHODES

HARVEST HOUSE PUBLISHERS

EUGENE, OREGON

Cover by Dugan Design Group, Bloomington, Minnesota

Cover photos © iStockphoto / TebNad

THE COMING OIL STORM
Copyright © 2010 by Ron Rhodes
Published by Harvest House Publishers
Eugene, Oregon 97402
www.harvesthousepublishers.com

Library of Congress Cataloging-in-Publication Data
  Rhodes, Ron.
  The coming oil storm / Ron Rhodes.
       p. cm.
  Includes bibliographical references (p.   ).
  ISBN 978-0-7369-2846-5 (pbk.)
  1. Bible—Prophecies—Middle East. 2. Bible—Prophecies—Petroleum industry and trade.
3. Bible—Prophecies—End of the world. 4. Middle East—History—Prophecies. 5. Petroleum
industry and trade—Biblical teaching. 6. End of the world—Biblical teaching. I. Title.
  BS649.N45R46 2010
  236'.9—dc22

                                                                    2009049155

In loving memory of Thomas Paul Rhodes

Acknowledgments

Kerri, David, and Kylie—as always, I couldn't have written this book without your continued support. The three of you are a rich treasure to me!

Contents

Introduction

"Oil Storm"

As we begin our journey together, it is important that we listen to what cultural observers have long told us: *The world runs on oil.* Certainly America runs on oil. The entire American infrastructure—from transportation to manufacturing to farming—is built upon oil. Today Americans consume approximately twenty-one million barrels of oil per day. That amounts to a quarter of the world's total of 84 million barrels per day. We are guzzling nearly a million barrels an hour!

Our cars, trucks, buses, trains, ships, and jets require oil. Without oil, transportation—at least *fast* transportation—shuts down. If that happens, no one can quickly get anywhere of any substantial distance. Moreover, food—indeed, products of all kinds—cannot be transported anywhere, at least not fast. Eighteen-wheel tractor-trailers become a thing of the past. Trains become a thing of the past. The frightening reality is that if we run out of oil, and we have not made adjustments so that our infrastructure can utilize alternative energies, we could find ourselves reverting to the transportation options of the nineteenth century, such as a horse and buggy!

Bulldozers and various kinds of construction equipment also require oil. Without oil, our efforts to build new houses and buildings is greatly impeded.

Tractors and other kinds of equipment that are a necessity on today's large farms also require oil. Without oil, the equipment does not run, and if it does not run, we must now do *by hand* what used to be done *by machine.* That slows things down dramatically. The food produced on our farms could be diminished and become much more expensive.

All of our industrial machines require oil. If the machines do not run, then the production of multiple thousands of products comes to a standstill. Machine operators lose their jobs. Even if we adapt and start making such products by hand, mass production is greatly impeded, and whatever products are made cannot easily be distributed throughout the country because our rapid transportation system has been shut down. The economy plummets.

Edwin Black wrote a book titled *The Plan: How to Rescue Society When the Oil Stops—Or the Day Before*. In it he points out how oil is used for all kinds of very important things on this tiny planet:

> Every time an impoverished African nation builds a two-lane road to help starving tanners, every time a family in Peru gathers enough wealth to purchase their first car, every time a Chinese businessman installs another noisy diesel generator to supplement flagging electrical power, every time a California developer builds a new home in the suburbs of San Diego requiring a longer commute, every time a Polish entrepreneur opens a new store, *humanity requires more oil to make it work.*
>
> As the world modernizes and industrializes—as it must…as the world rescues more populations from the brink of famine and isolation—as it must…as society proliferates the intelligent use of fertilizers and pharmaceuticals to improve crop yields and cure illnesses everywhere—as it must, the pivotal lubricant is petroleum. *Oil has become the very oxygen of progress.*[1]

Not to belabor the point, but the United States military also runs on oil. Without oil, our military jeeps, trucks, tanks, fighter jets, helicopters, and aircraft carriers will not run. If our military shuts down, we cannot protect ourselves. We become vulnerable. That is bad news, because there are many—particularly among today's oil-rich Middle Eastern countries—who do not like Americans today.

On a broader geopolitical note, the United States and other nations of the world want to protect their interests in oil not only because oil is "the very oxygen of progress," but also because *oil is power.* Kjell Aleklett, president of the Association for the Study of Peak Oil and Gas (ASPO), correctly observed that "countries are always drilling and exploring for oil (despite political turmoil), because there is power in having oil."[2] No wonder the nations of the world are positioning themselves to protect their shrinking pieces of oil pie. Many today are ominously forecasting that things could get nasty in the not-too-distant future.

Are We Really Running Out?

Many of the top experts in the oil business, as well as economists and even government leaders, are telling us that nations around the world—especially the United States, but in more recent days China and India as well—are collectively using oil faster than it is being found. Moreover, the oil that exists is getting much harder to find. Because it is getting harder to find, we have to spend more money to find it. That, in turn, makes oil a much more expensive proposition. Warren Brown, in his *Washington Post* article "We're Running Out of Oil," asserts that "oil is running out, and it is running out as global demand for available energy resources is growing rapidly. That means per barrel prices and pump prices are going up and will stay up."[3] Economists tell us that regardless of any temporary drops in oil prices we may experience day-to-day (mostly as a result of economic factors), future forecasts are sobering—even frightening—and the day *will* come when we are face-to-face with an "oil storm." As Matt Simmons put it, the global demand for oil is fast becoming a classic runaway train.[4]

Consider that in 1985, the United States imported less than 30 percent of its oil. Just five years later, in 1990, the United States was importing almost 50 percent of its needed oil. James Woolsey, foreign policy specialist and former director of the Central Intelligence Agency (CIA), says that at present "the United States gives about $4 billion a week to the outside world in order to finance its oil product consumption," and that "we import now about 60 percent of our oil."[5] If the current (2010) rate of growth continues, by 2015 America will be importing up to 75 percent—maybe even 80 percent—of its oil. Again, though, the problem is that oil is becoming *harder* to find—and thus *more expensive* to find.[6] We have a steadily increasing appetite for increasingly expensive finite resources. Economically, this spells D-A-N-G-E-R.

It is in view of this danger that Mark Hitchcock, in his intriguing book *Iran: The Coming Crisis*, warns:

> The margin between oil supply and demand today is razor thin.
> At present, we are pumping out crude oil at about the same rate

we're consuming it—1,000 barrels a second. The level of spare capacity (known as the world's safety blanket) is only about two million barrels a day. This means that the world's oil supply chains are operating at an unbelievable 97.5 percent capacity. This leaves almost no margin for error for such things as natural disasters, accidents, terrorist attacks, geopolitical stress, or whatever else could disrupt the fragile supply chain.[7]

The million dollar question then becomes, when will "peak oil" be upon us? "Peak oil" refers to that point at which we have used up half of the available oil reserves in the earth. If the world's total supply of oil is 3 trillion barrels (an optimistic estimate, according to many experts), then peaking would occur when we have drawn about 1.5 trillion barrels out of the ground.[8]

No one is precisely sure when peak oil will intrude upon us. However, innumerable experts have affirmed that peak oil *will* come,[9] whether five years from now or thirty.[10] One day we will reach a peak in the supply of cheap oil, after which we will have a dwindling supply of increasingly expensive oil.[11]

Some experts believe we reached peak oil back in 2004. The Association for the Study of Peak Oil and Gas (ASPO), a European network of scientists, projected peak oil in 2007. Independent experts Matthew Simmons, Colin Campbell, and Kenneth Deffeyes projected peak oil in 2010. The French oil company TotalFinaElf also projected 2010. The official position of the U.S. Geological Survey says peak oil will occur between 2011 and 2015. A number of major oil companies project dates sometime after 2015.[12] The US Energy Department is optimistically— some might say *foolishly*—holding out for 2037.[13]

Dr. Gal Luft, executive director of the Institute for the Analysis of Global Security, and Anne Korin, codirector of the Institute, note that "even the major U.S. oil companies have begun to acknowledge that the growth in world demand is expected easily to exceed available world supplies for the foreseeable future."[14] David O'Reilly, the chairman and CEO of Chevron Corporation, tells us that the days of easy oil are over, for many of the world's oil and gas fields are "maturing." O'Reilly says that "new energy discoveries are mainly occurring in places where resources are difficult to extract—physically, technically, economically, and politically."[15]

Mike Bowlin, chairman and CEO of ARCO, likewise says "we have embarked on the beginning of the last days of the age of oil."[16] Dr. Colin Campbell, who wrote "The World Oil Supply 1930-2050," agrees, noting: "The major oil companies are merging, downsizing and outsourcing, and not investing in new refineries because they know full well that production is set to decline and that exploration opportunities are getting less and less. We have depleted most of our high-quality resources."[17]

Stephen Leeb, a respected investment analyst who consistently finishes among the leaders in the annual stock-picking contests of the *Wall Street Journal* and *Forbes*, wrote a book titled *The Coming Economic Collapse* in which he warned:

> The world's demand for oil is growing faster than oil production can increase. Some petroleum geologists…now believe that worldwide oil production may be close to its permanent long-term peak and will soon start to decline. Even if the peak is farther away than they think, demand for oil, especially from large developing nations such as India and China, is rising faster than production. If this trend continues—and we fully expect it will—the result will be an inevitable clash between supply and demand that will send oil prices soaring to unprecedented levels.[18]

Experts are increasingly warning that the gap between oil demand and supply, once considerable, has steadily narrowed to the point that today it is almost negligible. Economically, an oil shortfall could cause a global recession, and the typical American lifestyle could quickly become unaffordable, even in two-income families.[19] At the time I am writing (early 2010), economic hard times are upon our country. I hesitate to ponder how an oil crisis would further damage the fragile economy.

It is foolish to ignore the problem or pretend it does not exist. The crisis might not hit us this week or next month, *but it is coming.* Leeb put it this way:

> No one is one hundred percent certain how much oil is left in the ground, how expensive it will be to extract, or how high demand for oil will grow long-term. While the world will never completely run out of oil, oil will become increasingly difficult and expensive to extract, to the point where diminishing returns make further production increases unaffordable, and worldwide production begins to decline.[20]

Dark Clouds on the Horizon

In view of the warnings of oil experts, economic advisors, and government officials, it is hard to be optimistic about global prospects regarding oil, the economy, and how all this will affect us on a national and even personal level. In the next twenty-five years, our projected need for oil will be astronomical, and many people in the know are warning there will be an insufficient supply to meet the growing demand.

Current growth rates indicate that by the year 2035 humanity will need about 140 million barrels of oil a day, week after week, month after month, year after year. Anything less than that and people are going to be deprived. Because the age of "easy oil" is over, meeting this need for oil—*if it's even possible*—will involve a staggeringly high cost.

Paul Roberts, in his sobering book *The End of Oil*, put it this way:

> Simply building that much new production capacity (to say nothing of maintaining it or defending it) will mean spending perhaps a trillion dollars in additional capital and will require oil companies to venture into places, like the Arctic, that are extremely expensive to exploit. Repeat the exercise for gas and coal, and you begin to understand why even optimistic energy experts go gray in the face when you ask them what we will use to fill up our tanks thirty years from now.[21]

Some may be tempted to think, "Well, we'll just worry about all that later. We'll start conserving in the years to come, and then everything will be fine!" However, oil expert Kenneth Deffeyes provides a "reality check" in his assertion that "after you drive a car off a cliff, it's too late to hit the brakes. In effect, we have gone over the edge of the cliff."[22] A growing chorus of people today think we have *already hit* peak oil (more on this in a later chapter), and hence it is inevitable that we will have to "face the music" sooner rather than later.

Cultural observers also warn us of a false sense of security that is all too easy for people to develop in modern times. Here is the problem we face: While many respected oil experts are warning that we are running out of oil, some others are very optimistic and claim we've got nothing to worry about, at least in the immediate future. "There are a host of experts on the *supply* side, and a host of experts on the *demand* side—and a raging debate between them. Some think that we're running out of oil; others say we've got plenty left."[23]

The problem, as Deffeyes puts it, is that "when the experts disagree, the public usually thinks that no valid knowledge exists."[24] That is shortsighted thinking! Let us be clear: Even if you are one of those optimists who says that peak oil is still decades away, today's margin between supply and demand is razor thin, and by every reasonable gauge, *demand will soon overtake supply*—and that's when we're going to feel the weight of the dilemma. As one analyst put it, "We are facing an unprecedented problem. World oil production has stopped growing; declines in production are about to begin. For the first time since the Industrial Revolution, the geological supply of an essential resource will not meet the demand."[25] Many who recognize this fact are understandably living day-to-day with a strong sense of angst.[26]

Dependence on Middle Eastern Nations

President Obama and his administration are strongly campaigning to break America's oil dependence on foreign nations—especially nations in the Middle East that are hostile to American interests ("Death to America" is a common slogan in such nations). The sad reality is that much of the world's oil reserves are in the custody of unstable and sometimes hostile regimes. Despite this, President Obama hopes to succeed where many previous administrations have failed—including those of Presidents Ford, Carter, Reagan, Bush (Sr.), Clinton, and Bush (Jr.).

In a separate chapter, I will discuss in detail how Muslim and Arab oil money is not only funding terrorism, but is also funding the Muslim attempt to bring America into its religious fold. I want to offer a preliminary introduction to this issue here, however, for it has implications for everything else I will say in this book.

Briefly put, those who have studied Muslim literature (including purpose statements of Muslim organizations in the United States) tell us that Muslims have designs on undermining and overcoming America *from within*. The ultimate goal is to do away with all other religions in America—especially Christianity—so that Islam alone will be predominant. Many of the Muslim associations that support this policy portray themselves to the public as moderate Muslim groups. In reality, many of the leaders and members of these groups have been prosecuted on terror charges, and in some cases have been shown to have connections with such groups as Hamas. The collective goal of these various Muslims is that America will one day be a Muslim country.

Consider the following[27]:

- A common goal of radical Muslims is the establishment of a global Islamic State. This would certainly include the United States.

- Zakir Naik, the founder and president of the Islamic Research Foundation, cites Koran 3:85 in support of the idea that God will never accept any religion other than Islam.

- Abu Yahya al-Libi, a leading high-ranking official within al-Qaeda, asserts that "the whole world must be under the rule of Islam, without exception."

- Omar Bakri Mohammed, who was instrumental in developing the Islamist organization Hizb ut-Tahrir, says that "Jihad is a foreign-policy to expand the Islamic authority all over the world."

- Imam Johari Abdul Malik, the chairman of the Coordinating Council of Muslim Organizations, stated: "Before Allah closes our eyes for the last time you will see Islam move from being the second largest religion in America—that's where we are now—to being the first religion in America."

- Abdul Alim Musa, a well-known imam in Washington, DC, says that an Islamic State of North America will be a reality no later than 2050. This man is also an outspoken supporter of Hamas, as well as an admirer of Israel-and-U.S.-hating Iranian president Mahmoud Ahmadinejad. It is a bit disconcerting to ponder that this man lives in Washington, DC, where our own government is headquartered.

The work of many of these individuals and their respective Islamic organizations is being financed by Muslim oil money. Later in the book, I will address how Americans are spending mega-dollars buying oil from Muslim countries, and how those same dollars are subsequently being used by Muslims to undermine America, either through terrorism or supporting Islamic groups in America who seek to convert all of America to Islam.

While it is true that most of these activities are being carried out only by *radical* Muslims, one must realize that according to recent polls, some 26 percent of American Muslims are on the radical side, in favor of suicide bombings against civilians.[28] Hence, the radicals are not an insignificant group. They are large and they are growing.

Not "Newspaper Exegesis"

Throughout this book I will demonstrate how the impending oil crisis relates specifically to biblical prophecy. Not unexpectedly, whenever an author relates current events to biblical prophecy, naysayers and mockers claim this is nothing but "newspaper exegesis." So, before beginning chapter 1, I want to briefly comment on this.

Arnold Fruchtenbaum, in his book *The Footsteps of the Messiah*, commented that "current events must never be the means of interpreting the Scriptures, but the Scriptures must interpret current events."[29] Fruchtenbaum is correct. The wrong approach would be to take a newspaper's headlines and then force them into biblical prophecies. Such forced exegesis is unworthy of Bible students. The proper approach is to first study the Scriptures to find out what God has revealed about the future, and then—in seeking to accurately discern the times, something Christ Himself clearly desires of us (Matthew 16:1-3; Luke 21:29-33)—measure current events against what the Bible reveals in order to give thoughtful consideration as to whether there is a legitimate correlation. If we conclude there is, we can rejoice in God's sovereign control of human history while at the same time resist the temptation to set dates regarding end-time events, recognizing that this is something God forbids (Acts 1:7). All the while, we avoid sensationalism, recognizing that Christ calls His followers to live soberly and alertly as they await His coming (Mark 13:32-37).

A Note on Methodology

While I will draw a connection between the impending oil crisis and biblical prophecy, it is critically important that I thoroughly establish the case for an impending oil crisis. Only after I make this case will

I be able to demonstrate its relevance to biblical prophecy. So—*hang with me till the end!*

Also, as you read the book, you will likely notice that the earlier chapters are closely related to each other. They are like "close cousin" chapters that focus on the impending oil dilemma from different angles. The book is organized in this way so you will be better able to grasp the full impact of the crisis that lies before us.

Having laid this foundation, strap on your seat belt and let's begin our journey.

The Global Addiction to Oil

Some experts who have assessed the declining oil in the world are now warning humankind that "the party is over." Kjell Aleklett, president of the Association for the Study of Peak Oil (ASPO) and a physics professor at Uppsala University in Sweden, warns that "we have all been enjoying the greatest party the world has ever seen: the great oil party... After the climax comes the decline, when we have to sober up and face the fact that the party is coming to an end." Not only could the end of the party severely damage the global economy, he warns, but it could also lead to social and political unrest as various countries try to keep the party going even as the oil disappears.[1]

It is a fact of life in the United States that more and more oil is consumed every year. Today Americans are using something in the vicinity of twenty-one million barrels of oil each and every day.[2] This amounts to approximately one-fourth of the oil being used in the world.

During the energy-crisis days of the early 1970s, President Richard Nixon made a very pro-American statement that in more modern days would not be so well-received. He put it bluntly:

> There are only seven percent of the people of the world living in the United States, and we use thirty percent of all the energy. That isn't bad; that is good. That means we are the richest, strongest people in the world and that we have the highest standard of living in the world. That is why we need so much energy, and may it always be that way.[3]

There was a time when America produced all the oil it needed. In

1946, however, America found itself in the surprising position of having to import oil to meet its energy needs. As one analyst put it, "Americans would now understand firsthand the anxiety and insecurity that had long afflicted Britain, Europe, and Japan." The United States had now become an "economic and military giant whose life-blood was controlled in other parts of the world."[4]

It is a sad fact that drug addicts often end up taking increasing doses of their drugs of choice. The United States is an *oil* addict. From 1995 to 2005, this addiction increased by three million barrels of oil per day. At present the United States imports about three times as much oil as it produces. That is, the United States produces about seven million barrels of oil per day while it uses twenty-one million barrels per day. In contrast to 1985 when the United States imported just 30 percent of its oil, and the mid-1990s when the United States imported 50 percent of its oil, today we import between 60 and 70 percent of the oil we consume.

Today's trends are staggering. Assuming the same rate of current growth, Americans will consume twenty-seven million barrels per day by 2020. By 2030, Americans will need about 34 percent more oil than they need today—that is, they will need some thirty million barrels each and every day. Americans seem to have a steadily increasing appetite for increasingly expensive finite resources.

Many energy analysts and economists are concerned that the margin between today's oil supply and current demand is alarmingly thin. Measuring current oil output against consumption, the world is essentially pumping out oil at the same rate we are consuming it—a thousand barrels a second.[5] This is obviously a great risk, for there is only a very small safety net ("spare capacity" in oil lingo) of about two million barrels a day. This means that 97.5 percent of the oil being pumped out of the ground is being devoured by modern society, and hardly any is being saved to cushion us against possible natural disasters, terrorist attacks, or anything else that could disrupt the delicate supply-demand ratio.[6]

In keeping with this, Edwin Black warns that "the international system of production and distribution contains very little cushion for normal day-to-day disruptions, such as industrial accidents, infrastructure disruptions, or natural disasters."[7] The production of oil is just barely keeping pace with actual usage. Such production, however, will not keep pace with actual usage for very long. Indeed, Black warns:

Soon, the oil supply-to-demand ratio will lose its cushion or even become outstripped. At the point when demand completely exceeds production—whether that occurs by 2015 or 2030, depending upon prognostication—the Middle East will possess the dominant remaining reserves. That condition will only magnify the West's utter dependence upon that troubled region's cooperation for day-to-day existence.[8]

Sounding ominous regarding how demand will soon exceed supply, *USA Today* reports:

> There's no question that demand is rising...The U.S. Energy Information Administration projects [worldwide] demand rising from the current 84 million barrels a day to 103 million barrels by 2015. If China and India—where cars and factories are proliferating madly—start consuming oil at just one-half of current U.S. per-capita levels, global demand would jump 96 percent...Such forecasts put the doom in doomsday.[9]

A look at the oil fields in nations that collectively produce about a third of the world's oil shows definite cause for concern. One analyst notes that according to a study published in the highly respected *Petroleum Review*, "in Indonesia, the United Kingdom, Gabon, and fifteen other nations that together supply nearly a third of the world's daily oil needs, production is now falling by 5 percent a year—more than twice the rate of decline of the year before." Other oil-producing nations such as Saudi Arabia, Russia, and Venezuela must now pump increasing volumes of oil just to keep global supplies flowing at a steady pace, to say nothing of increasing production to meet ever-increasing demand.[10]

Chris Skrebowski, editor of the *Petroleum Review*, hit the nail on the head when he said that "those producers still with expansion potential are having to work harder and harder just to make up for the accelerating losses of the large number that have clearly peaked and are now in continuous decline."[11] This is not a healthy state of affairs.

Even our federal government has signaled that things are not going well. The federal Energy Information Administration (EIA) now concedes that "all or nearly all of the largest oil fields have already been discovered and are being produced. Production is, indeed, clearly past its peak in some of the most prolific basins."[12]

Moreover, a 2004 publication produced by the Department of Energy affirms that world discoveries of oil peaked before the 1970s. The document concedes that no new major field discoveries have been made in decades. As well, "presently, world oil reserves are being depleted three times as fast as they are being discovered." The document affirms that "the disparity between increasing production and declining reserves can have only one outcome: a practical supply limit will be reached and future supply to meet conventional oil demand will not be available." The document concludes that "the nation must start now to respond to peaking global oil production to offset adverse economic and national security impacts."[13]

This assessment is confirmed by Michael Rodgers, an ex-oil geologist who is now senior director of PFC Energy. He states that "over the last 20 years, the size of oil discoveries has fallen off dramatically. We are finding more fields than in the '60s and '70s, but they're much smaller."[14]

What has caused the current addiction to oil? Lots and lots of oil is needed to heat our homes during winter months, cool our offices during summer months, and lubricate our large fuel-inefficient SUVs. The United States is heavily transportation-oriented. In fact, over 85 percent of the American workforce commutes to work by car, and many American cars are—let's face it—*gas and oil guzzlers*. (It is far different in other countries, where many of the cars are much smaller.) Some 70 percent of the oil imported into the United States is consumed by transportation costs. Understandably, then, experts warn that without such imported oil, the U.S. transportation system—as well as the entire U.S. economy—is in danger of collapsing. If Middle Eastern countries were to suddenly pull the trigger on the flow of oil, it is impossible to see how the U.S. could dodge the bullet.

Because the United States uses more oil than any other country, its citizens are also more vulnerable than those in any other country to changes in the price of oil. This vulnerability becomes amplified when we realize that much of the oil presently imported comes from some of the most volatile and unstable countries in the world. The United States presently derives *almost half* (around 45 percent) of its oil from Middle Eastern countries such as Saudi Arabia, Iraq, and Kuwait, as well as from North Africa, which, combined, control a whopping two-thirds of the remaining oil reserves in the world.[15] That is not a healthy state of affairs for the United States.

It is therefore little wonder that recent President George W. Bush (known as an oil-friendly leader) commented that "America is addicted to oil" in his January 2006 State of the Union address. After all, our freeways are jam-packed with large SUVs, many Americans commute long distances to their jobs (sometimes over a hundred miles each way), and we are forced to feed our addiction by buying oil from people who don't like us and would like to see us harmed.

Many are finally beginning to realize that change needs to be made. But change cannot happen overnight. It is not as if the president can just make a quick policy change and, voila, the problem is solved. In Peter Tertzakian's eye-opening book, *A Thousand Barrels a Second*, he suggests that "North American addiction to cheap energy is too strong, and the technological standards of the last century too entrenched, for any new or different approach to be easily or painlessly (let alone quickly) adopted." Our culture is about to experience a major energy paradigm shift, he says, and there are some tough choices ahead of us. Indeed, we will soon need to give serious consideration to "potential changes to our lifestyles, the trade-off between cheap energy and clean energy, the necessity of building new refineries and power plants in our own backyards, and even the impact on national security. Our birthright of abundant, reliable energy is coming to an end."[16]

Global Addiction

While the United States presently guzzles about twenty-one million barrels of oil per day, the world guzzles some eighty-six million barrels per day. That amounts to a staggering thousand barrels per second. Hon Edward Schreyer, former governor general of Canada, comments that "the idea that eventually there will be a point reached where the global oil supply would not meet demand is not a new idea." However, he says, today the scale of the global problem "is dreadfully large."[17] Clearly, the United States is not the only oil addict in the world. Current figures indicate that every one of the 192 nations on this planet is addicted to oil in varying degrees. In newly industrializing countries, such as those in Asia, more and more citizens are driving cars, and hence the "substance abuse" is growing at a staggering rate in such parts of the world.[18] With so many addicts on the planet, the concern is, *How will we all feed our addictions?*

Christian author Mark Hitchcock suggests a word picture to help us understand the magnitude of the oil being guzzled globally. Imagine an Olympic-size swimming pool, which holds over 660,000 gallons of water. Instead of water, imagine such a pool filled with oil. In our present world, one of these pools is being drained of oil every fifteen seconds; 5,760 of these pools are being drained of oil every day. And every day that passes, we use *ever-more* oil.[19]

While in the past the United States has been *the* major culprit as an oil guzzler, other countries are hopping on the bandwagon. The surging demand from China and other developing nations, such as India, is outpacing new production.[20] With 1.3 billion people, China is the world's most populous country. China's oil addiction has steadily grown by 8 percent a year since 2002. This is in keeping with China's ever-increasing car sales in what has been a thriving economy. The impending oil crisis, however, will affect China's economy just as it will affect every other nation.

A BBC report tells us that world demand for oil is set to increase by 37 percent by the year 2030. This estimate is based on the Energy Information Administration's (EIA) annual report. Global demand will hit 118 million barrels per day, up from today's 86 million barrels per day. This escalation will largely result from today's transportation needs.[21]

Demand Outstripping Supply

Drug counselors tell us that when a heroin addict does not receive the amount of drugs he or she is accustomed to, he or she goes into withdrawal and suffers greatly. When the demand for oil outstrips the supply of oil, we will all experience oil withdrawal.

This idea of oil demand outstripping oil supply is not something many in the United States seem to want to hear about. Paul Roberts observes that the oil economy, and American dominance in it, has in the past always been predicated on a ready supply of oil, as well as on the ability to meet increasing demand simply by pumping more oil or searching for more oil fields.[22] Yet this paradigm is failing before our very eyes. Times are changing!

Of great concern to many in the West is that almost 60 percent of China's oil imports and 70 percent of India's come from Saudi Arabia and Iran. Analyst Frank Gaffney, who often advises U.S. government leaders, warns us that "there is an ominous strategic aspect" to China's and India's "budding relationships with the two leading Islamist regimes, Saudi Arabia and Iran. China and India are cementing multibillion dollar energy deals with these suppliers, affording them in return political protection, non-Western revenue streams, and arms."[23] This is obviously not good news for the United States.

On top of all this, Colin J. Campbell and Jean H. Laherrère note that since 1985 energy use is up about 30 percent in Latin America and 40 percent in Africa.[24] So while the demand for oil is rapidly increasing globally, our supply of oil continues to be depleted. Economically, this means that oil prices will—at some point in the not-too-distant future—increase to near-prohibitive levels.

Chuck Taylor warns us that "in four years, the equivalent of a new Saudi Arabia will be needed just to keep pace." He observes that "in every year since 1988, more petroleum has been used than found. In 2007, 31.5 billion barrels were burned and only 8 billion found." He warns that global demand for oil will continue to increase 2 percent per year, but the supply of oil will not keep up with that demand.[25]

This lack of oil supply spells trouble for the United States and the rest of the world. Ronald G. Nelson says that "in the face of supply shortages, it is likely that the oil-exporting countries would begin to restrict the volumes previously available for export, to ensure that their own economies and people will be spared immediate shortages. Shrinking exports will adversely impact the global economy. The aftermath of peak oil will have major ripple effects for everyone on the planet, and these will only grow in intensity."[26]

U.S. Failure to Solve the Problem

When President George W. Bush was in office, he urged that it was time for the U.S. to "move beyond a petroleum-based economy and make our dependence on Middle Eastern oil a thing of the past." His goal was to "replace more than 75 percent of our oil imports from the Middle East by 2025."[27] Of course, a lot can happen between now and 2025.

Despite Bush's good intentions, it is disconcerting that past presidents have likewise sought energy independence but failed to achieve their goals. This does not bode well for the future. In 1973, during the Arab oil embargo, President Richard Nixon urged, "In the last third of this century, our independence will depend on maintaining and achieving self-sufficiency in energy." He referred to Project Independence 1980, with the goal of ensuring "that by the end of this decade, Americans will not have to rely on any source of energy beyond our own."[28] Under President Gerald Ford's leadership, the date was pushed back to 1985 when he signed the Energy Policy and Conservation Act. Of course, this did not solve the problem.

President Jimmy Carter in 1977 declared that energy independence was of such vital national interest that it was the "moral equivalent of war." Later that year he signed a law that brought into being the U.S. Department of Energy to manage America's ongoing energy crisis. In his July 1979 nationally televised speech, after the doubling of oil prices due to the Iranian oil crisis, Carter flatly asserted: "Beginning this moment, this nation will never use more foreign oil than we did in 1977—never." He came up with a new plan designed to achieve energy independence by 1990.[29]

The year after, in 1991, President George H. W. Bush announced an energy strategy engineered to reduce "our dependence on foreign oil." The year after that, President Bill Clinton proposed a tax on crude oil designed to discourage dependence on foreign oil. The year after that, in 1993, he launched a partnership with automakers to produce a car at least three times more fuel-efficient than then-existing cars.

No one can deny that efforts have been made by past administrations. Despite all such efforts, however, the United States today is more dependent on foreign oil than ever before. Certainly there is good reason to be skeptical about the current administration's plan.

Blind Optimism?

There is a crisis on the horizon. The dark clouds are gathering, and it does not seem as if anyone is preparing for the storm. Many authorities blindly continue to claim there is a limitless supply of oil, and that supply will outpace demand into the distant future—some say at least forty years. This, however, seems to be an outright contradiction of the facts. "The trends in place for the last thirty years show declining returns from oil exploration, peaking or declining oil production everywhere but in a few OPEC nations, and increasing demand for energy, especially among the world's largest developing nations."[30]

Oil experts Campbell and Laherrère warn that folks who are holding out for an endless supply of oil over the next forty years are making some critical errors in their analysis. For example:

■ This viewpoint relies on distorted estimates of current oil reserves.

■ This viewpoint falsely assumes that production at the various oil fields will remain constant—something that cannot possibly be the case if oil peak has been reached.

■ This viewpoint falsely assumes that the last barrel of oil can be pumped out of the ground just as easily and quickly as barrels today. Once peak oil is reached, every respective oil field steadily declines in its output, and it is *harder* and *more expensive* to retrieve remaining oil from those fields.[31]

Though not easy to swallow, the truth is that some of the top oil experts in the world are warning that we will all soon suffer extreme withdrawal pains from our oil addiction. Those who deny the addiction or the problem it will cause are much like heroin addicts who deny they have an addiction.

Prophetic Significance of Oil Addiction

I previously noted that one out of every four barrels of oil produced in the world is burned in America. Roberts warns that this "enormous, apparently limitless appetite exerts a ceaseless pull on the rest of the world's oil players and on the shape of the world political order." He rightly observes that this heavy dependence on foreign oil "makes the United States vulnerable to disruptions in supply and to energy 'blackmail.'"[32] I think Roberts is correct.

It is precisely here that we begin to see prophetic significance in global peak oil. In this book, I will seek to answer the following questions:

■ Will this oil crisis contribute to the weakening of America in the end-times, with an economic and political shift in power from the United States of America to the United States of Europe—the revived Roman Empire over which the Antichrist will rule (see Daniel 2 and 7)?

■ Will this oil crisis contribute to the weakening of America so that she is unable to come to the rescue of Israel when the invasion of Muslim nations into Israel takes place? This northern invading coalition includes Russia, Iran, Turkey, Libya, Sudan, and other Muslim nations (see Ezekiel 38–39). Since the biblical text tells us that God *alone* delivers Israel, perhaps the implication is that America does not help Israel because she is too weak to do so.

■ Or is it possible that Middle Eastern, Israel-hating countries will engage in "oil blackmail" against the United States, forcing the United States to back off of its support of Israel in the end-times in exchange for precious oil? (Addicts often engage in acts of desperation in order to feed their addictions.)

All such scenarios are entirely possible.

Understanding Peak Oil

I noted in the introduction that the age of *easy* oil is over. Even the best-case scenario is that the oil that remains in the earth is more difficult to get to, more expensive to extract, and less dependable to count on.[1]

The end of cheap, easy oil has implications for each of us. As one CNN reporter put it, "The end of cheap oil may mean more than just higher gas prices for Americans. It may mean the end of the oil age as we know it...We're using oil faster than we can ever hope to find it."[2] This clash between supply and demand will one day—in the not-too-distant future—send oil prices soaring like never before.[3]

While I introduced the subject of peak oil in chapter 1, I will in this chapter expand on that foundation with important background and supplemental data. This chapter is engineered to help you better grasp the big picture on the peak oil dilemma.

Peak Oil and Overpopulation

Among the factors propelling growth in world demand for oil is "an expanding global population."[4] Kenneth Deffeyes notes that "since 1979, the world has been producing people faster than we have been producing oil." His solution—not palatable to many—is that in the long haul, "we have to stabilize our population at a level that the earth can support."[5] In other words, we need to practice effective birth control and keep the population in check. But even if we were to somehow keep the population at its current level, we'd still be singing the oil blues. How do we know this is so? For the answer, we turn to Dr. M. King Hubbert.

The Groundbreaking Work of Dr. M. King Hubbert

Dr. Hubbert, a former Shell geophysicist, observed that in any large region, the unrestrained extraction of a finite resource (such as oil) rises along a bell-shaped curve that peaks when about half of that resource is gone. Because of Hubbert's groundbreaking work, *predictability* became a part of the oil world. His model was able to predict with reasonable accuracy the peak and decline of production from oil wells, fields, regions, and even countries.

According to Hubbert's model, early in the bell-shaped curve (*pre-peak*), the production rate of oil increases, while late in the bell-shaped curve (*post-peak*), the production of oil declines because of resource depletion. Put another way, a rapid period of exponential growth in an oil field is followed by an inflection point (a *peak*), after which growth tapers off. More specifically, "oil fields go through predictable depletion. Production increases until roughly half the oil is pumped and then falls back down the slope to zero."[6]

Hubbert based his forecast model on the history of oil exploration success in the United States up to 1956. To prove his theory, he fitted a bell curve to production statistics and projected that crude oil production in the lower forty-eight states would rise for thirteen more years, and then peak around 1970.

Hubbert hit the nail right on the head, and he quickly became a big star in the oil world—a bona fide black-gold celebrity. The production of oil did indeed peak in 1970, and then continued to follow a bell-shaped curve on the decline, with only minor variations along the way. For example, by the mid-2000s oil production in these forty-eight states had fallen to 1940s levels.

How sweet all this must have been for Hubbert, for he had been ridiculed for his views for years by peers in the oil industry.[7] As research continued, it became clear that the flow of oil fields in the former Soviet Union and oil fields outside of the Middle East have also followed this bell-shaped curve, a model that became known as "Hubbert's Peak." The "peak" is reached after approximately 50 percent of the oil field's resource base is extracted. One oil expert explains that "this holds true whether you're talking about a single oil well or the collective behavior of all oil wells on the planet: with half the supply gone, it simply gets harder and harder to maintain the same levels of production—the same number of barrels per day—and eventually, production falls."[8]

This model has been used to predict global peak oil. Ronald G. Nelson notes that "in analyzing global oil production, the methodology consists of backdating all oil reserves to their original year of discovery, and then constructing the production curve to project the same volumes of oil that are likely to be produced ultimately. In this way, scientists can make informed assumptions about peak oil production."[9]

The OPEC nations, however, threw a wrench into the works in the 1970s when they deliberately reduced their oil exports while all other nations continued producing oil at full capacity. This skewed the global forecasts a bit. Nevertheless, various geologists have used Hubbert's methodology to analyze the global oil scene, and their results are amazingly similar. David Goodstein, author of *Out of Gas*, notes that "recently, a number of oil geologists have applied Hubbert's techniques to the oil supply of the entire world. They have each used different data, different assumptions, and somewhat different methods, but their answers have been remarkably similar. The worldwide Hubbert peak, they say, will occur very soon—most probably within this decade."[10]

To be fair, some today challenge the Hubbert predictive model. I will address this in chapter 3, "A World in Denial."

Peak Oil—When?

The question presently being hotly debated by the experts—briefly introduced in chapter 1—relates to precisely when peak oil will be upon us. An article in *National Geographic* magazine noted that while no one is precisely sure *when* the peak will come, everyone is sure *that* it will come,[11] whether five years from now or fifty.[12]

Let's consider what some of the experts have said:

Already Happened. Some experts believe we have already reached peak oil. A primary proponent of this position is the Association for the Study of Peak Oil and Gas (ASPO), a European network of scientists.

Happening Now—2010. Others—including Matthew Simmons, Colin Campbell, and Kenneth Deffeyes, as well as the French oil company TotalFinaElf—say we are presently experiencing peak oil. Campbell and Jean H. Laherrère tell us that a great deal of the oil we are presently

pumping from the ground comes from old oil fields, many that were
found before 1973. A great majority of these fields are declining. They
therefore caution us that peak oil is upon us.[13]

Between 2011 and 2015. UK-based Energy Institute researcher Chris
Skrebowski says we will hit peak oil by 2011: "Peak oil is real; peak oil
is imminent and will occur sooner than we think." He argues that the
falling discovery rate of new reserves is an indication that "we are close
to peak oil."[14] The U.S. Geological Survey is ever-so-slightly more optimistic, suggesting that peak oil will occur between 2011 and 2015.

Sometime After 2015. A number of major oil companies project peak
oil sometime after 2015.[15]

By 2020. The International Energy Agency (IEA) believes peak oil
will come perhaps by 2020. It also stipulates that we are headed toward
an even earlier "oil crunch" because demand after 2010 is likely to exceed
dwindling supplies.[16]

In the Very Near Future. Steve Yetiv notes that "a growing number
of oil industry executives, including the CEOs of ConocoPhillips and
Total, believe peak global oil production will hit at 100 million barrels
per day. We're at 85 million barrels per day already."[17] The day is coming soon.

Let's Be Optimistic: 2037. Meanwhile, the U.S. Energy Department
has its metaphorical fingers crossed for 2037.[18] This 2037 estimate has
been widely criticized as grossly underestimating oil demand in the
coming decades.[19] A realistic view of growing demand places peak oil
much sooner—some (as noted previously) even say the day is past. As
one expert put it, "This extra demand simply cannot be met. We would
have to find and develop the equivalent of 10 new North Sea oil fields
in just a decade. Even if Iraq's oil fields are fully developed, with almost
unlimited new investment and new technology, it could only produce an
extra 6 million barrels, or a mere one-tenth of the amount needed."[20]

By 2050. Some are gleefully optimistic, saying we have perhaps another
forty years of oil. However, this view, too, is highly disputed.[21] David
Goodstein warns:

> Some say that the world has enough oil to last for another forty
> years or more, but that view is almost surely mistaken…When
> the peak occurs, increasing demand will meet decreasing supply,

possibly with disastrous results. We had a foretaste of the consequences in 1973, when some Middle Eastern nations took advantage of declining U.S. supplies and created a temporary, artificial shortage. The immediate result was long lines at the gas stations, accompanied by panic and despair for the future of the American way of life. After the worldwide Hubbert's peak, the shortage will not be artificial and it will not be temporary.[22]

What Smart People Are Saying

It is sobering to consider what people in the know are saying about all this. For example, an article published in *Energy Resource*, an industry insider publication, found that "48 percent of chief financial officers at U.S. oil and gas exploration and production companies agree that the world has reached its peak petroleum production rate or will reach it within the next few years."[23]

William J. Cummings, a spokesperson for Exxon-Mobil, concedes that "all the easy oil and gas in the world has pretty much been found. Now comes the harder work in finding and producing oil from more challenging environments and work areas."[24]

Steve Connor reports that "the first detailed assessment of more than 800 oil fields in the world, covering three quarters of global reserves, has found that most of the biggest fields have already peaked and that the rate of decline in oil production is now running at nearly twice the pace as calculated just two years ago."[25]

In keeping with this, Richard Heinberg, author of *The Party's Over*, warned in a televised interview that "we're seeing the world's largest oil fields, the super-giant oil fields…going into decline. Nor are the small fields going to replace production from these giant fields. We're on an accelerating treadmill here. And the signs are, I think, pretty obvious for all to see that we're not going to be able to keep up with that treadmill much longer."[26]

Michael Ruppert, author of *Crossing the Rubicon: The Decline of the American Empire at the End of the Age of Oil*, likewise warns: "Thirty-three of the largest oil producing nations are in permanent, irrevocable, and in some cases very very steep decline."[27] These are ominous words.

Certainly a number of major investors believe we have reached global peak oil. Billionaire oil investor T. Boone Pickens, who heads BP Capital

Hedge Fund with more than $4 billion under management, testified to the Senate Energy and Natural Resources Committee: "I do believe you have peaked out at 85 million barrels a day globally."[28]

Heinberg laments that almost everyone has seemingly bought into a mind-set of "business as usual." No one wants to think outside that box. The problem, he says, is that the box is about to be blown apart by peak oil.[29]

Let's be honest: A "business as usual" mentality involves a state of denial. Many people seem to be dealing with the peak oil issue the way they deal with death and dying. People get stuck for a time in *denial*, and then they transition into *bargaining*—that is, bargaining with God for a timely rescue. Only eventually will they come to the point of *acceptance*.

Why Are There Differing Estimates?

Many oil experts say three vital numbers enable us to make projections about future oil production:

1. A tally of how much oil has been extracted from the ground so far, a figure known as *cumulative production*.

2. An estimate of oil reserves, which refers to the amount of oil that can be pumped out of known oil fields before having to abandon them.

3. An educated guess at the quantity of conventional oil that remains to be discovered and exploited.

Adding these three numbers together gives us an approximation of the barrels of oil that will have been extracted from the ground when production ceases many decades from now.[30]

It is relatively easy to come up with the cumulative production statistic, for this is a matter of looking up this data in publications produced by the oil community. Estimating reserves is much more difficult, however. The data we have on this is reported in two primary journals: *Oil and Gas Journal* and *World Oil*. These journals annually query oil companies and governments of oil-producing countries.

The problem is that the reporting by companies and governments is often not accurate and not verifiable. Oil experts Campbell and Laherrère tell us that "in practice, companies and countries are often deliberately vague about the likelihood of the reserves they report, preferring instead to publicize whichever figure...best suits them. Exaggerated estimates can, for instance, raise the price of an oil company's stock."[31] Without that accurate information, different experts make different guesstimates as to when peak oil will be upon us. They all agree, however, that the day is coming. "While panic is not the prescription, experts are warning that the time to begin taking Peak Oil seriously is past."[32]

No New Substantive Discoveries

Some people may be tempted to think that we will be saved by discovering new oil fields. However, Professor Goodstein of the California Institute of Technology tells us that, for the most part, we're just not finding new sources of oil. "Better to believe in the tooth fairy than in future supply of new sources of oil." He notes that most of the planet has been extensively explored, and even if new fields were discovered, they will not delay global peak oil by more than a few years.[33] Oil geologists have gone all over the world searching for oil. There likely is not enough unexplored land to contain a spectacularly productive unknown oil field. Despite intense worldwide effort, the rate of oil discovery began declining decades ago, and has been in steady decline ever since.[34] Goodstein thus muses:

> Let us suppose for one euphoric moment that one more really big one is still out there waiting to be discovered. The largest oil field ever found is the Ghawar field in Saudi Arabia, whose eighty-seven billion barrels were discovered in 1948. If someone were to stumble onto another ninety-billion-barrel field tomorrow, Hubbert's peak would be delayed by a year or two, well within the uncertainty of the present estimates of when it will occur. It would hardly make any difference at all.[35]

Jane Bryant Quinn likewise affirms that "we're running out of the capacity to produce surpluses of oil. Demand for crude is expected to rise much faster than new supplies...Most producer nations can't find enough new oil, or drill out more from their reserves, to replace what we're using up. Production from most of the large, older fields is in *irreversible decline*."[36] Analyst Richard Vodra agrees, adding that "no huge fields have been discovered since the North Sea in the 1970s, and the world's annual production has exceeded annual discoveries for more than 25 years."[37]

Will Saudi Arabia Rescue Us?

One might also be tempted to think that oil-rich Saudi Arabia will come to the rescue. Based on the best data we have, however, this is nothing more than wishful thinking. Analysts Edward Morse and James Richard tell us why:

> Global demand for oil has been increasing by between 1.5 and 2 mbd [million barrels a day] each year, a rate of growth with alarming long-term consequences. The U.S. Department of Energy and the International Energy Agency both project that global oil demand could grow...to 120 mbd [million barrels a day] in 20 years, driven by the United States and emerging markets of South and East Asia. The agencies assume that most of the supply required to meet this demand must come from OPEC... Virtually all of this increase would come from the Middle East, especially Saudi Arabia.[38]

The problem, Morse and Richard tell us, is that such expectations for Saudi Arabia's growth do not fit the facts. Indeed, Saudi Arabia has been unable to increase its production capacity over the past twenty years. Truth be told, few OPEC countries in the 2000s have more production capacity than they did in 1990 or 1980.[39] In order for the world to obtain the increasing level of oil it needs, the very countries that have been unable to raise their production capacity for more than twenty years must more than double their oil production over the next twenty years.[40] Dark clouds are gathering on the horizon.

Matthew Simmons in his book, *Twilight in the Desert: The Coming Saudi Oil Shock and the World Economy*, documents how secretive the Saudis have been about how much oil they really have. In the process, they have given a false sense of hope to their customers—including the United States:

> By veiling its oil operations in secrecy and refusing to provide credible data to support its claims about reserves, production

rates, and costs, Saudi Arabia (and other producers) served its customers, the consuming nations, poorly. Energy planners the world over were forced to base their calculations on assumptions rather than verifiable information, a circumstance that has undoubtedly had harmful consequences for all energy stakeholders, producers and consumers alike. Most importantly, this secrecy concealed the true condition and extent of aging of Saudi Arabia's principal fields.[41]

A detailed study of over two hundred technical papers about Saudi Arabia's petroleum resources and production operations, published by the Society of Petroleum Engineers, found that oil industry folks in Saudi Arabia began observing serious signs of aging in its oil fields over thirty years ago. Ever since, they have been struggling to overcome problems brought about by the increasing maturity of those oil fields. This calls into question whether the Saudis will be physically able to produce what they have promised through the years.[42]

Insiders at Saudi Arabia's oil company, Aramco, told Simmons that the most productive parts of three key fields—Ghawar, Abqaiq, and Berri—passed peak oil levels years ago. There is still much oil left in Saudi Arabia, but what has vanished is the easy-to-produce light grade of oil that consuming nations want to purchase. The oil that remains is heavier, the reservoir rocks are less porous, and they have far less permeability.[43]

Placing hopes in the possibility of new oil field discoveries in Saudi Arabia is not wise. The truth is, the Saudis have been exploring its territories over the past thirty-five years with substantial fervor, but the results are highly disappointing. Our best information tells us that the odds of finding another giant oil field in Saudi Arabia are remote.[44]

Here, then, is the big problem: All the important Saudi Arabian oil fields—including Abqaiq and Ghawar—are having difficulty keeping oil production from declining. And yet, long-term energy-supply forecasts have always assumed that the Saudi oil fields could boost output to meet *any level* the world would demand. Demand for oil is forecast to grow phenomenally in coming years (the United States, China, and India are the three biggest culprits), and yet the Saudi oil fields are having difficulty maintaining a "flat" level of production, let alone increasing production. It is a recipe for a disaster.

What About Other Oil Countries?

If Saudi Arabia will not rescue us, might some of the other oil countries have good news? Don't hold your breath! Mexico's oil output has been declining since 2004. Venezuela's oil output is also declining, and will only decline more rapidly as a result of new exports to China, the second largest oil-guzzler on the globe.[45]

Venezuela's president, Hugo Chavez, is meanwhile openly criticizing the "imperialist policies" of the United States. He has signed a series of energy accords with Iran, including a $2 billion investment fund to finance some "special projects."

Consider the implications of this. If the United States stands with Israel against Iran's nuclear policy and military buildup, will Venezuela retaliate by withholding its much-needed oil? Some folks are more than a little concerned that this is a real possibility.[46]

Life After Peak Oil

Once peak oil does take place, the world's production of oil will continue to decline, never to rise again. This does not mean that earth will utterly run out of energy. It does mean, however, that we will have to develop alternative energy sources. The problem is, the entire infrastructure of human society—not just in the United States but in other nations as well—is built upon oil (transportation, industrial machinery, farming equipment, construction equipment, and the like). So it's not just a matter of switching to a different energy source. It's a matter of rebuilding the infrastructure. This will put an incredible strain on the global economy.[47]

Some say the transition will be merely uncomfortable; others say it will be downright horrific. As one researcher put it: "Peak Oil doesn't mean we have run out of the stuff. It means that we have crested the top of a bell curve of supply. Then it's a roller-coaster ride down. Depending on who you ask, that ride will either be slow and uncomfortable, or teeth-rattling and destructive."[48]

Any way one chooses to look at it, there will be some measure of public unrest on a global level. Such unrest is already evident in some parts of the world. One report indicates that "recent riots in Myanmar were touched off by high prices for energy." Moreover, "the Nigerian government is struggling to pacify its citizens, who are striking for a larger share of the oil revenue from exports to the U.S." Such unrest is likely to continue and further escalate as increasing numbers of people wake up to the sobering implications of peak oil.

(I will discuss specific consequences of peak oil in chapter 4.)

Implications for the United States

It is disconcerting to witness how little attention is being paid by both the media and the general population to the impending oil crisis. One case in point involves a 2007 meeting of the World Oil Conference of the Association for the Study of Peak Oil and Gas, held in Houston, Texas. There were four days of presentations and hundreds of highly qualified participants, all pointing to peak oil occurring within the decade. Amazingly, there was very little press coverage and even less public interest. One analyst thus laments:

> We have had plenty of warnings about the consequences of an early peak in global oil production, but no one in Washington is listening. A premature topping plateau in global oil production would wipe out most, if not all, economic and policy plans on offer by politicians and "think tanks" in our nation's capital. Such plans assume continued growth in supplies of generally affordable oil, but a surprised world could instead soon be facing rapidly dwindling supplies of increasingly unaffordable oil.[49]

Meanwhile, even in the best-case scenario—even if by some strange fluke a forty-year supply of oil is left in the ground—the fact remains that oil is a finite resource that is running out, and the United States is increasingly dependent on hostile and potentially unstable nations to meet its needs. Moreover, we are presently spending billions of dollars on oil purchased from Middle Eastern countries who then use some of that same money to finance terrorism against us.

We are literally funding our own destruction. We are rapidly moving toward a day of reckoning. The days are prophetic.

A World in Denial

Many experts have presented substantive evidence that peak oil has either already taken place, is presently taking place, or will take place in the very near future. Surprisingly, however, many Americans—both government officials and citizens—have an attitude of "no worries." They seem to think there is nothing to be concerned about. In this chapter, I will briefly address some of the reasons for this attitude.

People Have Cried Wolf Before

Some in recent days have suggested that we have nothing to worry about because various people have been claiming we are running out of oil for a very long time. For example, when the wells ran dry in western Pennsylvania back in the 1880s, many claimed the age of oil was about to end. Following World War I, the head of the U.S. Geological Survey delivered a verdict of gloom in 1919: The country will likely run out of oil in the next nine years! Consequently, President Coolidge set up the Federal Oil Conservation Board in 1924 to draft legislation to preserve national resources.[1] Similar concerns were raised following World War II, especially since oil was a necessity in keeping the American war machine functioning. Certainly panic gripped the oil industry when Middle Eastern nations inflicted an oil embargo on the United States in the early 1970s.

In each of these cases, it is argued, new technologies emerged that were able to banish the fears of people within a few short years. In each case, *shortage* gave way to *surplus*. Many today claim the same will be true regarding current fears of the end of the age of oil.[2]

The million-dollar question is this: *Is it different this time around?* One must answer this question with studied consideration, for the stakes are very high. Some analysts are hesitant but hopeful that we have nothing to worry about—at least in the next few years. But they are also forthright in admitting that geopolitics, costs, government decision making, oil industry complexity, restrictions on access to key oil fields, and investments can hamper development and lead to both dwindling supplies and very high prices.[3] Add to this the recent insatiable oil appetites of China (where there will be 1.1 billion cars on their roads by 2050, up from 20 million three years ago) and India (not to mention the United States), and the "cry wolf" argument begins to sound hollow. In fact, one publication that warned of impending peak oil has the amusing title, "This Time the Wolf Really *Is* at the Door."[4]

The book you are holding in your hands provides substantive evidence that the "cry wolf" argument does not apply to the present impending crisis. This is one reason I provided so many quotes from geologists, oil experts, CEOs of oil companies, economists, researchers, and government leaders in chapters 1 and 2. The cumulative weight of their assessments is profoundly convincing.

Oil Exploration Has Declined Because of a Booming Oil Surplus

Some optimists have suggested that the only reason the discovery of oil has declined in recent decades is that so much oil had previously been discovered that no more oil was needed for a very long time. For this reason, exploration came to a standstill. Now that the need for oil has emerged again, exploration can begin anew and all will be well.

Such thinking is incalculably naive. Exploration has been a continuous effort, and the oil discoveries that have taken place in recent decades have fallen far short of global consumption. The world is now consuming oil at such a breathtaking rate, with staggering estimates for future demand, that no discoveries—past, present, or future—are going to keep up with demand. Peter Tertzakian warns that "with global demand for oil rising every year, global production declining in the absence of massive investment, and with over one billion new consumers in China awakening with their own powerful thirst, the world is going to need every extra barrel of oil the industry can find."[5] Peak oil is knocking at the door.

Differing Estimates

Some peak oil theorists say that peak oil has already occurred, some say it is presently occurring, and others say it will occur in the future— perhaps in 2011, or 2020, or 2037, or sometime later. Because there are such differing opinions, with no one being absolutely sure, some people reason that we need not take the claims of such theorists seriously.

This is a silly objection, for although different theorists may offer different suggestions as to *when* peak oil will occur, they all agree *that* peak oil will occur. To ignore this fact is to imperil oneself.

I once saw a plaque in a doctor's office that said: THE FIVE MOST DANGEROUS WORDS IN THE WORLD: "Maybe it will go away." I fear that many today are saying the same thing about the impending oil crisis, and are not taking the current symptoms seriously only because peak oil theorists have different opinions on the timing. Not wise!

"Don't Rain on My Parade"

Some people have apparently chosen to reject the Hubbert's Peak predictive model for what one might call emotional reasons. More specifically, the oil business is highly profitable, with many people making truckloads of money. Investors who pour their cash into that business do not want to hear that the profits are just about to dry up. They have a "don't rain on my parade" attitude. They continue to live in denial as they continue to hope in astronomical profits. They are ultimately blinded by desire.

"Peak Theorists Make Mistakes"

Some anti-peak critics say that despite how convincing many pro-peak arguments may initially sound, and despite the tremendous number of geologists and economists issuing warnings, "careful examination of the data and methods, as well as extensive perusal of the writings, suggests that the opacity of the work is at best obscuring the inconclusive nature of their research."[6]

If that last statement flew right over your head, don't be concerned. This critic's main point is that, in his opinion, Hubbert's bell-curve model was simplistic, and the production of oil in some locations does not necessarily follow this model.[7]

More specifically, some claim that aside from the lower forty-eight states, "the pattern of production is not rendered by a bell curve but is marked by large discontinuities."[8] Some geologists claim that Hubbert's model is no longer definitive because technology has changed the equation, "allowing oil companies to produce more oil from reservoirs than was previously possible."[9]

Not unexpectedly, there is much debate on this. Pro-Hubbert geologists respond that technology has indeed improved immensely, but the existence of such technology does not invalidate the peak oil theory; *it simply causes each oil field to reach "peak" faster than it would have otherwise.* The geologists, oil experts, CEOs of oil companies, economists, researchers, and government leaders cited in chapters 1 and 2 are all aware of the newest technologies, and yet they still warn that peak oil has either already taken place, is now taking place, or will soon take place.

"There's Lots of Oil Left"

Peak oil theorists have suggested that between 850 billion and 1.2 trillion barrels of oil are left in the ground. However, at least one analysis put together by Cambridge Energy Research Associates (CERA) claims there are 3.74 trillion barrels left. In view of this, we are told, policymakers who base their actions on peak oil theorists may well make inappropriate decisions and end up inadvertently hurting the economy.[10] It is claimed that the peak oil estimate of 1.2 trillion barrels is pessimistic because "it excludes the enormous contribution likely from probable and possible resources, those yet to be found, and plays down the importance of unconventional reserves in the Canadian oil sands, the Orinoco tar belt, [and] oil shale…"[11]

Peak oil geologists respond by casting doubt on the idea that we will be saved by oil sands, tar belts, and oil shale. Let's briefly consider each of these.

Oil Shale

Shale oil comes from oil shale. What is oil shale? Oil experts tell us that conventional oil gets created when source rock that is loaded with organic matter sinks deep enough into the earth for the organics to be cooked into oil. "Oil shale" refers to source rock that has *not* sunk deep enough for oil to be produced.[12] We are told that there is significant shale oil (from oil shale) in Colorado, Wyoming, and Utah, and this no doubt contributes to the bloated estimates of CERA that are stated above.

The problem, experts point out, is that shale oil is not really oil at all, but has been called oil by folks who seek investors. It is more accurate to describe shale oil as a wax-like substance that can be converted into usable oil if the rock containing it is mined, crushed, and heated. Contrary to the "easy oil" that is quickly pumped out of the ground, shale oil is not easy (it is a couple of miles underground) and it is not fast (it has to go through a production process). To derive oil from oil shale is expensive, slow, and damaging to the environment (lots of pollution is emitted into the atmosphere in the process). CERA failed to mention the multiyear time frame and colossal investment required to develop such resources.[13]

Moreover, experts tell us that it requires a great deal of energy to convert this form of energy into a usable form.[14] As researcher Richard Gwyn put it, "more than half as much energy is used extracting this oil as the energy value of the oil produced."[15] We're not getting much benefit for our efforts—not too much "bang for the buck."

In the coming years, it is going to take progressively more energy to find energy. Oil specialists call this the "energy return on investment." Historically, the energy return-on-investment ratio has been 50 to 1, meaning that we derive about 50 parts energy for expending 1 part of energy. That is a substantial return on investment, and it has enabled Americans to create the amazing way of life we so take for granted. But the oil is running out. The return on investment has been fabulous as long as it has lasted, but that return is about to vanish. It's as if we inherited a million dollars from a rich aunt, and now we're down to our last few thousand dollars. We have created an expensive lifestyle that can no longer be sustained.[16]

Another consideration is the need for new machinery. Robert Hirsch, former senior energy program adviser for Science Applications International Corporation, says "it takes a very long time to build the machinery that is necessary to exploit oil shale."[17] Colin J. Campbell and Jean H. Laherrère agree, noting that "the industry will be hard-pressed for the time and money needed to ramp up production of unconventional oil quickly enough."[18]

Oil Sands/Tar Sands

Oil sands, also known as tar sands, are naturally occurring mixtures of sand, water, and bitumen, which is an extremely dense and viscous form of petroleum. Though found throughout the world, there are heavy concentrations in Canada and Venezuela. Oil sands or tar sands are often referred to as "unconventional oil," which distinguishes it from the free-flowing oil that can be pumped out of the ground. As noted previously, some believe that tar sands will make a huge contribution toward solving our oil dilemma.[19]

Though at first glance the oil sands or tar sands might seem like a solution to the impending oil shortage, in reality these sands contribute little. The world presently guzzles down 86 million barrels of oil each and every day, and the tar sands in Canada and Venezuela produce 1.7 million barrels per day. Yes, they make a contribution, but they come nowhere near making a contribution that will "save the day." Oil industry leaders concede that the impact of these sands on the skyrocketing demand for oil is negligible.[20] What we need, these oil executives say, are brand new gigantic gushers the likes of which we see in Saudi Arabia or the Alaskan North Slope. Global demand for oil dwarfs any oil that can be produced from tar sands.

Besides, as was true with shale oil, deriving oil from the tar sands is difficult and costly. It also requires the use of massive quantities of water and natural gas, itself a costly form of energy. Further, the process takes a long time—a multiyear commitment.[21]

There is also the problem of pollution.[22] As Steve Connor warns, "this oil is dirty and will produce vast amounts of carbon dioxide which will make a nonsense of any climate change agreement."[23] He says that processing the tar sands "would be immensely damaging to the environment because of the amount of energy needed to recover a barrel of tar-sand oil compared to the energy needed to collect the same amount of crude oil."[24]

The delay factor is another critical consideration. Robert Hirsch speaks in sobering terms about the consequences of delays in dealing with the impending oil crisis:

> In our 2005 analysis we looked at a worldwide crash program to
> bring these things [processing oil from tar sands] into being as

fast as possible. We made a number of aggressive assumptions, because a crash program is different from business as usual.

But the problem is that the magnitude of oil production loss each year will be so large and the time required to implement these alternatives is so long that the problem runs away from you if we wait too long. And we have waited too long to seriously start...Right now, we are looking at a global recession that deepens each year for more than a decade because we are not prepared.[25]

What About Ethanol?

Some people believe that ethanol will be a huge part of the solution to the impending oil crisis. No one denies that ethanol can contribute to meeting our energy needs, but it will not be the savior for the current crisis. Consider the hard facts.

On the positive side, ethanol can be produced using the infrastructure already in place in the United States. There are currently 150 ethanol plants with more planned. As well, we already have gas stations providing a mix of ethanol and gasoline. So it *already is* a part of the solution.

But there is no way that ethanol can meet the fuel demands in America because current consumption levels dwarf the supply. Moreover, there are problems to consider:

- The very process of producing fuel from America's crops expends more energy than it produces. We do not receive a good energy return on investment. Ultimately it is self-defeating.

- John F. Walvoord and Mark Hitchcock note that America in 2006 utilized 14 percent of the country's corn production to produce ethanol, and even then it made little difference regarding our dependence on fossil fuels. That figure rose to 20 percent in 2007, with little contribution to meeting the staggering need.

To use any more of the country's food supply to produce ethanol could create food shortages worldwide—and the supply would *still* not meet the demand. "It takes eleven acres of land to grow enough corn to power one car with ethanol for one year (ten thousand miles). That's the same amount of land required to feed seven people for one year."[26] Further, "even if 100 percent of U.S. corn and soybean production were turned into fuel, it would only offset 20 percent of on-road fuel consumption. The bottom line is that biofuels aren't a real solution for America's growing energy needs for the foreseeable future."[27]

What About Coal?

Still others place their hopes in coal as a solution to the impending oil crisis. America is rich in coal. In fact, the United States has the largest recoverable coal deposits on the planet. The good news is that coal is cheap, and there are six hundred power plants in the United States that burn coal and produce about half the country's electricity.[28]

The bad news is that this coal does nothing to fuel our cars, trucks, buses, and other forms of transportation. As well, there is an environmental hazard. As energy expert Kenneth Deffeyes puts it, "the environmental problems with increased coal burning are not easily solved. Research efforts to solve coal's sulfur, carbon dioxide, and other environmental problems go back more than twenty years. We cannot pretend that coal's problems will be solved in a year or two by a crash research program."[29]

The pollution consideration should not be taken lightly. Economist Stephen Leeb notes that coal is the dirtiest of all fossil fuels. *The Economist* branded it "Environmental Enemy Number 1" in its July 6, 2002, issue, and most environmentally conscious people recoil at the idea of its continued use.[30] Dr. Jeremy Leggett, a former oil-industry consultant and now a green entrepreneur with Solar Century, says that extracting oil from coal is a carbon-intensive process and will deepen the climate problem.[31]

Still, because coal is a plentiful resource, it remains a viable energy option. And since the technology exists for converting coal into motor fuel, this may be a temporary solution to the oil crisis. Deffeyes suggests that the time may soon come when we simply have to choose between *diminished* energy with little pollution or *sufficient* energy with more pollution.[32] Robert Hirsch is sensitive to this issue, noting:

> Using and liquefying coal is an available technology, but under current conditions, there would be a great deal of CO_2 released

from making liquids out of coal. So people say, "no, we are not going do these things because of CO_2." They do not recognize that if we don't take action on the impending oil decline, populations are going to suffer beyond what most can imagine.[33]

Even then, the use of coal merely pushes back the inevitable. For, as Leeb notes, "coal—like oil—is a fossil fuel whose production is subject to similar diminishing returns. One study that applied Hubbert's Peak to North American coal production found that coal production will likely peak in the year 2035."[34]

What About Nuclear Power?

Some may be tempted to ask: Can't we solve our energy problem with nuclear power? Answering this question requires that we make a critical qualification. Our problem is not an *energy* problem, per se. It is a *liquid fuels* problem—a fuel that is used not just for transportation, but also in industrial machinery, farm machinery, manufacturing machinery, and much more.[35] As noted previously, a large part of the infrastructure of the United States is built to utilize oil. Simply because we have access to nuclear technology will not solve that problem. We will need to completely rebuild our infrastructure, which will require lots of time and lots of money.

What About Renewable Energy?

Is renewable energy—such as solar cells deriving energy from the sun, as well as wind energy—the solution to the impending oil crisis? Many might think so. However, renewable energy is very limited. The sun does not shine at night.[36] Nor does the wind blow all the time. Renewable energy can be a part of our energy program, but it does not solve the problem of our infrastructure's requirement of oil. Renewable energy will not fuel our countless cars and SUVs.[37]

Will New Technologies Save Us?

A primary argument of those who deny that peak oil is upon us is that new technologies will save the day. These new technologies include such things as 3-D seismic imaging and deepwater drilling techniques and equipment. Such technologies will allegedly enable us to greatly increase oil production so that supply will meet demand. Economics also plays a role. We are told that "if you pay smart people enough money, they'll figure out all sorts of ways to get the oil you need."[38]

Other economists warn that this argument would be valid if we were seeking to build a better contraption, such as a mousetrap. When it comes to finding oil, however, the argument is invalid for there is only so much oil that can be pumped out of the earth. Once it is gone, no amount of brains or money will cause oil to materialize because it is simply *no longer there!*[39] *Something* cannot come from *nothing*.

Moreover, new technologies constitute a double-edged sword. Addressing the use of new technologies over the past few decades, one analyst says that "while the technology did make it possible to extract oil and gas reserves far faster, it simultaneously created far higher decline rates in existing production areas. The accelerating decline rates were an unintended consequence of the new technology."[40]

At best, new technologies have bought us a little more time. But that time is rapidly running out. Oil peak is knocking at the door!

The Global Consequences of Oil Depletion

In reading chapters 1–3, I'm sure that you've not missed the point that difficult days may be ahead. I can attest that reading the opinions of some experts is downright disconcerting. As an example, Princeton professor and geologist Kenneth S. Deffeyes says that once oil supply begins to dwindle, the years to follow will see shortages that at best will cause "global recession, possibly worse than the 1930s Great Depression." He suggests that all this could lead to "war, famine, pestilence and death."[1] That sounds alarmingly like the book of Revelation.

It becomes even more disconcerting when we hear a growing chorus of energy experts and academics who fear that Deffeyes's comments may have merit. James Schlesinger, the country's first secretary of energy, asserts that "a growing consensus accepts that the peak is not that far off." He warns that "the inability readily to expand the supply of oil, given rising demand, will in the future impose a severe economic shock."[2]

A report prepared for the U.S. Department of Energy's National Technology Laboratory laments that "the world has never faced a problem like this." Although oil companies have searched intensively for new oil fields around the world, the "results have been disappointing," the report says, and the resulting "oil peaking will be abrupt and revolutionary."[3] That word *revolutionary* concerns me, for it carries the meaning: "involving or causing a complete or dramatic change."[4] I do not think any of us are prepared for a "complete or dramatic change."

I do not have a doomsday mentality. I am not an alarmist. I am not a sensationalist. Yet, I realize that when we take a hard look at what *could* happen should a sudden oil crisis hit the globe—as well could be the case in view of the peak oil phenomenon—it may *sound* doomsdayish or alarmist or sensationalistic. That is not my intention. Rather, my intention is to soberly demonstrate what is at stake *if* (or *when*) the demand for oil significantly exceeds supply in a world in which every nation is seeking to protect its vital interests. Later in the book, I will suggest how all this may relate to biblical end-times prophecy.

Sheer Disbelief

The American expectation is that there will always be more land, more wealth, more business, more energy, more oil, and more of everything we need or want. Some Americans respond with disbelief that we may now be facing a wall of limits that will royally cramp our style.[5] We can no longer build our society on the ideology of endless growth.

Disbelief or not, we are headed toward a day of reckoning, even though many are attempting to delay the inevitable. Thomas Homer-Dixon, a professor in the Centre for Environment and Business in the Faculty of Environment at the University of Waterloo and editor of the book *Carbon Shift: How the Twin Crises of Oil Depletion and Climate Change Will Define the Future*, suggested in an interview that "we're coming up to an energy transition that is as significant as anything that humankind has ever seen." He warns: "I think that it's likely that the pressures that we see developing in various parts of the world, including energy pressures, are going to produce some kinds of system shocks— for instance energy shock—in the future." The most alarming thing, Homer-Dixon says, is this:

> There's a fundamental resistance in the United States to the idea that endless growth may not be feasible. And anybody who has raised that idea up to this point—especially in political circles—has found that their political life span is very limited. Which is why we see such extraordinary resistance to the idea or suggestion that we may be facing peak oil, and to the suggestion that there may be significant climate changes...These things centrally threaten the enormous power and wealth of the...vested interests in our societies.[6]

Significant Side Effects of the Peak Oil Crisis

The problem is that a lack of *belief* yields a lack of *preparedness*. Some people will maintain disbelief up to the moment that peak oil punches them in the nose. By then, they will be fully aware of some rather unpleasant side effects of the peak oil crisis. In what follows, I note some of the more significant of these.

Population Concerns

Consider two important facts. The number of people on this planet *increases* with every passing minute. The amount of oil on this planet *decreases* with every passing minute. Therein lies a key component of our problem. *More people, less oil; more consumers, less to consume.* If the population of earth in 2030 is twice what it was in 1980 (as projections indicate), and if oil production in 2030 is at 1980 levels (as projected by peak oil theorists), then, considering that today oil production is barely keeping pace with demand, those living in 2030 are in for a tough time.[7]

Fewer Cars, More Expensive Cars

In the short term, an increasing number of energy-efficient cars will likely come on the market. There may also be some hydrogen-powered vehicles. Further, it may be that fewer cars will be built, for fewer people will likely be able to afford them. This, of course, will not be good for the economy.

Transportation Concerns

Experts tell us that oil shortages will affect every emerging and traditional industry. After all, oil powers industrial machinery and lubricates all the engines in the world. So here is the question of concern: If there is diminished oil, with a subsequent diminishing of lubricated trains and trucks and jets to distribute our products, then how will such products be transported from one state to the next? Horse and buggy?[8]

Adam Porter is spot on in his assessment that a significant increase in oil prices, due to a significant shortage, will "fundamentally change transport in general. Every single internal combustion engine, every single turbo engine, every single turbine will find its running costs dramatically increased. You want to replace them? *With what?*"[9]

As a result of a diminishing supply of oil, many cars, vans, SUVs, buses, jets, trains, and other forms of transportation will remain parked in garages and hangers, monuments to our collective irresponsibility for not acting sooner to alleviate the crisis. I've said it before: The infrastructure of our entire transportation system depends heavily on oil. Without that oil, the infrastructure collapses. The decreasing amounts of available oil will likely be used for luxury transportation that is unaffordable to most in the middle class. David Goodstein says that "we can all too easily envision a dying civilization, the landscape littered with the rusting hulks of useless SUVs."[10]

The only way to avert such an outcome is to *start today* in preparing for the peak oil crisis, and commit to rebuilding and tweaking our infrastructure. Yet many today live in perpetual denial that there will even be a crisis, despite all the warnings from geologists, oil experts, CEOs of oil companies, economists, researchers, and even government leaders.

Highway and Road Building Curtailed

Over the past century, countless miles of roads and highways have been built in this and other countries for car and truck traffic. The amount of money that has been spent is incalculable. Consider that in the Los Angeles area alone, taxpayers have coughed up some $127 million for each mile of highway construction. Over a decade ago, our government spent a staggering $80 billion on roads and highways, and the figure has only increased since then.

Of course, the production of asphalt requires large amounts of oil, and the equipment needed to build highways runs on oil as well. Once the oil supply becomes diminished, road building may also diminish, as will road repairs.[11]

Increasing Expense Concerns

Whether one is talking about transportation or products or services, things will get much more expensive following peak oil. Richard Heinberg tells us that "nearly everything that is genuinely useful will become relatively more expensive because the energy employed in its...production will have grown more rare and valuable."[12] Economists tell us that, as a result, the have-nots will have even less.

Concerns for the Poor

Should the oil crisis hit suddenly, and society has not made sufficient preparations, the poor will likely suffer the severest and the fastest. This will be true on both an individual and a national level. Rich people will be more likely than poor people to initially weather the storm, just as rich nations will as opposed to poorer nations. Eventually, however, *every person* and *every nation*—rich and poor and in between—will be affected.[13]

Community Service Concerns

When the demand for oil far exceeds the supply, some cultural observers are concerned that "cities and towns will start to struggle to provide basic services like police, firefighting, [and] school buses."[14] Think about what that might mean for your neighborhood. People may learn a whole new meaning of the word *angst*.

Social Unrest Concerns

Some experts have expressed concern that there could be significant social unrest when the demand for oil far exceeds the supply. British energy economist David Fleming warns, "Anticipated supply shortages could lead easily to disturbing scenes of mass unrest."[15] We have already witnessed such unrest in some parts of the world where there has been an ongoing struggle to attain and maintain sufficient energy to meet local needs.

Coal and Pollution: No Alternative

With a sudden depletion of oil, accompanied by skyrocketing costs for the oil that remains, we may have no alternative but to burn coal in mass quantities if only to stay warm, cook food, and engage in some form of industry. This will cause substantial damage to the environment. The change in the greenhouse effect as a result of coal burning will increasingly make the environment hostile to life.[16] As well, we will not see the stars so clearly anymore.

Manufacturing Concerns

An astonishing range of plastics, fibers, solvents, pesticides, coatings, and a multitude of other products are made from petrochemicals.[17] Adam Porter tells us:

Oil is the main ingredient in petrochemicals, and petrochemicals are everywhere. They make plastics and polyester: the clothes we wear, the carpets we walk on, frames for our computers, seats to sit on, bottles to drink from, and band-aids to salve our wounds. What will replace them—who will be able to afford them—as the price of oil starts to rise?[18]

The demise of the petrochemicals industry would further damage our already fragile economy. Here's a sobering scenario: When the oil decreases, industrial manufacturing decreases. When industrial manufacturing decreases, jobs decrease. When jobs decrease, the economy plummets. When the economy plummets, the country weakens. There is much *cause and effect* that we witness in the world of economics, and this will be nowhere better illustrated than in the decades following peak oil.

Distribution Concerns

As a result of a decrease in oil, and a subsequent dramatic escalation in price for the oil that remains, many truckers and shippers will be unable to carry out their distribution tasks. Food, water, medicine, clothing, and all other products will not be easily transportable to various states and cities. Shelves in our stores could become poorly stocked, perhaps even bare in some high-population areas. "It will be a slow deterioration in our quality of life, in the reliability of transportation, in the availability of certain foods, as well as price spikes for food."[19]

Unemployment Concerns

With manufacturing, transportation, and distribution diminished, many companies will suffer and some will go out of business. Many products may remain in warehouses. Many employees may not be able to drive to work. Further, since many companies utilize industrial equipment that requires oil, they may no longer be able to produce their products without paying astronomical costs for the oil that remains. The inevitable result is escalating unemployment rates.

Self-Sufficiency Concerns

Today we buy food from people who specialize in growing or processing food. We buy clothes from people who specialize in making clothes. Much of the food we eat is grown in other states. Many of the clothes we wear are made in other countries. If transportation and distribution are greatly reduced or (worst-case scenario) curtailed, people will be forced to do more for themselves. But few people today have the knowledge or the skills to grow food, make clothes, and the like.[20] Many people who live in a consumerist society haven't the foggiest idea how to be self-sufficient.

Increased Localization Concerns

Because transportation and distribution will be greatly affected, there may be a dramatically increased need for local businesses to produce the products that had formerly been distributed nationally by big corporations.[21] Or perhaps big corporations might establish local production plants throughout the country. The problem, of course, is that with the escalating price of scarce oil, how will *any* business or corporation be able to afford to use industrial machinery to produce products? Even if they somehow succeed in making such products, how will they make a profit in a country where many people can no longer afford to buy them?

Lessons Learned from Operation Shockwave

Back in 2005, oil experts got together with national security experts in a Washington hotel and engaged in "Operation Shockwave" to simulate a protracted disruption in the oil supply. The results of the simulation pointed to "panic and pain." Former CIA director Robert M. Gates, who played the role of national security adviser in this exercise, said that "the American people are going to pay a terrible price for not having had an energy strategy...The scenarios portrayed were absolutely not alarmist...They're realistic." We are told that when the flow of oil is disrupted, it will be much like a mushroom cloud that rises in the distance—a fiery atomic explosion whose shock wave will eventually hit us all. Following that, we will all suffer through the fallout as waves of misery engulf us all.[22]

These are strong words. Perhaps those who participated in Operation Shockwave used such strong words to awaken America from its stupor in the hopes that we will take the problem seriously.

U.S. Increased Dependence on the Middle East

With peak oil upon us (or occurring at some point in the coming decade or two), the United States will be increasingly dependent on Middle Eastern countries, such as Saudi Arabia. Some Middle Eastern nations do not do oil business with the United States, for they dislike everything we stand for.

Consider Iran, presently the fourth-leading exporter of oil. Iran's president Mahmoud Ahmadinejad thinks of the United States as the great Satan that must be destroyed along with Israel (the lesser Satan). He often states that we will soon know what it is like to live in a United States-free and Israel-free world. In the midst of an oil crisis, how likely would the United States be able to derive oil from Middle Eastern countries if Iran decided to get aggressive against us? If the United States continues to support Israel and to stand against Iran with its nuclear ambitions, is it possible that the "harm and pain" that Ahmadinejad has promised the U.S. might include thwarting the flow of Middle Eastern oil to the U.S.?

Some of our government officials are concerned that while the United States does not presently import any oil from Iran, Iran could stop virtually all Middle Eastern oil from being exported to the United States by blocking the narrow Strait of Hormuz, through which 40 percent of the world's oil flows each and every day. If that happened, the U.S. economy would suffer immense damage overnight.[23] (I will address the Strait of Hormuz in more detail in a later chapter.)

The United States learned the hard way what it's like to have an oil/economic war waged against it. Following the early 1970s, keeping the Persian Gulf open became a top security priority. President Jimmy Carter said that the United States must use "any means necessary, including military force," to maintain access to the Persian Gulf. It was a no-compromise issue because oil is the virtual lifeblood of America.

The Carter doctrine was put into action when Iraq's Saddam Hussein tried to take over the Kuwait oil fields in 1990. U.S. government leaders were understandably alarmed that Iraq could also possibly move against Saudi Arabia, which, if successful, would have put Hussein in control of almost half the world's proven oil reserves (Iraq, Kuwait, and Saudi Arabia). Dick Cheney informed the Senate Armed Services Committee that once Saddam acquired Kuwait, he would be in a position to dictate the future of worldwide energy policy and put a stranglehold on the U.S. economy. Not unexpectedly, the U.S. president responded militarily, noting that "our country now imports nearly half the oil it consumes and could face a major threat to its economic independence... The sovereign independence of Saudi Arabia is of vital interest to the United States."[24]

This episode demonstrated in no uncertain terms just how dependent the United States is on Middle Eastern countries for its oil fix. The phenomenon of peak oil, whenever it occurs, will fan this reality into a flame.

Nations Protecting Their Interests

Because oil is used in virtually every nation for transportation, farming, industry, and much more, it is entirely possible that at some point we will be faced with multiple nations vying against each other for increasingly scarce supplies. Imagine ten starving people around a table that has only a few pieces of bread on it. Everyone around the table contemplates strategies for securing their piece of the bread.

Things could get downright sinister—even violent—as nations seek to protect their own interests.[25] Fears about peak oil could "exacerbate tensions among great powers. For example, note China's obsessive concern about energy and Washington's growing concern about China's rising power. Imagine how tense Sino-U.S. relations could become against the backdrop of dwindling oil supplies or even the rising perception of such dwindling supplies."[26]

It does not require a vivid imagination to contemplate how nations might end up using force to protect their interests. One secular analyst suggests that if the world oil shortage becomes sufficiently painful, "there could be a temptation for a military seizure of the oil fields [in the Middle East] and the establishment of a 'world protectorate.' Some bureaucrat, even now, might be gathering euphemisms to justify an ugly scene."[27]

One begins to wonder how such a "world protectorate" might relate to the emergence of a global government, which the biblical prophets predicted of the end-times (see Revelation 13:1-6; 17:9-13). I find it highly revealing that secular experts are saying that the only thing that might suffice is a global solution. Another secular analyst, Matthew Simmons, likewise argues that "a global solution is needed to address how we can use oil far more efficiently than in our present system. A global solution is the only real option for addressing the energy gap."[28]

War Concerns

War may seem to be inevitable with national face-offs over oil. Of course, one would hope that oil wars will be waged merely with cash and not conventional weaponry.[29] However, many experts are concerned that the outbreak of weaponized war over oil remains a serious possibility.[30] One expert laments that "desperate attempts by one country or region to maintain its standard of living at the expense of others could lead to Oil War III."[31]

Consider the sobering role the lack of oil played in World War II. Recall that both Nazi Germany and Imperial Japan lacked domestic oil fields to fuel not just their industrial machinery and transportation, but also their military machinery. The choice they faced was to either curb their appetites and their ambitions or go looking for oil elsewhere. Both chose the latter. Adolph Hitler went after the oil fields of the Middle East and Russia, while Hirohito sought control of the oil-rich East Indies. One analyst notes that "when the Japanese bombed Pearl Harbor in December 1941, a primary objective was to sink any U.S. warships that might otherwise have prevented Japanese tankers from reaching Indonesia."[32]

Once the war was over, it became clear that oil played a major part in the success of the victors. By the time American forces dropped an atomic bomb on Hiroshima, Japan's air force was completely out of fuel. The winners had been those "best able to keep the oil flowing." Put another way, the allied forces "floated to victory on a wave of oil."[33]

And as I mentioned previously, when Saddam Hussein invaded Kuwait to seize control of the oil fields there, the United States had no other option but to militarily rescue Kuwait and protect the oil trade. Mark Hitchcock documents that "as much as 40 percent of the entire U.S. military budget can be attributed to protecting the oil trade."[34]

While it is disconcerting to think about, one could easily envision black oil being mixed with the red blood of young soldiers as we all begin to feel the stab of peak oil. Paul Roberts delivers the sobering news that there could be a "dangerous and escalating competition among the big oil-importing nations over the remaining reserves in the Middle East."[35] Edwin Black is convinced that "those who crave the oil will fight to get it. Those who possess it will fight to withhold it."[36]

Overall Mortality Concerns

Even at present, when we still have oil, some 770 people die annually from extreme cold and 380 from extreme heat. Serious ongoing fuel shortages could lead to a substantial increase in mortality rates from both of these temperature extremes.[37]

Experts suggest other ways people might die as a result of such a shortage. For example, as a result of a plummeting economy, people may not have enough money to buy sufficient food and medicine, which could lead to increased malnutrition and disease. Even if people have money, in a worst-case scenario they might not be able to buy sufficient food and medicine due to the diminished capacity of our distribution system. In addition, some fighting may erupt in the face of a shrinking food supply.

There will also likely be an increase in hoarders of oil, and some hostile encounters could occur as angry folks seek access to some of that hoarded oil. Still further, if someone has a medical emergency, how (in a worst-case scenario) will he quickly get to the hospital if there's insufficient oil for ambulances or cars? If a building is burning down, how will fire trucks get there if there's insufficient oil? Deaths could result from these and dozens of other possible scenarios.[38]

The Domino Effect

We may well witness the domino effect when peak oil hits.[39] As soon as fuel supplies decline, one of the first things we will witness is long lines at the gas pumps. Eventually "sold out" signs will appear at gas stations across America. Some of them may have broken windows from angry customers unable to get gas. Gas containers will disappear from stores nationwide. People will begin to hoard fuel.[40] Countries, too, will begin to hoard fuel. The richer countries will likely build massive petroleum reserves to ensure survival. A fuel black market will inevitably emerge. People will be forced to contemplate the extremes to which they are willing to go to heat their homes during the winter and to keep their children warm and fed. All this *and more* may result from peak oil pressures.

1973: A Preview

Many will never forget 1973, the year the Arab nations united in a joint effort to use oil as a weapon, reducing its production below the norm in order to embargo nations—principal target, the United States—that favored Israel. The price of oil quadrupled to twelve dollars per barrel. Higher gas prices resulted in a worldwide economic slowdown.[41] With long lines at the gas pumps, Americans soon realized that a new kind of war was being waged—an economic war. America was brought to its knees by way of the gas pump.[42] That was Act 1. Peak oil theorists say we will soon witness Act 2, which will be considerably more intense.

The Need to Act Now

Some experts believe that if we wait until the peak oil problem emerges in full swing, it may be too late to do anything substantive about it in the short term. Such experts believe we will encounter some of the problems listed above *not* when we fully run out of oil, but *once peak oil arrives*. These experts warn that once we have used up half the oil, "all efforts to produce, distribute, and consume alternative fuels fast enough to fill the gap between falling supplies and rising demand fail."[43] Problems could then escalate quickly.

Other experts deny the likelihood of sudden catastrophe, but they also warn against a false sense of security. Richard Heinberg is representative:

> Because the shift will be incremental, it would be a mistake to assume that the effects...will all occur soon or in an instantaneous fashion. However, it would also be a mistake to assume that they will be so gradual in their appearance that they will accumulate to truly dramatic proportions only in our grandchildren's lifetimes or later. The early effects of the net-energy peak are already upon us and will probably begin to cascade within the next two decades or even the next few years.[44]

Humanity on a Collision Course

I am fully aware of how awful much of this sounds. Keep in mind, however, that these warnings are coming from knowledgeable people—geologists, oil experts, CEOs of oil companies, economists, researchers, and government leaders. Many people are beginning to see dark clouds ahead. At least some are beginning to recognize that our energy system is in serious jeopardy, and that without a fundamentally new approach, we are almost assured of a painful failure.[45] At present no comprehensive plan is in place to deal with an oil shortfall. Congressman Roscoe Bartlett said: "If you ask the question, 'Do we have a plan for what we're going to do when we reach peak oil?' the answer is certainly no."[46] This means that the economic consequences of this crisis will be dire once it finally and fully hits.[47] Only by acting quickly can steps be taken to avert some of these consequences.

Tim Appenzeller, the science editor of *National Geographic*, believes "the world's oil addiction is hastening a day of reckoning." He warns that "humanity's way of life is on a collision course with geology—with the stark fact that the earth holds a finite supply of oil."[48]

Economist Stephen Leeb likewise warns that civilizations throughout history have suffered catastrophic consequences precisely because of the same type of situation we are in today—a shortage of a crucial resource and government leaders unwilling to acknowledge or deal with the problem. It is past time for people to open their eyes![49]

While I am convinced that the phenomenon of peak oil will have serious global consequences, and while I relate all of this to end-times biblical prophecy, I am also a socially concerned Christian who wants the very best for my children and my children's children. It is my hope that my readers will not only become more knowledgeable about how current events may relate to biblical prophecy, but also become actively involved citizens who can be salt and light in our society (Matthew 5:13-14), thereby contributing to positive change.

5

Running on Fumes:
Oil and Our Fragile Economy

The recipe is now in place for a massive economic upheaval in the United States. At present this country is guzzling down oil at an unprecedented rate. In 1985, the United States imported less than 30 percent of its oil. Just five years later, the U.S. imported almost 50 percent of its oil. Today, the U.S. imports 60 percent of its oil. If the current rate of growth continues, by 2015 the U.S. will be importing up to 75 percent of its oil (possibly more). We have a steadily increasing appetite for an increasingly expensive finite resource.

Meanwhile, amazingly, recent news reports reveal that small economical cars are no longer selling well. Americans are buying lots of SUVs—the bigger, the better. Of course, these SUVs do not have near the fuel economy that smaller cars have. At the same time, the consumption of oil in countries such as China and India is increasing explosively, with through-the-roof projections for the coming decades. Because the demand for oil will soon outpace the supply by a large margin, dark economic clouds are gathering on the horizon. The world is barely producing enough oil to supply its present demand. We are nearing a breaking point. We are nearing an oil storm. An economic storm will soon follow.

Joerg Schindler, of the Energy Watch Group, warns that "the world is at the beginning of a structural change of its economic system. This change will be triggered by declining fossil fuel supplies and will influence almost all aspects of our daily life."[1] I documented some aspects of this change in the previous chapter.

Where Is the Payoff?

An economic sign of the times is that oil companies are spending lots of money looking for new oil fields, but there is no real payoff. Robert Beriault, a retired biotechnology laboratory manager who was instrumental in founding the Ottawa-Gatineau Peak Oil Group, observes that exploration does not pay anymore. In recent days, "oil companies spent $8 billion on exploration and discovered only $4 billion worth of new reserves."[2] By necessity, our dependence on Middle Eastern oil will continue to escalate in coming decades.

Significant Declines

It is sobering that the highly respected International Energy Agency (IEA) now acknowledges that the decline in oil in existing oil fields is running at 6.7 percent per year. This is notably worse than the 3.7 percent decline the IEA estimated as recently as 2007. Dr. Fatih Birol, the chief economist at the IEA, said that "if we see a tightness of the markets, people in the street will see it in terms of higher prices, much higher than we see now. It will have an impact on the economy, definitely, especially if we see this tightness in the markets in the next few years." Dr. Birol also said that "even if demand remained steady, the world would have to find the equivalent of four Saudi Arabias to maintain production, and six Saudi Arabias if it is to keep up with the expected increase in demand between now and 2030." He warned that this is "a big challenge in terms of the geology, in terms of the investment, and in terms of the geopolitics. So this is a big risk, and it's mainly because of the rates of the declining oil fields."[3] Birol concluded that the world is heading for a catastrophic energy crunch that could cripple a global economic recovery.[4]

The economic formula is not complicated:

Damage to industry due to a shortage of oil

+

Damage to transportation and
distribution due to a shortage of oil

=

A plummeting economy

The Terrorist Agenda

The picture gets worse, however. Today's terrorists recognize how damaging it could be to the American economy to lose its supply of precious oil. For that reason, they have been trying to gain control of various oil fields. It is well known that Osama bin Laden plotted to overthrow the Saudi Arabian monarchy in 2001 and wrest control of the oil that the West so desperately craves. Had he succeeded, he could have set any oil price he wanted, thereby crippling the West economically.

In 2006, al-Qaeda terrorists sought to wrest control of the Abqaiq oil-processing facility in Saudi Arabia. Though they failed in their effort, they may one day succeed—and if they do, the United States will have no choice but to respond militarily. Many in the Middle East seek the West's economic ruin, and their weapon of choice is oil.

Wealth Continues to Flood Out of the U.S.

Meanwhile, as our own economy is even now suffering, we continue to flood monetary wealth to oil-producing nations that are not big fans of the West. These include Russia, Saudi Arabia, and Venezuela (which owns Citgo), the latter ruled by staunch anti-American Hugo Chavez, who has in recent days been seeking closer ties with Iranian president, Mahmoud Ahmadinejad.

T. Boone Pickens, who announced a $2 billion investment in wind energy in 2008, and who is widely respected for his economic savvy, informed U.S. lawmakers during a hearing on renewable electricity that he expected "the price of oil will go up further." Without alternatives, the cost of foreign oil will continually drain the United States of more resources, he said. "In 10 years, we will have exported close to $10 trillion out of the country if we continue on the same basis we're going now. It is the greatest transfer of wealth in the history of mankind."[5] Pickens indicated that things simply cannot continue as they are.

The last decade provides more than ample proof of the economic danger the United States is in. Back in the late 1990s the price of oil was just ten dollars per barrel. While prices have fluctuated up and down since then, at the time of this writing a barrel costs over eight times as much. Meanwhile, the profits of the OPEC nations have quadrupled over the past decade. The United States is quickly becoming poorer and Middle Eastern nations are getting richer, and at the heart of it all is oil.

No wonder American presidents, one after the other, have been fever-ishly seeking to break America's oil addiction.

This Western infusion of cash into the Middle East has actually been going on for some time. Indeed, award-winning author Edwin Black notes that "the systematic transfer of American wealth and financial health to the Middle East and OPEC has been under way since the Yom Kippur War when the first Arab Oil Embargo was triggered."[6] Mean-while, Hugo Chavez is threatening to raise oil prices to two hundred dollars per barrel if the United States moves against Iran over her pres-ent nuclear ambitions.[7]

The Growing Dilemma with Iran

If the United States *does not* take a stand against Iran's develop-ment of nuclear weaponry, our economy will eventually be even worse off. After all, our best national security experts are saying that the risk of attack by weapons of mass destruction within the next decade may be as high as 70 percent. Senator Richard Lugar, chair of the Senate Foreign Relations Committee, has said that the United States faces an existential threat from terrorists who may get their hands on weapons of mass destruction. In the next decade, we face the very real possibil-ity of nuclear jihad.

This is the primary reason so many are concerned today about Iran. The Bush administration's 2006 foreign policy doctrine affirmed: "We face no greater challenge from a single country than from Iran. We will continue to take all necessary measures to protect our national and economic security against the adverse consequences of their bad con-duct."[8] Iran is a rogue state headed by a fanatical apocalypse-minded leader who is seeking to acquire nuclear weaponry. If Iran ever succeeded in detonating a nuclear weapon in the United States—or if a third-party terrorist group derived such a weapon from Iran and detonated it on U.S. soil—the economic shock would be incalculable.

Economy Killers

Both the nuclear threat *and* the oil threat can potentially be economy-killers. One might be tempted to think that a foreign country's actions related to oil could not do too much damage to those of us here in the mighty United States. However, such a view shows a shallow understanding of global economics. Paul Roberts, in his book *The End of Oil*, speaks of how easily world events can cause severe fluctuations in the oil market. He points out how a single oil "event"—the explosion of an oil pipeline in Iraq, or perhaps political unrest in Venezuela, or hostile words between Russian and Saudi Arabian oil ministers—constitute oil *earthquakes* whose shock waves reverberate throughout the global economic community. Such oil events can push oil prices up or down and set off "tectonic shifts in global wealth and power."[9]

Again, given the central role oil plays in day-to-day life in the United States, if the oil supply is even just threatened verbally by a Middle Eastern leader, significant price fluctuations could occur in the oil markets.

Today oil is so critically important—both politically and economically—that governments of major industrial nations keep as close an eye on the oil markets as they used to on the spread of communism. Why is this? It is primarily because spikes in the price of oil preceded six of the last seven global recessions. For this reason, more than a few economists and policymakers believe that in today's energy-intensive global economy, oil price volatility may be a greater threat than actual terrorist activity. Of course, today the goal of many terrorists is to use oil as a weapon to inflict damage on the U.S. economy, and they may well succeed. If terrorists were able to cause a drop in oil production, and thus block the flow of Middle Eastern oil to the U.S., the economy would suffer immense damage. As one analyst put it, a drop in oil production "will pull one of the blocks out from underneath the pyramid."[10] If that block is removed, everything else collapses.

Is Anyone Listening?

In view of this, one is led to ask: *Is anyone listening?* In previous chapters I noted that many people in the United States are living in denial about the peak oil issue, and they need to be awakened from their stupor. Substantial evidence exists that an unprecedented crisis is just over the horizon. This crisis will cause chaos in the oil industry, in the overall business community, in governments around the world, and in the global economy.[11] People must be made to listen.

Jeremy Leggett, one of the United Kingdom's leading environmentalists and the author of the book *Half Gone* (a book about peak oil), says that both the UK government and the energy industry in general are in "institutionalized denial" regarding peak oil. "For those of us who know that premature peak oil is a clear and present danger, it is impossible to understand such complacency."[12] After all, as a result of oil demand exceeding supply, "major oil-consuming countries will experience crippling inflation, unemployment, and economic instability."[13]

Dr. Fatih Birol at the International Energy Agency says that "many governments now are more and more aware that at least the day of cheap and easy oil is over...[However,] I'm not very optimistic about governments being aware of the difficulties we may face in the oil supply."[14]

Chuck Taylor shares the same concern, noting that "experts say mitigation efforts to minimize the pain of peak oil should have begun 20 or 30 years ago. We missed that window, so what happens now?... Over the next few years, costs of $200 to $500 per barrel are realistic and probable."[15]

Very few political leaders seem to be paying much attention to the peak oil issue. The coming oil storm will have enormous effects on the global economy. In the near future, we may well witness industrialized nations bidding against each other—*bidding higher and higher*—for the dwindling oil supply. Such bidding alone will send shock waves through the global economy.

Meanwhile, Nations Jockey for Control

Inevitably, the ongoing depletion of world oil will eventually create a state of affairs in which nations are literally vying for control of the world's oil fields. As Joel Bainerman put it, "the subsequent decline in availability of fossil fuels could plunge the world into global conflicts as nations struggle to capture their piece of a shrinking pie."[16] *Newsweek* magazine reports:

> We're all jockeying for control of oil fields, in a vast game that runs the risk of turning mean. China and Japan are running warships near disputed oil and natural-gas deposits in the East China Sea. China is doing deals in Sudan, Venezuela, and Iran (our "bad guys"). Russia looks less friendly as we continue to invest in the oil countries around the Caspian Sea—Azerbaijan, Kazakhstan, Turkmenistan.[17]

We are told that "China signed a $100 billion deal with Iran to import 10 million tons of liquefied natural gas over a 25-year period in exchange for a Chinese stake of 50 percent in the development of the Yahavaran oil field in Iran. China is also exploring the feasibility of a direct pipeline to Iran via Kazakhstan."[18] China has also been hosting leaders from Saudi Arabia and Kuwait.

Meanwhile, "Russia is expected to increase the use of its vast energy resources to realize its national objectives, an effort some analysts believe will become more of a 'lever for blackmail.'" Indeed, "the plan to use its energy resources to leverage its national security and foreign policy ambitions comes in a report just issued by the Russian Security Council titled 'National Security Strategy of the Russian Federation up to 2020.'"[19]

All this has particular relevance to the United States, the world's single remaining superpower. One analyst has noted that "oil must remain at the center of U.S. foreign policy because any superpower that wants to *remain* a superpower will do whatever is necessary to ensure this goal."[20] The problem is, of course, that most of the oil-rich countries do not like the United States. "The bad news is that much of the world's oil reserves are in the custody of unstable and sometimes hostile regimes."[21] No wonder there are those who warn that in the near future, "we'll be paying in both treasure and blood, as we fight and parley to keep ever-tighter supplies of world oil flowing our way."[22]

Time Running Out

Governments need to take preemptive steps *now*, for the economic threat is real. Dr. Robert Hirsch, an energy advisor and lead author of a groundbreaking 2005 study on future oil production and declining reserves, was recently asked if the situation had changed any since 2005. He responded that "today, the situation is worse, and the reason for this is that it is now obvious that world oil production is already on a plateau. It has reached a high level, and has leveled off. The point at which oil production will decline is probably not far away."

Hirsch then asserted that if the world had started to implement solutions perhaps 20 years before the peak oil problem, we perhaps could have avoided significant negative consequences for our economy. "As it turns out, we now don't have 20 years; we don't even have 10. It wouldn't surprise me at all if oil production begins to decline within the next few years." He understandably warns that "we are racing towards a future that will be very difficult, and we have to do what is necessary to not economically kill ourselves."[23]

Top Priority: A New Infrastructure

It is not a simple matter of quickly switching from oil to another form of energy. I dealt with this issue earlier in the book. We need to build a new infrastructure that is not oil-based. As oil prices escalate in the coming years, research will continue on affordable alternatives to oil, but it will take a long time for alternatives to penetrate the marketplace. It is impossible to switch from an oil-based infrastructure to another kind of infrastructure overnight.[24] No wonder some analysts have said that the changes in our society as a result of peak oil will be "revolutionary."[25]

Is anyone listening? I fear not. It reminds me of the way it must have been in Noah's time. Noah warned people that the flood was coming, but no one listened.

Addressing the end-times, Jesus warned in Matthew 24:37-39: "For the coming of the Son of Man will be just like the days of Noah. For as in those days before the flood they were eating and drinking, marrying and giving in marriage, until the day that Noah entered the ark and they did not understand until the flood came and took them all away; so will the coming of the Son of Man be." Though I believe this passage has specific reference to the future tribulation period, it is nevertheless noteworthy that one characteristic of people living in the end-times is that they will be calloused toward impending danger.

Oil and the Funding of Terrorism

Radical extremist Islam is growing on a global level. No one—*any-where*—can afford to ignore it. The European Muslim community is an example. Alex Alexiev is vice president for research at the Center for Security Policy and has for several decades directed numerous research projects for the U.S. Defense Department. In a recent work, Alexiev thoroughly documents that an intolerant and violent extremist creed has taken hold throughout Muslim communities in Europe. He is convinced that the fast-spreading anti-Western Islamofascist strain is steadily becoming the dominant face of Islam throughout Europe.[1]

Alexiev documents that "many European Muslims are increasingly willing to engage in violence against their democratic host societies." He notes that 13 percent of British Muslims approve of terrorism, and 1 percent—amounting to sixteen thousand Muslims—said they had "engaged in terrorist activity at home or abroad, or supported such activity." Moreover, some 25 percent of German Muslim school students openly claim they are prepared to use violence on behalf of Islam.[2]

In the Middle East, Islamic radicalism rises to a fever pitch. Anyone even remotely aware of current news headlines knows that radical Islam is pouring—indeed, flooding—out of Iran. This has been thoroughly documented by Ali Ansari, who has written numerous books on the history and politics of Iran and the Middle East. He contends that "Iran is not simply a problem, it's *the* problem. It's not just a member of the Axis of Evil, but the founding member, the chief sponsor of state terrorism, or to use a more recent characterization, the central banker for terrorism."[3]

A *U.S. News and World Report* article provides substantive evidence that "Iran today is the mother of Islamic terrorism." We are told that "Tehran openly provides funding, training, and weapons to the world's worst terrorists, including Hezbollah, Hamas, the Palestinian Islamic Jihad, and the Popular Front for the Liberation of Palestine, and it has a cozy relationship with al Qaeda."[4]

In today's Islamic radicalism in Iran, there is an apocalyptic strain of Muslim theology that has many political leaders concerned. This strain has been thoroughly documented by Dore Gold, who has served as Israel's ambassador to the United Nations (1997–1999), was a foreign policy advisor to Prime Minister Benjamin Netanyahu of Israel, and has served as a diplomatic envoy to the leaders of Egypt, Jordan, the Persian Gulf states, and the Palestinian Authority. In a recent book, Gold speaks about this apocalyptic aspect of Islam:

> According to Islamic doctrine of recent centuries, the concept of jihad has evolved into an eschatological [end-times] concept reserved for the future. Accordingly, pious Muslims are expected to proselytize their religion and gain converts worldwide, an activity known as da'wa. Then, at the apocalyptic end of days, mainstream Muslims envision that a great, armed jihad will result in the subjugation of the entire world to Islam. Militant Wahhabism, however, reverses the order of da'wa and jihad, advancing jihad to the present day as a precursor for spreading Islam.

> Hence, almost by definition, militant Islam is an apocalyptic movement preparing in the present for a final confrontation with the West and with others opposed to its agenda. It brings scenarios from the end of days to the here and now. It is therefore not surprising to find apocalyptic references in the speeches of jihadist leaders like Abu Musab al-Zarqawi, the former head of al-Qaeda in Iraq.[5]

A look at Islamic history reveals that Shiite Muslims have long believed in the eventual return of the Twelfth Imam, believed to be a direct (bloodline) descendant of Muhammad's son-in-law, Ali, whose family, it is believed, constitutes the only legitimate successors to Muhammad. The Twelfth Imam—who allegedly disappeared as a child in A.D.

941—will return in the future as the Mahdi ("the rightly guided One"). He will allegedly create a messianic-like era of global order and justice for Shiites in which Islam will be triumphant.

It is believed that the time of the appearance of the Twelfth Imam can be hastened through apocalyptic chaos and violence—that is, by unleashing an apocalyptic holy war against Christians and Jews. It is thus believed that it is within man's power to bring about the end of days. It is within man's power to influence the divine timetable. Interestingly, a number of Shiite leaders in Iran claim they have seen the Twelfth Imam and that he will reveal himself to the world soon, presumably following the imminent eruption in chaos and violence.

This alarming aspect of extremist Muslim theology relates directly to current Iranian president Mahmoud Ahmadinejad, who boasts: "Our revolution's main mission is to pave the way for the reappearance of the Twelfth Imam, the Mahdi."[6] Ahmadinejad apparently informed his cabinet that in just a few more years the Twelfth Imam will appear. He makes this bold claim because of his own intention to play the critical role in ousting the Jews from Israel. Gold warns that "for Ahmadinejad, the destruction of Israel is one of the key global developments that will trigger the appearance of the Mahdi."[7] Indeed, Ahmadinejad seeks to "wipe Israel off the map"—a phrase he borrowed from the deceased mullah, Ayatollah Khomeini.[8]

The Muslim goal is to attain "a world without America and Zionism," and once this goal is reached, the Twelfth Imam can be expected to return. Ahmadinejad is sure that humanity will soon know what it is like to live in a Jew-free and USA-free world. He has assured the world that "the United States and the Zionist regime of Israel will soon come to the end of their lives," according to the Islamic Republic of Iran Broadcasting's website.[9] Iran's state-run television network has in recent years been airing a series of programs that delineate the signs of the end of the world. These programs are designed to prepare Iran for the arrival of the Mahdi.[10]

During a military parade, Ahmadinejad had a banner proclaiming "Death to America" draped over one of Iran's long-range missiles.[11] He seems sure that the world will soon be without the Great Satan (the USA) and the Little Satan (Israel), and this will give rise to the emergence of the Twelfth Imam.

Ahmadinejad is convinced that this apocalyptic event will occur in his lifetime. He believes he was chosen by Allah himself to play a role in ushering in the end of days. Indeed, he claims to be one of a select group of elite men specifically chosen by the Twelfth Imam to be his representatives in the world prior to his return.

Ahmadinejad has no intention or desire to be secretive about his extremist Islamic views. His speech at the United Nations several years back even invoked the soon arrival of the Islamic Messiah: "O mighty Lord, I pray to you to hasten the emergence of your last repository, the Promised One, that perfect and pure human being, the One that will fill this world with justice and peace." Once back in Iran, as documented in a videotaped meeting with a prominent ayatollah in Tehran, Ahmadinejad waxed mystical, claiming that during his U.N. speech he was surrounded by a light that utterly changed the atmosphere: "For 27 or 28 minutes all the leaders did not blink; it's not an exaggeration, because I was looking. They were astonished, as if a hand held them there and made them sit. It had opened their eyes and ears for the message of the Islamic Republic."[12] More recently, during Ahmadinejad's 2009 speech at the U.N., he again invoked the soon coming of the Mahdi.

There is good reason to be alarmed at such statements. Kenneth Timmerman, one of the world's top experts on Iran, comments that "Ahmadinejad's 'vision' at the United Nations could be dismissed as pure political posturing if it weren't for a string of similar statements and actions that clearly suggest he believes he is destined to bring about the End Times—the end of the world—by paving the way for the return of the Shia Muslim messiah...Given the fact that the Islamic Republic of Iran continues to pursue suspect nuclear programs, having a leader with a messianic vision is no cause to rejoice."[13] It is frightening to ponder that Ahmadinejad, in his warped thinking, may be convinced he can invoke the coming of the Islamic messiah by the mere push of a button.

There is no doubt that Iran—at this moment—is using some of its oil profits to fund terrorist activities around the world. Its oil revenues are financing its version of Islamofascism and underwriting Tehran's support of the world's most dangerous Islamist movements—not the least of which is the Lebanon-based terrorist group Hezbollah[14] (more on this below). Thomas D. Kraemer, of the Strategic Studies Institute of the U.S. Army War College, expresses concern that "America is buying billions of dollars of oil from nations that are sponsors of, or allied with, radical Islamists who foment hatred against the United States. The dollars we provide such nations contribute materially to the terrorist threats facing America."[15]

The horrific irony is that at present the United States finds itself in the untenable position of spending great amounts of money to fight terrorism while at the same time spending great amounts of money to purchase oil that ends up funding terrorism.[16] How in the world did such a state of affairs come to be? Kraemer laments that "in the war on terror, the United States is financing both sides. While spending billions of dollars on U.S. military efforts in the war, we are sending billions more to nations such as Saudi Arabia, Iran, and the Sudan, where the cash is used to finance training centers for terrorists, pay bounties to the families of suicide bombers, and fund the purchase of weapons and explosives."[17] How tragic to recognize that Americans, with their own money, are subsidizing acts of war *against themselves*.

The Jihad Backdrop

Jihad has become a household word in America today. We read about it in our magazines and newspapers and hear about it on the evening news. Bestselling books have been written on it. Television specials on the issue have received high ratings. We will see below that a strong connection exists between oil money in Middle Eastern countries and jihad in its various expressions around the world.

Early in Muhammad's career, when he was living in Mecca, he never made mention of jihad. Scholars have suggested that the reason for this is that during those early years he lacked a strong following and any military might whatsoever. Once in Medina, however, he was able to build a strong following and a strong military. Jihad suddenly became a topic of major Quranic revelation.[18]

Eventually Muhammad's movement took on the character of religious militarism. He transformed his followers into fanatical fighters by teaching them that if they died fighting Allah's cause, they would be instantly admitted to paradise. Also during this time, Muhammad's followers were given divine sanction to raid caravans en route to Mecca. The spoils were divided among Muhammad's men, with Muhammad keeping one-fifth of everything. Not unexpectedly, these caravan raids led to war with the Meccans.

It was not long before jihad became an emphasis in Muhammad's teaching. Jihad comes from the Arabic word *jahada*, which principally means "to struggle" or "to strive in the path of Allah." The term has been used in recent years in connection with terrorist activities around the world. It seems that whenever the United States takes a stand against terrorist Muslims, a jihad or "holy war" is declared against the States. The term is more generally taken among Muslims to refer to armed fighting and warfare in defending Islam and standing against evil.

To be accurate, however, some Muslims have held to less dangerous forms of jihad. One example of this is a jihad of the pen, which involves engaging in a written defense of Islam.[19] Scholar Frederick Mathewson Denny thus clarifies that "holy war" doesn't fully capture the meaning of jihad, although that is certainly part of it. Denny says that for Muslims there is a greater jihad and a lesser jihad.[20] A person's struggle with his own vices, the evil tendencies in his soul, and his lack of faith is considered the greater jihad. Jihad in this sense is more of a spiritual struggle or striving.

The lesser jihad involves engaging in armed struggle against the enemies of Islam.[21] Islam scholar Jamal Elias claims that for most Muslims today, "any war that is viewed as a defense of one's own country, home, or community is called a jihad. This understanding is very similar to what is called 'just war' in Western society."[22]

In modern times, radical Islamic fundamentalists are well known for their use of arms and explosives in defending their version of Islam. Jihad, in their thinking, has the goal of terrorizing perceived enemies of Islam into submission and retreat.[23] Such Muslims seek to emulate the behavior of Muhammad (Sura 33:21), for he often led Islamic forces into battle to make Islam dominant during his time. He shed other people's blood to bolster Islam throughout the Arabian Peninsula.[24] As one Islamic expert put it, "Muhammad's mission was to conquer the world for Allah. The goal of jihad, or holy war, is to establish Islamic authority over the whole world. Islam teaches that Allah is the only authority, and all political systems must be based on Allah's teaching."[25] Islamic history clearly reveals that jihad has been a primary tool of religious expansionism for Muhammad's religion.

It is wise to take this radical form of jihad seriously given the sheer number of radical Muslims threatening it and the growing availability of weapons of mass destruction. Though radical Islamic fundamentalists constitute a minority of Muslims, even a minority can be a substantial threat. As one researcher put it, "Since we are talking about 1.3 billion adherents to Islam, even a 'very small minority' can involve tens of millions of people who have the potential to cause a great deal of trouble in the world, not only for America, but for moderate Muslim governments as well."[26]

The Quran is often cited by Islamic fundamentalists in support of their view that armed conflict is permissible and even compulsory in the defense of Islam. In Sura 2:216 we read, "Fighting is prescribed for you, and ye dislike it. But it is possible that ye dislike a thing which is good for you." In Sura 47:4 we read, "Therefore, when ye meet the unbelievers (in fight), smite at their necks; At length, when ye have thoroughly subdued them, bind a bond firmly (on them)." Sura 9:5 says, "But when the forbidden months are past, then fight and slay the pagans wherever ye find them, and seize them, beleaguer them, and lie in wait for them in every stratagem (of war)."

Verses such as these no doubt led five Muslim caliphates (governments), representing five radical Muslim factions, to sign a *fatwa* (written decision) in 1998 declaring a holy war against the United States. The document they signed contains the following words:

> For over seven years the United States has been occupying the lands of Islam and the holiest of places, the Arabian Peninsula, plundering its riches, dictating to its rulers, humiliating its people, terrorizing its neighbors, and turning its bases in the Peninsula into a spearhead through which to fight the neighboring Muslim peoples...[There has been] aggression against the Iraqi people...[Their aim has been to] serve the Jews' petty state...[They express] eagerness to destroy Iraq...All these crimes and sins committed by the Americans are a clear declaration of war on Allah, his messenger, and Muslims...The ruling to kill the Americans and their allies—civilians and military—is an individual duty for every Muslim who can do it in any country in which it is possible to do it...This is in accordance with the words of Almighty Allah, "and fight the pagans altogether

as they fight you altogether," and "fight them until there is no
more tumult or oppression, and there prevail justice and faith
in Allah."[27]

There is little doubt that the September 11, 2001, attack against the
World Trade Center and the Pentagon was a manifestation of this *fatwa*,
written just three years earlier. Americans have taken jihad very seriously
since that day. They also take jihad more seriously in view of Ahmadinejad's campaign of jihad terror against Israel, and his continued threats
of "harm and pain" against the United States.

A religious motivation exists for many Muslims to participate in jihad,
for any Muslim who loses his or her life in service to Allah is guaranteed
entrance into paradise (Hadith 9:459). According to Muslim tradition,
Muhammad said: "The person who participates in (Holy battles) in
Allah's cause and nothing compels him to do so except belief in Allah
and His Apostles, will be recompensed by Allah either with a reward,
or booty (if he survives) or will be admitted to Paradise (if he is killed
in the battle as a martyr)" (Hadith 1:35). This is highly significant to
Muslims, for there is virtually *no other way* a Muslim can be assured of
going to heaven or paradise. Aside from this, it is also often taught that
a Muslim martyr (a suicide bomber, for example) can vouch for family
members and friends so that they, too, go to paradise for his "heroic"
and "religious" act.

Islamic Motivations

At the heart of Muslim hostilities against Israel (and the United
States) is the fact that Jerusalem is the holiest of cities for the Jews and
the third holiest city for Muslims, behind Mecca and Medina. Jews
believe Jerusalem belongs to them alone, by divine right. Muslims, too,
believe Jerusalem belongs to them alone, by divine right. Since neither
side will budge, conflict is inevitable.

On the Arab or Muslim side, Anwar Sadat once proclaimed that
"Jerusalem is the property of the Muslim nation...Nobody can ever
decide the fate of Jerusalem. We shall re-take it with the help of Allah."
Likewise, Yasser Arafat once promised that "whoever does not accept the
fact that Jerusalem will be the capital of a Palestinian state, and only that
state, can go drink from the Dead Sea." On the Jewish side, Benjamin

Netanyahu—with equal vigor—promised: "I will never allow Jerusalem to be divided again. Never! Never! We will keep Jerusalem united and... we will never surrender those ramparts." Israel—and anyone who supports Israel (such as the United States)—is thus now targeted by Muslims, especially the extremists.

Ever since the Jews returned to their homeland in 1948, they have been at great risk from the Arab/Muslim nations that surround them. Had Israel not developed a powerful military, and had the United States not remained a committed ally of Israel, Israel probably would not be around today.

Walid Phares, author of a fascinating book titled *Future Jihad*, says that "as the Jewish state became a reality and prospered, Islamists viewed the entire existence of Israel as an aggression. The initial settlement was illegitimate to start with; Jews had no right to 'return' or come back to an Islamic land." Muslim resentment toward the Jews is based on "the principle of a non-Muslim state reemerging on a Muslim land. Following the logic of the Fatah and of jihad, any territory that was at some time 'opened' by a legitimate Islamic authority cannot revert to a non-Islamic authority."[28] Clearly, then, Islamic resentment toward the Jews in Israel is in the first place religiously motivated, not politically motivated.

It is with this backdrop in mind that the ever-increasing hostilities of Iran against Israel are of such grave concern to many today. Since 2000, Iran has assumed the leading role in the Palestinian insurgency against Israel. Iran funnels both arms and money to terrorists active in the West Bank and the Gaza Strip. Iran even offers $50,000 to the families of Palestinian suicide bombers. In a country where many citizens are not "rolling in cash," that is a strong motivation.

There is also grave concern over Iran's escalating military capabilities. Ilan Berman tells us that "over the past several years, Israeli military planners have viewed Iran's burgeoning strategic arsenal with mounting alarm. According to top Israeli intelligence officials, Iran's nuclear program now constitutes the single greatest 'threat to the existence of Israel' since the Jewish state's founding in 1948."[29] All eyes are understandably on the Middle East today.

Conflicting Ideologies

During the nineteenth and twentieth centuries, three significant ideologies emerged in the Middle East: Zionism, Arab Nationalism, and Islamic Fundamentalism. Understanding these ideologies gives us a handle on current Arab/Muslim and Israeli hostilities.

Zionism. Zionism gets its name from Mount Zion, the hill in ancient Jerusalem where King David's palace once stood. Zion became a symbol for Jerusalem during David's reign (see 2 Samuel 5:7). Zionism is another name for a type of Jewish nationalism whose goal is to reestablish the Jewish ancestral homeland. It involves not just the idea that the Jews have returned to the Land, but includes the return of Jewish sovereignty to the ancestral homeland. Zionism, then, is essentially a national liberation movement of the Jewish people. Christians who uphold the right of the Jewish people to return to the Land and establish an independent state are often referred to as "Christian Zionists."

Arab Nationalism. Arab Nationalism emerged as a movement that seeks to unify Arabs as one people by appealing to their common history, culture, and language. This movement is secular, and its goal is to gain and maintain Arab power in the Arab lands of the Middle East. Arab nationalists seek to end, or at least minimize, direct Western influence in the Arab world. As well, Israel is viewed as a cancerous tumor that must be removed.

Islamic Fundamentalism. Islamic fundamentalism is a religious philosophy that seeks to establish Islamic dominance in the Middle East and eventually the rest of the world. Israel, a symbol of Jewish power, is viewed as a grievous insult to Allah and cannot be allowed to exist. Israel must therefore be pushed into the sea.

Mix these three ideologies together and you've got an explosive situation on your hands. That is precisely what we are witnessing today! Alarmingly, the Arab and Muslim fanatics in this battle are finding monetary support from the oil-rich nations of the Middle East.

The Funding of Terrorism

The evidence is massive and it is thoroughly convincing. As Wayne Simmons, former CIA operative, put it: "The major funding of terror is definitely oil."[30] In what follows, I will briefly consider some specific ways that oil money has been used to spread Islam, especially radical Islam and terrorism.

Saudi Arabia and Influence on U.S. Education

Oil-rich Saudi Arabia spends immense amounts of oil money to influence American policy and education. The Saudis are interested in exporting not only their *oil* but also their *Islamic ideology*. Cultural critic Mark Steyn, the author of *America Alone: The End of the World as We Know It*, said in an interview that we tend to think that "Saudi Arabia's principal export is oil. It's not, it's ideology. All oil does is enable them to have the money to export their ideology."[31] Let us be clear on this one fundamental fact: *The Saudis want to change the way people think. And they are using their money toward that end.*

Clare Lopez, a former CIA analyst, reveals that one of the principal means the Saudis use to spread Islamic influence is to endow academic departments of Middle Eastern studies at various respected universities throughout the United States. "The Saudis have given tens of millions of dollars to American universities. In the case of Georgetown and Harvard, it was in the amount of $20 million." The students who go to these universities are taught the Saudi point of view on Islam.

Dr. Juhdi Jasser, president of the American Islamic Forum for Democracy, suggests that the Saudis have been successful in penetrating American universities by portraying their goal in a politically correct way. Such Saudi-funded courses are portrayed as "bridging the gap between Islam and Christianity." The absurdity of this, Jasser says, is more than evident when one considers that "there isn't even one church in all of Saudi Arabia," and that "it is an offense for a non-Muslim to even set foot in Mecca, Islam's holiest city."[32]

It would appear that the Saudis are seeking to influence the future leaders of the United States, and they are using oil money to accomplish this task. In the documentary film *The Third Jihad: Radical Islam's Vision for America*, we are told that "petrodollars are invested on campuses"—classrooms where America's future diplomats are being trained. Once they join the ranks of the U.S. government, they apply the principles they were taught by the instructors and professors who are "sitting on Jihadhi grants." This video categorizes this as "diplomatic jihad."

As a backdrop, one must not forget that America is a country well known for its freedom of thought and freedom of expression. Today the enemies of America are using this freedom to their own advantage by seeking to influence the minds of our young people more favorably toward Islam and Islamic goals. It is time for America to wake up to what is going on here.

At the same time, Islamic apologists scattered all over America are training fellow Muslims with arguments against the Bible, against the deity of Christ, against the work of Christ on the cross, against the Trinity, and against the Christian gospel. Meanwhile, American Christians often go about with nary a concern, oblivious to what is going on around them. It is time for Christians to awaken from this stupor and stand boldly for the truth of Jesus Christ.

Saudi Arabia, Islamic Proselytizing, and Wahhabism

As documented throughout the book, Saudi Arabia is raking in hundreds of billions of dollars every year in oil revenues. Where is the money being used? According to Bernard Lewis, professor emeritus of Near Eastern studies at Princeton University, at least two of the ways the money is being used are to 1) promote the Saudi version of Islam, and 2) to fund terrorist movements. Lewis emphasizes that fifteen of the nineteen hijackers on the 9/11 jets were of Saudi origin.[33]

It also seems clear that some of the Saudi money goes to colleges for Islamic instruction called *madrassas*. In an interview with Larry King, former Secretary of Defense Donald Rumsfeld pointed out:

> There's a lot of money going into these so-called madrassas—and they aren't training people in mathematics or languages or sciences or whatever, humanities—they're training people to kill. They're training people to go out and kill innocent men, women, and children. And we need to see that those schools are closed down, and we need to see that those schools provided [are] teaching the right things, so that people can live a constructive life in this world.[34]

A Saudi publication, *Ain-al-Yaqeen*, boasts that the royal family and the Saudi Kingdom have spent billions of dollars to spread Islam around the globe. For example, they have underwritten Islamic Centers in Brussels, Belgium ($5 million), Geneva, Switzerland ($7 million), and Madrid, Spain ($8 million). All told, Saudi oil money has underwritten over two hundred Islamic centers, over fifteen hundred mosques, over two hundred colleges, and over two thousand schools for educating Muslim children in non-Islamic countries.[35] Saudi oil money supports Islamic education on a massive global level.

Despite U.S. requests that the Saudis stop funding extremist groups, they have in reality taken only baby steps in that direction. The Saudis continue to promote Wahhabism, a strictly orthodox and extremist form of Sunni Islam that advocates a return to the early Islam of the Quran and Sunna (tradition), rejecting all later innovations.[36] This form of Islam is named after Muhammad ihn Abd al Wahhab, who lived from 1703 to 1792. Former CIA director R. James Woolsey says that it is in this hostile Wahhabism soil that anti-Western and anti-American terrorist weeds grow.

Wahhabism advocates jihad to spread Islam and to defeat all enemies. Brigitte Gabriel, in her book *Because They Hate: A Survivor of Islamic Terror Warns America*, tells us that the Wahhabi teachings are like a "toxic tsunami of religious hatred that Saudi Arabia has unleashed here in the United States." She notes that Wahhabis "say that all religions but Islam are false, and that it is the religious duty of every Muslim to impose functionally Islamic governments on every country in the world."[37] The Islamic Society of North America (ISNA) is the front organization through which the Saudis promote Wahhabism in the U.S.[38]

The Funding of Al-Qaeda

Al-Qaeda is a term that literally means "the base" (or military base) in Arabic. Al-Qaeda has sought to diminish American influence in the Middle East, particularly in Israel and Iraq, and has sought to oust American troops from Saudi Arabian soil. The al-Qaeda network seeks to fund, recruit, train, and coordinate Islamic militants and extremist organizations across the globe. Many members of al-Qaeda envision the establishment of a caliphate—a single Islamic state ruled by a caliph, a successor of Muhammad—across all Muslim lands, similar to the Taliban model. While al-Qaeda has been on the run from the U.S. military, the organization is still alive and well.

Al-Qaeda was first established in Afghanistan in 1982 by Palestinian sheikh Abdallah Yussuf Azzam and Osama bin Laden, the seventeenth of fifty-two children of a wealthy Saudi construction magnate. The bin Laden family wealth is calculated to hover around $5 billion, with Osama's cut being in the vicinity of $300 million.

To date, bin Laden's al-Qaeda terrorist cells have penetrated ninety-four countries around the world, and they are growing. Al-Qaeda training camps in Afghanistan and Pakistan have equipped around seventy thousand Islamic fighters from some fifty-five countries. They spread like a hidden virus, forging alliances with both Muslim and non-Muslim terrorists, as well as with organized crime. U.S. deputy secretary of defense Paul Wolfowitz thus testified before the Senate that "al Qaeda is not a snake that can be killed by lopping off its head...it is more analogous to a disease that has infected many parts of a healthy body."[39]

As for the funding of al-Qaeda, the "smoking gun" clearly points to the Saudis. Rachel Ehrenfeld, author of a ground-breaking book titled *Funding Evil: How Terrorism Is Financed—and How to Stop It*, says al-Qaeda funding includes the oil-rich Saudi royal family, Saudi charitable organizations, Saudi banks and financial networks, Saudi businesses (including real estate, publishing, software, and construction companies), and Saudi criminal activities (for example, credit card fraud, the pirating of compact discs, prostitution rings, and the sale of illegal drugs). Despite multiple sources of funding, the lion's share is rooted in Saudi oil money, clear and simple.[40]

One might be surprised that Saudi charitable organizations are helping to fund al-Qaeda. The truth is, such charities do not operate the way you might think. Muslims are expected to give alms (*zakat*) to the Muslim community that amount to one-fortieth (or 2.5 percent) of one's income. *Zakat* literally means "to be pure," and signifies the purifying of one's soul.[41] The offering is supposed to benefit widows, orphans, and the sick, or it can be used toward furthering Islam (for example, building mosques and religious schools). Giving to charity is considered an extremely meritorious act in Islam (see Suras 24:56; 57:18). The gift is to be done with the conscious awareness that all things ultimately belong to Allah, and that each person is a mere trustee for a limited time on earth.[42]

Muslim tradition affirms that Allah withholds his blessing from those who withhold alms (Hadith 2:515). Tradition also indicates that one can nullify salvation by withholding charity (Hadith 2:486). "Save yourself from Hell-fire even by giving half a date-fruit in charity" (Hadith 2:498). Muhammad said almsgiving was important because society is like a body with many parts. If one part of the society suffers, all of society suffers, and hence the other "body parts" of society rally in response.[43]

Different Muslim communities handle charity in different ways. In some communities it is up to the individual Muslim to make a charitable contribution to the Islamic cause of his choice—generally a local charity. Some Muslims give the money to their local mosque or to a respected Islamic leader, who then applies the funds to good use. In other Muslim communities a *zakat* tax is collected by the government. The income derived from this tax is then used either for social benefit (building schools, for example) or for religious purposes.

In Saudi Arabia, as well as in Kuwait, the United Arab Emirates, and other oil-rich Islamic countries, *the respective governments control the charities and actually make substantial contributions to them.* We are talking major bucks here, for these charities collectively have a treasure chest worth over $4 billion. Although much of the money has gone to support humanitarian tasks in Islamic territories, "a significant amount of money has been diverted, directly or indirectly, to fund terrorism."[44] More to the point, Saudi charities have helped to fund al-Qaeda and jihad! Al-Qaeda thus remains alive and well because the finances are there to fuel it.

The Funding of Hamas

Hamas is an Arabic term that literally means "Islamic Resistance Movement." The organization was founded by Sheikh Ahmed Yassin in 1987 in order to wage jihad to liberate Palestine and to establish an Islamic Palestinian state. It has both a military wing and a sociopolitical wing, the latter engaging in such activities as building hospitals, running health clinics and schools, and aiding the poor.

Members of Hamas believe that negotiations with the Israelis are a waste of time because the Arabs and the Israelis cannot coexist. The military wing has committed countless terrorist attacks against Israel, including hundreds of suicide bombings. Yassin once called on Iraqis to "become human bombs, using belts and suitcases aimed at killing every enemy that walks on the earth and pollutes it."[45] President George W. Bush categorized Hamas as one of the deadliest terrorist organizations in the world. One often finds supporters carrying signs saying, "Death to USA."

There is no question that Hamas has widespread funding, including from Iran, Saudi Arabia, the Gulf States, the United Arab Emirates, Syria, and Iraq, among others. Untold millions upon millions of oil dollars are funneled to Hamas by these nations in order to continue its jihad. This is clearly oil-sponsored terrorism.

The Funding of Hezbollah

Hezbollah, literally, the "party of God," is a Lebanese umbrella organization of radical Islamic Shiites who hate Israel and oppose the West. Founded in 1982, they are deeply entrenched in terrorism. They believe Israel occupies land that belongs only to the Muslims, and they will resort to any level of violence and terror to rectify the situation. They advocate the establishment of Shiite Islamic rule in Lebanon and the liberation of all "occupied Arab lands," including Jerusalem. Hezbollah has continually vowed to destroy Israel and establish an Islamic state in Lebanon. They also seek to eliminate Jews worldwide.

From the inception of the organization, it has had deep ties to both Iran and Syria. This is highly significant, for Yossef Bodansky, the director of the Congressional Task Force on Terrorism and Unconventional Warfare, tells us that "ultimately the key to effective terrorism in and out of the Arab world is firmly in the hands of the two main sponsoring states—Iran and Syria."[46] Large infusions of cash come into Hezbollah from these two states.

Hezbollah's Secretary-General Hassan Nasrallah has openly acknowledged that it receives funds from oil-rich Tehran to support its terrorist activities. In earlier years, Iran provided some $60 to $100 million annually to Hezbollah, and then increased the amount in 2001 to $10 million per month. This money is provided by Iran specifically to be used in terrorist activities against Israel. Iran also assists in providing weaponry, explosives, organizational aid, instructors, and political support.[47]

Multiple news reports have indicated that Syria provides not only shelter and financing to Hezbollah, it also supplies the group with weaponry, as well as thousands of long-range rockets, from its own stockpiles. Training facilities are also provided, along with logistical and technological support for attacks against Israel.

The Funding of Palestinian Islamic Jihad

The Palestinian Islamic Jihad is a militant Islamic group based in Damascus, Syria. They are dedicated to the destruction of Israel and the establishment of an Islamic state in Palestine. It emerged in the 1970s and has engaged in large-scale suicide bombing attacks against Israeli civilians as well as military targets.

Not surprisingly, Iran's oil money helps to underwrite this organization. As well, Syria has provided safe haven, finances, arms, and training for the group. One Damascus radio broadcast boasted that "Syria has turned its land into a training camp, a safe haven and an arms depot for the Palestinian revolutionaries."[48] According to Palestinian intelligence documents discovered by the Israelis in 2002, money transferred from Iran and Syria to Palestinian terrorist groups is used for preparing terrorist attacks against Israel, supporting families of dead and detained terrorists, procuring arms, and purchasing equipment for terrorist attacks.[49]

Are We Funding Our Own Demise?

The United States has been self-defeating in its policies, sending a veritable tidal wave of wealth to Middle Eastern nations as we purchase their oil. Much of that oil money is then used to fund terrorist acts against the U.S. It is no wonder that Jim Woolsey, former CIA director during the Clinton administration, suggested: "When we pull into the gasoline pump we probably ought to turn the mirror a little bit and look ourselves in the eye for just a second before we get the credit card out and charge it, because if we want to know who's paying for these madrassas around the world that are teaching little eight-year-old boys to be suicide bombers, and the oppression of everyone else, you and I are, as we pay for that gasoline."[50] Perhaps Woolsey is not the world's most eloquent man, but who would dare deny the wisdom of his words?

If I am correct that biblical prophecy implies that the United States may weaken and the United States of Europe will become the economic powerhouse in the end-times, ruled by the Antichrist, then the oil funding of terrorism has high relevance for how such a state of affairs might be brought about. I will discuss this further in the next chapter.

Will the Oil Card Be Played
Against the United States?

The Middle East/Persian Gulf area has close to 60 percent of the known oil reserves in the world. This not only means tremendous wealth for the Middle Eastern nations, but also makes the United States vulnerable to being blackmailed by these nations. The United States faces "serious geopolitical challenges: Most oil remaining is in unstable, hostile parts of the world."[1] Experts inform us that the oil in the Middle East "will be the last left as the rest of the world's production declines, from Africa to Russia and the United States."[2]

Our best estimates are that the proven oil reserves are around 1 trillion to 1.2 trillion barrels. If you can imagine a pie, Saudi Arabia controls about a fourth of the pie, with 26 percent of the remaining oil (260 billion barrels). Iraq has 11 percent (113 billion barrels), Kuwait has about 10 percent (97 billion barrels), and Iran has 10 percent (100 billion barrels). These four Middle Eastern nations control 57 percent of the remaining oil in the world. That is very good for the Middle East but very bad for the West. Some experts believe that Iraq has a lot more than 11 percent of the remaining oil reserves, perhaps as high as 25 percent. All these nations will be major players in the oil market in the end-times.

The very countries that possess the natural resources to help the United States with its immense consumption of oil are precisely those countries that have the most intense hatred of Americans. They may eventually play the "oil card" against the United States. Americans must come to realize that oil can function as part and parcel of the radical

Islamic arsenal of weapons. Because the Islamic mullahs recognize they are sitting on one of the massive pools of available oil, they believe they have power and leverage. One analyst suggests that "the prestige of having a corner on a commodity as important to the world economy as oil is only equaled in the eyes of the mullahs with the prestige they imagine they will have once they possess nuclear weapons. The prospect of possessing two weapons so powerful—oil plus nuclear weapons—is a terrorist's dream."[3]

In a stark warning to Western nations, Dr. Fatih Birol of the International Energy Agency said that "the market power of the very few oil-producing countries that hold substantial reserves of oil—mostly in the Middle East—would increase rapidly as the oil crisis begins to grip" in the very near future.[4] Bottom line: The Middle East will strengthen as the United States weakens.

Will the Middle Eastern nations be successful in using oil as a weapon to weaken the United States? Will the oil card really be played against this country? Will this country experience oil blackmail? There are many prophetic experts who think so.

In some of my previous books I have wrestled with the issue of America in Bible prophecy, and how America might relate to end-time events. In what follows, I will provide a brief summary of the basic interpretive options, and then I will zero in on the connection I see between oil and America's demise.

The Decline of America

The terms *America* and *United States* do not appear anywhere in Scripture. Some believe that America is only indirectly mentioned in Bible prophecy. For example, there are a number of general prophetic references to "the nations" in the Tribulation that may include the United States. Zechariah 12:2-3 is a good example, where God affirms: "Behold, I am going to make Jerusalem a cup that causes reeling to *all the peoples* around; and when the siege is against Jerusalem, it will also be against Judah. It will come about in that day that I will make Jerusalem a heavy stone for *all the peoples*; all who lift it will be severely injured. And *all the nations* of the earth will be gathered against it" (emphasis added). General passages such as this one, however, do not tell us anything specific about any possible unique role of the United States in the end-times.

Others believe that even though the United States is not specifically mentioned in biblical prophecy, perhaps the United States will, in the end-times, be in general cooperation with Europe—the revived Roman Empire headed by a powerful leader, the Antichrist. Since many U.S. citizens have come from Europe, it would be natural for the U.S. to become an ally of this Roman power in the end-times. I think this is a viable option, and I will address it a bit more later in the chapter.

Still other Bible students see parallels between Babylon the Great in the book of Revelation and the United States (or, more narrowly, New York City). After all, both Babylon and the United States are dominant, both are immoral, both are excessively rich, and both think they are invulnerable. However, most serious Bible interpreters do not give much credence to this theory. This view seems based more on *eisegesis* (reading a meaning into the text) than *exegesis* (deriving the meaning out of the text).

Some prophecy interpreters suggest that the United States may be the fulfillment of Isaiah 18:1-7, with its reference to a land "divided by rivers," since the U.S. is divided by the Mississippi River. The reference to this nation being feared because of its military conquests is seen as supportive evidence for this view. The big problem, however, is that the nation is explicitly identified in Isaiah 18:1-2 as ancient Cush, or modern Sudan.

Some of my prophecy-loving friends believe the reference to the land of Tarshish in Ezekiel 38:13 may involve the United States. Others argue that it refers to Spain, and others say Great Britain, and still others say it refers to all the western nations of the end-times. There is no consensus and no definitive proof in the context that this is a reference to the United States.

Still other Christians—I include myself in this group—think a good case can be made that America is not mentioned in Bible prophecy at all. If this is the case, the more immediate question becomes: *Why isn't* America mentioned in Bible prophecy? There are a number of viable possibilities.

Most Nations Not Mentioned

Perhaps the United States is not mentioned because, generally speaking, most nations of the world are not mentioned in biblical prophecy.

If this view is correct, then there is little significance in America not being mentioned in Bible prophecy. The problem I see with this view is that America is the world's only remaining superpower and is at the same time a powerful ally of Israel. Since Israel is at the very heart of biblical prophecy, one might naturally expect there to be at least some passing reference to its most powerful ally, especially with Israel being so endangered in the end-times.

No Significant Role

Another possibility is that the United States is not mentioned in biblical prophecy simply because it does not play a major role in end-times events. Still, as I noted above, the United States is the world's single remaining superpower that also happens to be Israel's principal ally, supporting Israel with vast sums of money and military aid. Hence, we might naturally expect the United States to be mentioned, at least minimally. So perhaps this is not the best explanation.

It is possible that America plays no significant role specifically because she is *no longer a superpower* in the end-times. My Dallas Theological Seminary prophecy mentor John F. Walvoord put it this way: "Although any conclusion about the role of America in the end times is necessarily tentative, the scriptural evidence is sufficient to conclude that America in that day will not be a superpower and apparently will not figure largely in either the political, economic, or religious leadership of the world."[5]

Implosion Due to Moral Degeneration

A view that is disturbing to think about is that perhaps America will continue on its slide into the gutter, morally and spiritually, so that the country eventually implodes. Few deny that the moral fiber of this country is eroding before our very eyes. If the trend continues, it is only a matter of time before the country collapses, like other great national powers of the past.

Lest the reader think this unlikely, consider the current state of the union from a moral perspective. Today there is widespread acceptance of homosexuality. Abortion—especially the barbaric practice of partial-birth abortion—continues to be widely practiced, with some 50 million unborn babies having been murdered since the enactment of *Roe v. Wade* in 1973. Pornography is pervasive and freely available on the Internet, enslaving millions as sex addicts. Drug abuse and alcoholism are pervasive as well, among both teenagers and adults. Promiscuity, fornication, and adultery continue to escalate to ever new heights, bringing about the carnage of sexually transmitted diseases, even among young teenagers. Over a fourth of American girls between the ages of fourteen and nineteen have at least one sexually transmitted disease. Meanwhile, the family unit continues to disintegrate before our eyes. The divorce rate continues to hover around 50 percent, and many today—including professing Christians—are living together outside of marriage. Out-of-wedlock births have escalated to new highs, with 40 percent of women not being married when they gave birth. As well, gay couples are adopting children, raising them in a homosexual atmosphere. A moral implosion of this country is a genuine possibility.[6]

Nuclear Attack

According to political advisors and government leaders, there is a strong possibility over the coming decade that America could suffer a nuclear attack. Such an attack would not likely destroy the entire country, but even if a nuclear weapon were detonated in only one major city, such as New York City or Los Angeles or Chicago, the economy would be in utter ruins for an indeterminate time.

Electromagnetic Pulse Attack

One form of attack that many Americans have not thought about much is an electromagnetic pulse (EMP) attack. Such an attack would quickly bring the country to its knees. The Commission to Assess the Threat to the United States from Electromagnetic Pulse Attack was created by Congress to study this issue. After hearing this report, some of our own government leaders lamented that the technology now exists to bring America's way of life to an end. The commission found that a single nuclear weapon, delivered by a missile to an altitude of a few hundred miles over the United States, would severely damage electrical power systems, electronics, and information systems—all of which Americans depend on for everyday life.

At high risk would be all forms of electronic control, the infrastructures for handling electric power, sensors and protective systems of all

kinds, computers, cell phones, telecommunications, cars, boats, air-
planes, trains, transportation, fuel and energy, banking and finance,
emergency services, and even food and water. Anything electrical is at
risk—and restoration could take a year or more. Such an attack could
be easily launched from a freighter off the coast of the United States. Of
great concern is that U.S. intelligence has discovered that oil-rich Iran
has performed tests on its Shahab-3 medium-range ballistic missiles in
a manner consistent with an EMP attack.

Economic Weakening Due to Peak Oil

It may well be that the United States—with its ever-increasing addiction to oil—will greatly weaken as a direct result of the declining oil
supply that appears to be imminent. Once supply begins to exceed
demand, the years to follow will see shortages that at best will cause
a severe global recession. To use an analogy of drug addiction, those
people with the worst addictions suffer the worst withdrawals. Because
no nation on earth is as severely addicted to oil as the United States, our
country will suffer more than most when the oil runs out.

We would also be increasingly vulnerable because the American military machine runs on oil. The power and mobility of the U.S. military
could diminish proportionally with the diminishing oil supply. If that
were to happen, how could America's military muscle be flexed on behalf
of Israel against Arab antagonists? There are also profound implications
for biblical prophecy, including the reality that the United States would
likely be less able to assist Israel when the future Ezekiel invasion occurs
at the hands of oil-rich Russia, Iran, Sudan, Turkey, Libya, and other
Muslim nations (Ezekiel 38–39). (I'll discuss this in greater detail in
the chapters that follow.)

The Rapture of the Church

It is also quite possible that the United States will suffer catastrophic
weakening following the rapture of the church. Because there are more
Christians in the United States than anywhere else in the world, the
United States will be affected more than any other nation by this event.
With a large part of America's work force not showing up for work—and
with their bills and loans no longer being paid—the economy is sure to
take a nosedive, and the country could easily go belly-up.

A Combination

Several of the above scenarios could take place, and their combined effect will greatly weaken the United States. I am an American patriot, and I want only the best for this country. However, the scenarios I have described are entirely possible and consistent with what we know of Bible prophecy.

Terror, Oil, and the United States

Make no mistake about it. Terrorists who hold to fanatical Islamic ideology have a long track regard of engaging in horrific acts against the United States. Take a moment to ponder this brief review:

- The Iranian hostage crisis took place in 1979.

- Hezbollah bombed the U.S. Embassy in Beirut in 1983, killing 63 people.

- A truck bomb crashed into the U.S. Marine barracks in Beirut in 1983, killing 241 U.S. soldiers.

- A truck bomb was exploded in the World Trade Center in New York City in 1993.

- The Twin Tower buildings in New York City were attacked by suicide pilots who flew themselves and innocent passengers into the buildings, bringing them both to the ground, with thousands of casualties.

In view of such facts, do not think for a second that extremist Muslim terrorists would hesitate to inflict damage on the United States via oil if they can accomplish it. In what follows, I explore several scenarios in which this could easily happen.

I begin with the strategic importance of the oil that flows from the Middle East. As Shibley Telhami, senior fellow in the Saban Center for Middle East Policy, put it:

> There is no escaping that the region that has grabbed the greatest global attention during the past half century in matters of oil, the Middle East, remains critical for future energy supplies. In a way, all the scrambling to develop resources around the world today

is intended to delay the day of reckoning. Although the Middle
East produces a quarter of world oil supplies, it holds between
two-thirds and three-quarters of all known oil reserves.[7]

Four of the top five nations with the greatest known oil reserves are
Arab nations. For the rest of the world to keep their oil needs met—
most notably the United States—lots of it will have to come from the
Middle East.

It is also sobering that Middle Eastern leaders themselves *recognize*
that the rest of the world is dependent on their oil and that oil can be
used as a weapon. Let us consider Iran as a prime example. Iran presently holds about 10 percent of the world's proven oil reserves and also
has the world's second-largest natural gas reserve. Frank Gaffney tells
us that Iran's oil revenues serve "to support its version of Islamofascism
and to underwrite the support Tehran gives to some of the world's most
dangerous Islamist movements. Notable among these is the Lebanon-
based terrorist group Hezbollah." Moreover, Gaffney notes, "Iran's mullahs are fully aware of the power of their oil. Their supreme leader, Ayatollah Ali Khamenei, warned in 2002: 'If the West did not receive oil,
their factories would grind to a halt. This will shake the world!'"[8] It is
the opinion of many that one day, Iran and other Middle Eastern oil
suppliers will indeed seek to "shake" the United States.

Consider the preview we had during the 1973 oil crisis. During that
year, the Arab nations united to use oil as a weapon, reducing oil production in order to embargo nations—principal target, the United States—
that favored Israel. These Arab nations wanted Israel to surrender all the
lands it had taken over by war. Even Jerusalem—or part of it—was to
be surrendered to the Arabs. The embargo, under the able leadership of
King Faisal of Saudi Arabia, created a temporary shortage and effectively
quadrupled the price of oil to twelve dollars per barrel.[9]

Higher gas prices produced a worldwide economic slowdown. With
long lines at the gas pumps, Americans soon realized that a new kind
of war was being waged—an *economic* war. America was brought to its
knees via the gas pump. There was panic and despair for the future of
the American way of life. The fastest transfer of money in the history
of planet earth took place. Cash gushed out of the United States to the
Middle East in order to satisfy its addiction. (Addicts can get desperate.)

Middle Eastern nations became wealthy beyond all possible expectations. From that point forward, we have lived in a new world.

In the coming years the Arabs could collectively decide to withhold oil from the West, much as they did in 1973, because the West continues its support of Israel. Yet another possibility is that Venezuela, with its anti-American, pro-Iranian president Hugo Chavez, might decide to stop selling oil to the United States and sell it instead to China, the second-largest guzzler of oil. Such activities would have profound implications for the global energy markets.[10] An economic shock of this nature could bring the United States to its knees.

Possible Terrorist Attacks Against the Oil Industry

Worse comes to worst if extremist Muslims attack oil fields or oil pipelines or an oil transportation route to inflict ruinous damage on the United States economy. John Kilduff, senior vice president for energy risk management at Fimat USA in New York, warns that "oil is just very much in the crosshairs around the world...There's no country, there's no production that can come to the rescue of any kind of terrorist attack."[11] John F. Walvoord makes the astute observation that "oil and terror, the two greatest issues facing the world today, are both centralized in the same part of the world—the Middle East. Since the oil and the terrorists are in the same location, it's easy to envision terrorist attacks that could damage or interrupt world oil production."[12]

Some countries might even attack their *own* oil fields just to keep that oil from the United States. Just a few years ago, Hugo Chavez claimed that "if the United States attacks, we won't have any other alternative [but to] blow up our own oil fields. They aren't going to take that oil."[13] The United States has imported significant oil from Venezuela in the past, but one can easily foresee a day when that will change, and Venezuela's leader, along with Iran and other Middle Eastern nations, will play the oil card against the United States.

The Ghawar Oil Field

Award-winning investigative journalist Edwin Black tells us that the apex of all oil terrorism targets is Saudi Arabia. He notes that this nation, which supplies over 11 percent of all U.S. oil imports, flows through a string of highly vulnerable choke points. (A "choke point" is a point of congestion or blockage.) The first choke point is the Ghawar Oil Field, the greatest petroleum repository on the globe. Ghawar is not Saudi Arabia's only oil field, but it is their most productive one and the one oil field that *absolutely must* remain operational to meet the global demand for oil. If a terrorist group either attacked or somehow took over the Ghawar Oil Field, it would be catastrophic for the United States.

Abqaiq Processing Facility

From the Ghawar Oil Field, the oil is then piped to the Abqaiq processing facility operated by Saudi Arabia's Aramco Oil Company. This is a second possible choke point. This facility processes two-thirds of all Saudi petroleum—up to 6.8 million barrels per day—for seaborne export. If Abqaiq were put out of action, the Saudi economy would be in great danger.

How might an attack against an oil choke point occur? There are a number of viable scenarios. The Abqaiq camp, for example, is populated by some thirty thousand workers (mainly foreign), and there are small armies of armed security personnel who (we are told) "react first and ask questions later." Instead of an overt outside attack against the facility, many are concerned about the possibility of an inside job designed by terrorists.

An even worse scenario involves the possibility of an airborne assault against the facility. Terrorists could attack using either short-range missiles or a hijacked airliner. These kinds of attacks could become regular events, with ongoing and escalating damage. This would interfere with oil production over an extended time, wreaking havoc on the world economy. While some of Saudi's fighter jets could bring down hijacked airliners before they hit their targets, the short-range missiles reach their targets with such speed that the damage is done before anyone can respond.[14]

Ras Tanura Facility

From the Abqaiq facility, the oil is then piped to the nearby tank farm and port facility at Ras Tanura on the Persian Gulf. This is yet another choke point, for here the crude is loaded onto supertankers for travel to other countries. If terrorists either attacked or took over this facility, the oil vein to the West is severed. Again, such attacks could be airborne in nature.

Strait of Hormuz

In order to reach the ocean, oil-bearing supertankers must traverse the Persian Gulf and pass through the most strategic—and most perilous—choke point, the six-mile wide Strait of Hormuz between Iran to the north and the United Arab Emirates and Oman to the south. Peter Tertzakian says that "while not all of the world's supply travels that narrow waterway, almost all of the world's spare capacity is behind that opening, including the great mother of all oil-supplying nations, Saudi Arabia."[15] Black tells us that "this funnel waterway is not only the exit ramp for Saudi oil, but also for the enormous flows of Iranian and Iraqi crude."[16] Indeed, some 18 million barrels per day traverse these waters. Muslim extremists would love to cut the flow of oil through the Strait of Hormuz.[17]

In recent days, Iran has warned that if the Israelis attack it because of Iran's nuclear ambitions, Iran will immediately close the Strait of Hormuz to shipping and then launch an attack against the Saudi Arabian oil facilities at Ras Tanura and Abqaiq. Ayatollah Ali Khamenei sternly warns that if Israel or the United States were to attack its nuclear facilities, then "the shipment of energy from this region will be seriously jeopardized."[18] A block of this strait would instantly rob America of a huge portion of its daily needed oil supply. The United States would have to tap its Strategic Petroleum Reserve and beg allies for any oil they can spare. "Oil Storm" may be more imminent than we think.

If the foregoing should take place, then gas prices could escalate dramatically overnight, severely damaging America's already-fragile economy. Further, the U.S.'s strained military may get sucked into yet another conflict in order to protect our vital interests in the Middle East.

It is highly significant that the Islamic Revolutionary Guard Corps (IRGC)—the most powerful military force in Iran and the praetorian guard of the Tehran regime—has installed "surface-to-air and anti-ship missile batteries along Iran's southern border facing the Strait. In addition, the IRGC is assessed to have several hundred Chinese-made C-801 anti-ship cruise missiles deployed along the waterway and on islands in the Strait and on its own warships. Iran also has a major naval base at Bandar Abbas at the bend in the Strait which also would be used in any anti-ship action."[19]

Further, Iran has small craft that can swarm merchant vessels and launch torpedoes at them. In addition to anti-ship missiles, the Iranians may possess Russian-made and Chinese-copied torpedoes capable of traveling some three hundred miles an hour.[20]

Military analysts inform us that over the past few years, "Tehran's naval forces have conducted repeated exercises simulating the takeover of the strait."[21] They would not be doing this unless there was a good possibility that they will one day attempt it.

One means of blocking the Strait would be to use sea mines. "Mining the waterway is considered the most likely method Tehran would employ—a tactic that was used to some effect during the so-called Tanker War between Iran and Iraq in their 1980-88 conflict." Analysts tell us "it would take weeks, possibly months, for them to clear safe passages in the strait if Iran was able to sow only 200-300 mines."[22]

Despite all this firepower, however, some analysts believe that all it would take to shut down this passageway would be for Iran to *threaten* military attack against any supertanker trying to make its way out. Iran could even fire off a few shots to let everyone know the seriousness of the threat.

Blocking the Strait of Hormuz is Iran's *ace in the hole*: "They know it and hold the world hostage by it," said Fariborz Saremi of the International Strategic Studies Association based in Washington, DC. "No one should or is ignoring the threat and strategic implications," he said. "If there is a strike against Iranian nuclear facilities, most likely they will play their ace."[23]

Ilan Berman, adjunct professor at the National Defense University in Washington, DC, and author of *Tehran Rising: Iran's Challenge to the United States*, states that "Tehran's ongoing military rearmament—and its resulting strategic control of the Strait of Hormuz—already gives it the power to control a substantial portion of the oil trade from the Persian Gulf."[24] It is sobering to ponder that disrupting the flow of oil from the Persian Gulf "can occur at any time, and will certainly have far more serious consequences as Middle East oil production becomes even more vital."[25]

It may seem hard to believe that blocking that little strait could impact the world economy. However, experts tell us that "even if a closure of the strait was relatively short, in the order of several weeks, the economic shock waves would still be substantial."[26] Caitlin Talmadge of the Security Studies Programme at the Massachusetts Institute of

Technology warned that "extended closure of the strait would remove roughly a quarter of the world's oil from the market, causing a supply shock of the type not seen since the glory days of OPEC."[27]

So these choke points—the Ghawar Old Field, the Abqaiq processing plant, the Ras Tanura tanker facility, and the Strait of Hormuz—constitute what one analyst called "the solar plexus of the planet." Choking off any one of these would cripple the world oil supply. Some say Iran could do it in mere hours. Moreover, "nearly every leading expert seems to agree that the question is not *how* or *if*, but *when* such a debacle would occur."[28]

Other Possible Targets

Terrorists might go after other possible targets, including the Strait of Malacca, the Druzhba Pipeline, and the Suez Canal. The Strait of Malacca is strategic because it provides the quickest passage between the Pacific and Indian Oceans. About 20 percent of all world trade moves through this strait. This area is vulnerable to both pirate activity and sea mines that can sink large ships. A disruption or blockage of this strait could cause economic panic in East Asia, cause serious shipping delays, escalate shipping costs, and render significant overall damage to the economy.

The Druzhba Pipeline is a Russian oil pipeline that is over twenty-four hundred miles long—the longest in the world. This pipeline distributes 1.2 million barrels of oil each day, supplying both the Ukraine and then Germany. A disruption in service due to a terrorist attack would cripple the economies of the countries the pipeline supplies, ultimately driving up global oil prices, which in turn would affect the U.S. economy.

The Suez Canal, located beside Egypt, is highly vulnerable, its narrowest point only a thousand feet wide. Some 1.3 million barrels of oil ship through the canal each day. Shut it down and incalculable damage is done to the Egyptian economy, which subsequently affects the global economy, which in turn affects the U.S. economy.

You get the picture. All kinds of oil targets exist that could easily disrupt the flow of oil. A petrol sword hangs over our heads. And if a sudden major disruption occurred in the oil supply, the U.S. economy would take a nosedive. Our thirst for oil is near-insatiable, and the only place that thirst can be quenched is the Middle East. Terrorist leaders recognize this and will exploit it to their best advantage.

These terrorist groups also recognize that the U.S. infrastructure is built upon oil and cannot be replaced overnight. Robert Hirsch is probably correct in his assessment that because of the enormity of the problem, true energy independence in the next three or four decades is impossible for most countries outside of OPEC.[29] This is not good news for the United States.

Why Do Muslims Hate Americans So?

Muslims hate Israel because in 1948 the Israeli state was reborn on land that Muslims believe Allah gave to them. Because the United States supports Israel with over $800 million in aid annually, both Israel and the United States are targeted by Muslim extremists.

Further resentment of Americans is rooted in America's alleged meddling in Middle Eastern affairs, such as positioning U.S. troops ("infidels") on Muslim soil (in Saudi Arabia and Iraq, for example). Still further, it is claimed that Americans are arrogant and imperialistic, trying to muscle their way around throughout the Middle East.

All of this is why Iran's vitriolic president, Mahmoud Ahmadinejad, boasts that humanity will soon know what it is like to live in a Jew-free and USA-free world.[30] He has assured the world that "the United States and the Zionist regime of Israel will soon come to the end of their lives," according to the Islamic Republic of Iran Broadcasting's website.[31]

Of course, it is no surprise to those interested in Bible prophecy that Israel is a sore spot in the world in the end-times, for this is prophesied in Zechariah 12:2-3: "Behold, I am going to make Jerusalem a cup that causes reeling to all the peoples around." What we are witnessing today is, I believe, a direct fulfillment of this biblical prophecy.

Will America Be Judged by God?

Whether the United States weakens due to a moral implosion, peak oil, oil blackmail, a nuclear attack, an EMP attack, the rapture, or a combination of these factors, one cannot help but wonder whether America will fall as a judgment from God, particularly as we near the end-times. The Bible is absolutely clear that God is in sovereign control of all nations, bar none. God rules the universe, controls all things, and is Lord over all (see Ephesians 1). Nothing can happen in this universe that is beyond the reach of His control. All forms of existence are within the scope of His absolute dominion.

Psalm 50:1 refers to God as the Mighty One who "speaks and summons the earth from the rising of the sun to the place where it sets." Psalm 66:7 affirms that "He rules forever by his power." We are assured in Psalm 93:1 that "the LORD reigns" and "is armed with strength." God asserts, "My purpose will stand, and I will do all that I please" (Isaiah 46:10). God assures us, "Surely, as I have planned, so it will be, and as I have purposed, so it will stand" (Isaiah 14:24). Proverbs 16:9 tells us, "In his heart a man plans his course, but the LORD determines his steps." Proverbs 19:21 says, "Many are the plans in a man's heart, but it is the LORD's purpose that prevails." (All references in this paragraph are from the NIV.)

In the book of Job we read, "He makes the nations great, then destroys them; He enlarges the nations, then leads them away" (Job 12:23). We are told that "from one man he created all the nations throughout the whole earth. He decided beforehand when they should rise and fall, and he determined their boundaries" (Acts 17:25-26 NLT). Daniel 2:21 tells us that "it is He who changes the times and the epochs; He removes kings and establishes kings."

The biblical God is also a God of judgment. J.I. Packer, in his classic *Knowing God*, forcefully reminds us of this sobering, oft-forgotten truth:

> The reality of divine judgment, as a fact, is set forth on page after page of Bible history. God judged Adam and Eve, expelling them from the Garden and pronouncing curses on their future earthly life (Gen. 3). God judged the corrupt world of Noah's day, sending a flood to destroy mankind (Gen. 6–8). God judged Sodom and Gomorrah, engulfing them in a volcanic catastrophe (Gen. 18–19). God judged Israel's Egyptian taskmasters, just as He foretold He would (see Gen. 15:14), unleashing against them the terrors of the ten plagues (Ex. 7–12). God judged those who worshipped the golden calf, using the Levites as His executioners (Ex. 32:26-35). God judged Nadab and Abihu for offering Him strange fire (Lev. 10:1ff.), as later He judged Korah, Dathan, and Abiram, who were swallowed up

in an earth tremor. God judged Achan for sacrilegious thiev-
ing; he and his family were wiped out (Josh. 7). God judged
Israel for unfaithfulness to Him after their entry into Canaan,
causing them to fall under the dominion of other nations (Judg.
2:11ff., 3:5ff., 4:1ff.).[32]

I have often heard people say that God in the Old Testament seems to
be characterized more by judgment, whereas God in the New Testament
is characterized by love. But while God is a God of love, He continues
to be a God of judgment even in the New Testament. Judgment falls
on the Jews for rejecting Jesus Christ (Matthew 21:43), on Ananias and
Sapphira for lying to God (Acts 5), on Herod for his self-exalting pride
(Acts 12:21-23), and on Christians in Corinth who were afflicted with
serious illness and even death in response to their irreverence with the
Lord's Supper (1 Corinthians 11:29-32; see also 1 John 5:16). Christians
will one day stand before the judgment seat of Christ (1 Corinthians
3:12-15; 2 Corinthians 5:10). Unbelievers, by contrast, will be judged at
the great white throne judgment (Revelation 20:11-15).

So then, let us be clear that *God is a God of judgment.* Since God
is absolutely sovereign over the nations and He is a God of judgment,
then is it possible that God may sovereignly judge America in the end-
times for turning away from Him? I'm not the only one who considers
this a possibility:

> One often-overlooked aspect of God's judgment is His deal-
> ing with nations. God has often judged entire nations in the
> past. Lengthy sections in the Old Testament are devoted to
> God's prophesied judgment against nations. God repeatedly
> pronounced judgment against Judah and Israel for their disobe-
> dience. The majority of the Old Testament prophets are devoted
> to this subject—Isaiah, Jeremiah, Hosea, Joel, Amos, Micah,
> Zephaniah, Habakkuk, Zechariah, Haggai, and Malachi. But
> Judah and Israel were not the sole recipients of God's just displea-
> sure. God also announced judgment on Gentile nations for their
> sin...In light of the biblical record, we would be shortsighted to
> believe that God no longer judges nations for their sin.[33]

Those who doubt this should consult what the apostle Paul says in
Romans 1:18-21,24-28:

For the wrath of God is revealed from heaven against all ungodliness and unrighteousness of men who suppress the truth in unrighteousness, because that which is known about God is evident within them; for God made it evident to them. For since the creation of the world His invisible attributes, His eternal power and divine nature, have been clearly seen, being understood through what has been made, so that they are without excuse. For even though they knew God, they did not honor Him as God or give thanks, but they became futile in their speculations, and their foolish heart was darkened...

Therefore God gave them over in the lusts of their hearts to impurity, so that their bodies would be dishonored among them. For they exchanged the truth of God for a lie, and worshiped and served the creature rather than the Creator, who is blessed forever. Amen.

For this reason God gave them over to degrading passions; for their women exchanged the natural function for that which is unnatural, and in the same way also the men abandoned the natural function of the woman and burned in their desire toward one another, men with men committing indecent acts and receiving in their own persons the due penalty of their error.

And just as they did not see fit to acknowledge God any longer, God gave them over to a depraved mind, to do those things which are not proper.

If this passage tells us anything, it is that when a nation willfully rejects God and His Word, God eventually reveals His wrath against it. God has a long track record of wrath against ungodly nations, and one way He reveals His wrath is by allowing the people to experience the full brunt of the ravaging consequences of their sin. God literally *hands them over* to the consequences of their sin.

It is a sobering reality that many great nations have risen and fallen throughout human history. In each case, the nation had no expectation of its impending demise. Those who lived within these nations thought their nation could never fall. But great nations do fall—and they fall hard.

The Babylonians never thought Babylon would fall, but its demise came in less than a century. The Persians never thought the Persian Empire would fall, but it finally collapsed after about two centuries. The Greeks never thought Greece would fall, but it waned in less than three centuries. No one thought the mighty Roman Empire would ever decline, but it, too, waned after holding out for nine centuries. One could legitimately argue that in each of these cases, the fall of these nations was preceded by a gross moral decline, and God rendered appropriate judgment.

The same may one day be true of America. If what we are witnessing in America today—pornography, premarital sex, extramarital sex, homosexuality, abortions, drinking, drugs, divorce, the disintegration of the family unit, and the like—were taking place in ancient Babylon, would you think that Babylon was ripe for judgment? I think so. The problem today is that many have become desensitized to moral issues because immorality is so rampant. That is a dangerous place to be, for God's patience will not last forever.

If God's judgment falls upon America for its moral and spiritual degeneracy, this is just one more reason why there will be a shift in power from the United States of America to the United States of Europe in the end-times. Rome will rise again, and the Antichrist will be her ruler.

Political Realignments in the End-Times: Rebirth of Israel

Biblical prophecy, in fairly broad strokes, informs us what the political landscape will look like in the last years prior to the second coming of Jesus Christ. I am talking about such things as a nation being reborn after many centuries of not being a nation, political and commercial shifts in the balance of power, new coalitions emerging with a common agenda, and other nations reacting against these new political shifts. And all of this—in one way or another—is related to oil. In this and the two chapters that follow, I will narrow attention to the issue of political realignments in the end-times, and how oil fits into the picture.

Earlier in the book, I noted that on the global front, nearly every one of the 192 nations on this planet is an oil addict. All told, the nations of the world now consume oil at the staggering rate of a thousand barrels a second.[1] And the trends indicate nearly incalculably large increases in demand for the future, while supplies will continue to dwindle.[2]

Because oil is used for transportation, farming, industry, and much more, the reality of peak oil may cause nations around the world to engage in a massive energy war as they compete against each other for increasingly scarce supplies. The ongoing rapid depletion of world oil will inevitably create a state of affairs in which nations are literally vying for control of the world's remaining oil fields. Each will try to capture its piece of a shrinking pie.[3] Tragically, war may be inevitable with such national face-offs.[4] Nations in the past have gone to war over oil, and history will likely repeat itself.

In discussing the political structure of the world in the end-times and its relation to peak oil, it makes sense to focus initial attention on the political sore spot of the world—*Israel*. Only then will we gain a proper understanding of the political shifts and alliances that will emerge in the end-times.

God's Unconditional Land Promises to Israel

It all began with Abraham. Abraham's name literally means "father of a multitude." He lived around 2000 BC, originating from the city of Ur, in Mesopotamia, on the River Euphrates. He was apparently a very wealthy and powerful man.

God called Abraham to leave Ur and go to a new land—the land of Canaan, which God was giving to Abraham and his descendants (Genesis 11:31). Abraham left with his wife, Sarai (God would later change her name to Sarah), and his nephew, Lot. Upon arriving in Canaan, his first act was to construct an altar and worship God. This was typical of Abraham; God is of first importance.

God made a pivotal covenant with Abraham around 2100 BC. In this covenant, God promised Abraham a son, and that his descendants would be as numerous as the stars in the sky (Genesis 12:1-3; 13:14-17). The promise may have seemed unbelievable to Abraham since his wife was childless (11:30). Yet Abraham did not doubt God; he knew God would faithfully give what He had promised. God reaffirmed the covenant in Genesis 15, perhaps to emphasize to Abraham that even in his advanced age, the promise would come to pass. God also promised Abraham that he would be personally blessed, that his name would become great, that those who bless him would be blessed and those who curse him would be cursed, and that all the families of the earth would be blessed through his posterity.

At one point, an impatient Sarai suggested that their heir might be procured through their Egyptian maid, Hagar. Ishmael was thus born to Abraham, through Hagar, when he was eighty-six years old. But Ishmael was not the child of promise. In God's perfect timing, His promise of a son to Abraham and Sarah was fulfilled when they were far beyond normal childbearing age—Abraham was a hundred years old and Sarah was ninety (Genesis 17:17; 21:5). Their son was named Isaac. As promised, the entire Jewish nation eventually developed from his line. Isaac means "laughter," which points to the joy derived from this child of promise. Recall that when Abraham and Sarah heard they would have a son in their old age, they laughed (see Genesis 17:17-19; 18:9-15).

Isaac would carry on the covenant first given to his father Abraham. The New Testament calls him a child of promise (Galatians 4:22-23), and he was a man of good character. He trusted in God (Genesis 22:6,9; Hebrews 11:20), practiced regular prayer (Genesis 26:25), and sought peace (Genesis 26:20-22).

In a famous episode in the Bible, Abraham's faith was stretched when God commanded him to sacrifice his beloved son of promise, Isaac. Abraham obeyed without hesitation. In his heart, he believed God would provide a substitute lamb for the burnt offering or else raise Isaac from the dead (Genesis 22:8; Hebrews 11:17-19). God, of course, intervened before Isaac was sacrificed, but the episode demonstrates the tremendous faith Abraham had in God. In God's providence, Isaac indeed was the son of promise.

God made specific land promises to Abraham. We read in Genesis 15:18-21 (NIV): "On that day the LORD made a covenant with Abram and said, 'To your descendants I give this land, from the river of Egypt to the great river, the Euphrates—the land of the Kenites, Kenizzites, Kadmonites, Hittites, Perizzites, Rephaites, Amorites, Canaanites, Girgashites and Jebusites.'" These are specific territories.

The land promises made to Abraham were then passed down through Isaac's line. Indeed, in Genesis 26:3-4 (NIV) we read the Lord's very words to Isaac: "Stay in this land for a while, and I will be with you and will bless you. For to you and your descendants I will give all these lands and will confirm the oath I swore to your father Abraham. I will make your descendants as numerous as the stars in the sky and will give them all these lands, and through your offspring all nations on earth will be blessed."

The land promises then passed from Isaac to Jacob (not to Esau, the firstborn). The Lord said to Jacob, "I am the LORD, the God of your father Abraham and the God of Isaac. I will give you and your descendants the land on which you are lying. Your descendants will be like the dust of the earth, and you will spread out to the west and to the east, to the north and to the south. All peoples on earth will be blessed through you and your offspring" (Genesis 28:13-14 NIV).

This distinct family line through which God's covenant promises were to be fulfilled is affirmed later in the Bible. For example, in Psalm 105:8-11 (NIV) we read:

> He remembers his covenant forever,
>   the word he commanded, for a thousand generations,
> the covenant he made with Abraham,
>   the oath he swore to Isaac.
> He confirmed it to Jacob as a decree,
>   to Israel as an everlasting covenant:
> *"To you I will give the land of Canaan*
>   *as the portion you will inherit."*
>   (emphasis added)

Clearly, then, the land promises made by God and recorded in the Bible are for the descendants of Abraham, Isaac, and Jacob—*the Jews*. From a biblical perspective, there is virtually no question about God's intended recipients of the holy land.

The Rebirth of Israel: A Super-Sign

When the modern self-governing nation of Israel was born in 1948, it represented the beginnings of an actual fulfillment of Bible prophecies about an international regathering of the Jews before the judgment of the tribulation period. This regathering was to take place after centuries of exile in various nations around the world.

In Ezekiel 36 God promised, "I will multiply the number of people upon you, even the whole house of Israel. The towns will be inhabited and the ruins rebuilt" (v. 10 NIV). God promised, "I will take you out of the nations; I will gather you from all the countries and bring you back into your own land" (v. 24 NIV). Israel would again be prosperous, for God "will increase the fruit of the trees and the crops of the field, so that you will no longer suffer disgrace among the nations because of famine" (v. 30 NIV).

Then, in the vision of dry bones in Ezekiel 37, the Lord is portrayed as miraculously bringing the bones back together to form a skeleton, and the skeleton becomes wrapped in muscles and tendons and flesh, and God then breathes life into the body. There is no doubt that this chapter in Ezekiel is speaking metaphorically about Israel, for we read: "Son of man, these bones are the whole house of Israel" (v. 11 NIV). Hence, this chapter portrays Israel as becoming a living, breathing nation, brought back from the dead, as it were.

Christian writers living in the sixteenth and seventeenth centuries were already writing about Jews coming back to the land, centuries before 1948. They wrote in this manner because they believed God's prophecies in Ezekiel would literally come to pass.

Therefore, 1948 is a year to remember. In AD 70, Titus and his Roman warriors trampled on and destroyed Jerusalem, definitively and thoroughly ending Israel as a political entity (see Luke 21:20). Since then, the Jews have been dispersed worldwide. In 1940, no one could have guessed that within a decade Israel would become a nation again. And yet it happened. Israel achieved statehood in 1948, and the Jews have been returning to their homeland ever since.

Consider the numbers. When Israel declared her independence on May 14, 1948, the country's population stood at only 806,000. Yet by the end of 2005, nearly 7 million people lived in Israel, 5.6 million of whom were Jewish. Thousands more arrive every year. In 2005 alone, some 19,000 Jews immigrated to Israel. Today more Jews live in the greater Tel Aviv area than in New York City, and as many Jews live in Israel as in the United States. It will not be long before more Jews live in Israel than Jews who do not.[5]

I have no interest in setting or implying dates for specific fulfillments of biblical prophecies, but it does appear that the divine program of restoring Israel is presently in progress. Key elements in recent history include:

- *1881–1900:* About 30,000 Jews who had been persecuted in Russia moved to Palestine.

- *1897:* The goal of establishing a home in Palestine for Jewish people received great impetus when the First Zionist Congress convened in Basel, Switzerland, and adopted Zionism as a program.

- *1904–1914:* 32,000 more Jews who had been persecuted in Russia moved to Palestine.

- *1924–1932:* 78,000 Polish Jews moved to Palestine.

- *1933–1939*: 230,000 Jews who had been persecuted in Germany and central Europe moved to Palestine.

- *1940–1948*: 95,000 Jews who had been persecuted in central Europe moved to Palestine. Meanwhile, more than 6 million Jews were murdered by Adolph Hitler and Nazi Germany.

- *1948*: The new state of Israel was born.

- *1967:* Israel captured Jerusalem and the West Bank during the Six-Day War, which was precipitated by an Arab invasion.[6]

In view of such facts, it would seem that since the late nineteenth century, God has been gradually fulfilling what He promised in Scripture. And one day, toward the end of the tribulation period, there will be a spiritual awakening in Israel.

Israel at the present time still remains in unbelief (that is, the Jews do not believe in Jesus the Messiah). But there is a day in the future, according to Joel 2:28-29, in which there will be a spiritual awakening in Israel. I believe that Armageddon will be the historical context in which Israel finally becomes converted (Zechariah 12:2–13:1). The restoration of Israel will include the confession of Israel's national sin (Leviticus 26:40-42; Jeremiah 3:11-18; Hosea 5:15), following which Israel will be saved, thereby fulfilling Paul's prophecy in Romans 11:25-27. In dire threat at Armageddon, Israel will plead for its newly found Messiah to return and deliver them (they will "mourn for Him, as one mourns for an only son"—Zechariah 12:10; Matthew 23:37-39; see also Isaiah 53:1-9), at which point their deliverance will surely come (see Romans 10:13-14). Israel's leaders will have finally realized why the tribulation has fallen on them—perhaps due to the Holy Spirit's enlightenment of their understanding of Scripture (see 1 Corinthians 2:9–3:2). Later, in the millennial kingdom, Israel will take full possession of the Promised Land and the reestablishment of the Davidic throne (2 Samuel 7:5-17). It will be a time of physical and spiritual blessing, the basis of which is the new covenant (Jeremiah 31:31-34).

Keep in mind that God's plan for the future hinges largely on Israel. Many prophecy interpreters believe that the reconstitution of Israel as a nation is a "super-sign" for the end-times (see Ezekiel 36–37; Romans 9–11). They say this because so many of the other biblical prophecies of the end-times relate in some way to Israel, and hence Israel *must exist* in order for these other prophecies to come to pass. Put another way, many of these other prophecies do not have meaning *until* and *unless* Israel is a nation (see below). Hence, 1948 is extremely significant from a prophetic standpoint, for that year Israel became a nation again.

Necessity of the Regathering of Jews to Their Homeland

The necessity of the regathering of the Jews to their homeland and Israel becoming a nation again is clearly implied in the peace covenant to be signed between the Antichrist and the leaders of Israel in the end-times. This relates to the seventy weeks of Daniel.

In Daniel 9, God provided a prophetic timetable for the nation of Israel. The prophetic clock began ticking when the command went out to restore and rebuild Jerusalem following its destruction by Babylon (Daniel 9:25). According to this verse, Israel's timetable was divided into seventy groups of 7 years, totaling 490 years.

The first sixty-nine groups of 7 years—or 483 years—counted the years "from the issuing of the decree to restore and rebuild Jerusalem until the Anointed One, the ruler, comes" (Daniel 9:25 NIV). The "Anointed One," of course, is Jesus Christ. "Anointed One" means Messiah. The day that Jesus rode into Jerusalem to proclaim Himself Israel's Messiah was exactly 483 years to the day after the command to restore and rebuild Jerusalem had been given.

At that point God's prophetic clock stopped. Daniel describes a gap between these 483 years and the final 7 years of Israel's prophetic timetable. Several events were to take place during this "gap," according to Daniel 9:26:

1. The Messiah will be killed.

2. The city of Jerusalem and its temple will be destroyed (which occurred in AD 70).

3. The Jews will encounter difficulty and hardship from that time forward.

The final "week" of 7 years will begin for Israel when the Antichrist confirms a "covenant" for 7 years (Daniel 9:27). When this peace pact is signed between the Antichrist and the leaders of Israel, it will signal the beginning of the tribulation period, the 7-year count-down to the second coming of Christ, which follows the tribulation period. However, such a treaty would make no sense if the Jews had not returned to their land and Israel were not a viable political entity. Israel *must* be regathered to the land before the beginning of the tribulation period. This is what makes the year 1948 so significant from a prophetic standpoint.

Scriptural prophecies about the rebuilding of the Jewish temple are another indication for the need for Israel's rebirth as a nation. For how can the Jewish temple be rebuilt if the Jewish nation did not first exist?

That the temple must be rebuilt by the middle of the seven-year tribulation is clear from Jesus' warning in the Olivet Discourse of a cata-strophic event that assumes the existence of the temple: "When you see the ABOMINATION OF DESOLATION which was spoken of through Daniel the prophet, standing in the holy place (let the reader understand), then those who are in Judea must flee to the mountains" (Matthew 24:15-16). This "abomination of desolation" refers to a desecration of the Jewish temple by the Antichrist.

It is significant that Jesus says this because just previously, in Matthew 24:1-2, Jesus affirmed that the great Temple built by Herod (the Jewish temple of Jesus' day) would be utterly destroyed: "Truly I say to you, not one stone here will be left upon another, which will not be thrown down." This prophecy was literally fulfilled in AD 70 when Titus and his Roman warriors overran Jerusalem and the Jewish temple. The only conclusion that can be reached is that though the temple of Jesus' day would be destroyed, the abomination of desolation would occur in a yet-future temple. This latter temple would be built by the middle of the tribulation period (see Daniel 9:27; 12:11).

Even today there are reports that various individuals and groups have been working behind the scenes to prepare materials for the future temple, including priestly robes, temple tapestries, and worship utensils.[7] These items are being prefabricated so that when the temple is finally rebuilt, everything will be ready for it. I reiterate that the temple does not need to be rebuilt until the middle of the tribulation period. Hence, the fact that many items are today already being prefabricated is all the more exciting to many prophecy enthusiasts.[8]

The Problem with "Replacement Theology"

When Israel finally took possession of the land of milk and honey, it was in direct fulfillment of God's promise to the nation. As we read in Joshua 21:43-45 (NIV):

> So the LORD gave Israel all the land he had sworn to give their forefathers, and they took possession of it and settled there. The LORD gave them rest on every side, just as he had sworn to their forefathers. Not one of their enemies withstood them; the LORD handed all their enemies over to them. Not one of all the LORD's good promises to the house of Israel failed; every one was fulfilled.

Today, however, proponents of "replacement theology" argue that because God gave the Israelites the land in Joshua 21:43-45, God's obligation regarding the land promises to Israel were completely fulfilled and *no future land promises are yet to be fulfilled*. After all, the text tells us that "not one of all the LORD's good promises to the house of Israel failed; every one was fulfilled." These proponents thus believe that the modern state of Israel has no legitimate biblical basis. They claim it is not a fulfillment of biblical prophecy. This theology also teaches that national Israel has been permanently replaced by the church—that is, the church is the new or true Israel that has permanently superseded Israel as God's people.

Historically, this kind of theology has been a motivation to some to engage in anti-Semitism. Prophecy expert Thomas Ice once said that "wherever replacement theology has flourished, the Jews have had to run for cover."[9]

Several pertinent points can be made in response to this theology. First, Joshua 21:43-45 is absolutely correct regarding God fulfilling His part in giving the Israelites the promised land. Israel, however, failed to take full possession of what God promised to the nation, and they failed to dispossess all the Canaanites. The gift of land was there for the taking. God had faithfully done for Israel what He promised, but Israel failed by faith to fully conquer all the land.

The idea that there are no further land promises to be fulfilled for Israel is proven to be false by the many prophecies written *far after* the time of Joshua that speak of Israel possessing the land *in the future* (see, for example, Isaiah 60:18,21; Jeremiah 23:6; 24:5-6; 30:18; 32:37-40; 33:6-9; Ezekiel 28:25-26; 34:11-13; 36:24-26; 37; 39:28; Hosea 3:4-5; Joel 2:18-29; Amos 9:14-15; Micah 2:12; 4:6-7; Zephaniah 3:19-20; Zechariah 8:7-8). In fact, every Old Testament prophet except Jonah speaks of a *permanent* return to the land of Israel by the Jews. Also, though Israel possessed the land at the time of Joshua, it was later dispossessed, whereas the Abrahamic Covenant promised Israel that she would possess the land *forever* (Genesis 17:8).

Also against replacement theology is the fact that the church and Israel are still distinct in the New Testament. For example, we are instructed in 1 Corinthians 10:32 (NIV), "Do not cause anyone to stumble, whether Jews, Greeks [Gentiles] or the church of God." Moreover, Israel and the church are distinct throughout the book of Acts, with *Israel* being used twenty times and *church* nineteen times.

The prophecies that have already been fulfilled in Scripture—such as the Old Testament messianic prophecies about the first coming of Jesus Christ—have been fulfilled literally. From the book of Genesis to the book of Malachi, the Old Testament abounds with anticipations of the coming Messiah. Numerous predictions fulfilled to the "crossing of the t" and the "dotting of the i" in the New Testament relate to His birth, life, ministry, death, resurrection, and glory (for example, Isaiah 7:14; Micah 5:2; Zechariah 12:10). The prophecies that have been fulfilled *completely* have been fulfilled *literally*, and this gives us strong confidence to expect that the prophecies not yet fulfilled will also end up being fulfilled literally. Hence, the land promises to Israel will be fulfilled literally.

Eventually, Israel will finally (wonderfully) recognize Jesus as the divine Messiah and take full possession of the promised land. At present, however, Israel's regathering to the land is only partial, and Israel is yet in unbelief. This partial regathering in unbelief is setting the stage for Israel to eventually go through the tribulation period—the "time of Jacob's trouble" (Jeremiah 30:7)—during which a remnant of Israel will be saved (see Romans 9–11). Israel will then come into full possession of her promised land in the millennial kingdom.

Meanwhile, replacement theology has done much damage to the cause of Israel. Many Christians are abandoning support for Israel and her right to stay in the land. Based on the Abrahamic covenant—an *unconditional* covenant—I believe the land unconditionally belongs to Israel, and I pray the United States remains committed to protecting Israel against her enemies.

Concurrent Muslim Resentment

Meanwhile, modern Arabs claim a long and continuous residency in the holy land. They assert that the land *does not* belong to Israel. Once a land has been under Muslim control, they claim, it cannot revert to non-Muslim control. Such is the will of Allah. Besides, Muslims say, the British McMahon-Hussein Agreement promised the land to the Arabs back in the early 1900s. In view of this, modern Palestinian authorities say the existence of "the Zionist state" is the entire cause of the Middle East conflict. The land belongs to the Arabs, and Israel cannot continue to exist.

So today, we have a massive Middle East conflict with a number of variables. While Jews view Israel as the land of Jewish people, Arabs believe Palestine belongs to the Arabs. While Jews believe Israel includes Transjordan (as stipulated in the Balfour Declaration of 1917), the Arabs have never accepted this declaration that recognized the Jewish people's right to a national home in the land of Israel.

The "Law of Return," an important piece of legislation adopted by the new state of Israel, provides all Jews the legal right to immigrate to Israel and immediately become citizens if they so choose. The Arabs, by contrast, say Jewish immigration to Palestine must stop.

As a result of the ongoing conflict between the Israelis and Arabs, many Palestinians have been displaced and have taken up residence in refugee camps in Jordan, the West Bank, and Gaza. Today there are millions of Palestinian refugees. While Jews from anywhere in the world are welcomed in Israel as Israeli citizens, Palestinian refugees are prevented from becoming citizens in neighboring Arab countries, except for in Jordan.

The Israelis are willing to participate in a limited way in solving the refugee problem, but they do not want to allow millions of unhappy Palestinians into the Jewish state who could later become allies with Arab nations seeking to attack Israel. The most they have been willing to do is to allow a limited number of Palestinians to live outside of Israel proper, segregate the Jews and Palestinians by a perimeter wall, and demilitarize the Palestinian area.

Palestinians, by contrast, want permission to return to their former homes or be given compensation for choosing not to return. They claim Israel is not honoring the U.N. Security Council Resolutions 194 and 242, which grant repatriation and war reparations to the ousted Palestinians.

Resentment among Arabs and Muslims is very high today. The extremist Muslims want to "wipe Israel off the map." They want to destroy this "lesser Satan," along with the "greater Satan" that supports Israel—the United States. The Middle East conflict continues to escalate, with no viable solution in sight.[10]

When we talk about political realignments in the end-times, then, we are concerned not only with the rebirth of Israel as a nation, but also how this rebirth has upset many other nations, primarily Muslim nations (see Zechariah 12:2-3). In the next chapter, I will demonstrate that a northern coalition of largely Muslim nations will emerge in order to move against Israel in the end-times. Even today, these nations are forming alliances with each other, and a commonality among them is a shared hatred for Israel. In chapter 10, I will discuss yet another motivating factor for this invasion into Israel: *Recent discoveries that there may be significant oil underneath the ground in Israel.*

Political Realignments in the End-Times: Israel Endangered

I t is not difficult to imagine how some in Israel might consider themselves all alone in seeking to defend their state. Aaron Klein tells us that Israel is "under relentless pressure from an international community that favors terrorist gangs over a forward-looking Westernized democracy; that balks at any assertion of Israeli self-defense; that pressures the tiny Jewish country to evacuate vital territory; that perpetuates the Israeli-Palestinian conflict by artificially maintaining a festering 'refugee' crisis; and that provides legitimacy, and at times money, weapons, and advanced training, to Israel's terrorist foes."[1]

The backdrop is that when Israel became a nation again in 1948 after a long and worldwide dispersion, the rest of the Middle East was utterly enraged. Klein tells us that "the declaration of the state of Israel set off the chain of events that has led to the modern terrorism we see today."[2] Moreover, "the Islamic-Arabic world erupted like a volcano. The call of jihad was pronounced throughout the Islamic-Arab world. The first call to jihad came from the founder of the Muslim Brotherhood in Egypt (the forerunner of today's terrorist organizations). Al-Azhar also openly condemned Israel. All the people in the Arab countries were pushing their governments to send their militaries to fight Israel."[3]

This land was viewed as the sole possession of Islam. "When the Jewish people declared the birth of the nation of Israel, it was an affront to every Islamic country because it took the land away from Islam."[4] Hamas, the largest, most active jihad group now fighting in Israel, has a thirty-six-article covenant that outlines its position toward Israel. In it we read: "The land of Palestine is an Islamic *Waqf* [Holy Possession] consecrated for future Moslem generations until Judgment Day" (Article 11). "Palestine is an Islamic land...Since this is the case, the liberation of Palestine is an individual duty for every Moslem wherever he may be" (Article 13).[5]

A large part of the problem, from the Islamic perspective, is that Israel presently contains the third most holy site of Islam—the al-Aqsa Mosque in Jerusalem. Many Westerners fail to understand how serious Muslims are about keeping their holy sites pure and undefiled. It is their firm conviction that a holy site must not be corrupted by the presence of non-Muslims—such as Jews—who are universally considered impure and unholy. The Muslims are especially protective knowing that the Jews wish to rebuild their own temple on the same site, something that Muslims have vowed never to allow happen. In fact, we are told that "if the third most holy mosque in the world were taken away from them [by the Jews], the whole Islamic world would be ignited."[6]

In the past, of course, Israel has not stood alone. The United States has long been an ally and supporter of Israel. I believe this is one reason God has blessed the United States throughout its history. In recent decades, however, the United States has tried to remain friends with Israel while at the same time befriending some of the Arab/Muslim nations. Richard Heinberg tells us: "For the past few decades, the U.S. has pursued a dual policy in the Middle East, the most oil-rich region of the planet. On the one hand, it has supported repressive Arab regimes in order to maintain access to petroleum reserves...On the other hand, the U.S. has supported Israel unquestioningly and with vast amounts of money and weaponry."[7]

Such a policy is like burning both ends of a candle. A conflict seems inevitable, and in today's hostile Middle East climate, it is like a powder keg waiting to explode. Increasingly, the United States is being attacked for its support of Israel, and one day, I fear that the U.S.'s support of Israel may wane. *In view of the reality of peak oil, will the United States continue to support Israel when it finds itself in increasingly desperate need of oil from the Persian Gulf?*

In direct fulfillment of biblical prophecy, Israel is today a thorn or sore spot in the world. God prophesied in Zechariah 12:2-3, "Behold, I am going to make Jerusalem a cup that causes reeling to all the peoples around; and when the siege is against Jerusalem, it will also be against Judah. It will come about in that day that I will make Jerusalem a heavy stone for all the peoples; all who lift it will be severely injured. And all the nations of the earth will be gathered against it." This passage reveals that in the end-times Israel will be hated by the nations of the earth. We also know that in the end-times, when the Muslim nations (with Russia) move against Israel in the Ezekiel invasion, God Himself will destroy the invaders (Ezekiel 39). This is apparently in direct fulfillment of Zechariah 12:2-3—that is, nations that launch a siege against Jerusalem end up "severely injured."

At present the Middle East conflict gives no indication of ever receding. There seems to be no hope for permanent peace. In view of Zechariah 12:2-3 and other prophecies, we would not expect permanent peace today, for Israel will continue to be a sore spot in the world up through the end of the tribulation.

Biblical prophecy is clear that there will not be lasting peace for Israel or the Middle East (or *for the world*, for that matter) until the Lord Jesus comes again at the second coming. President Barack Obama may seek to bring about a lasting peace in the Middle East, but I believe he, like all others, will fail; only the Lord Jesus will succeed.

Please do not get me wrong. We should do all we can to bring peace to the region and stop the bloodshed. Peace is always God's ideal (Isaiah 19:23-25), and the apostle Paul calls God the "God of peace" (Romans 15:33). Jesus is the "Prince of Peace" (Isaiah 9:6), and He affirmed, "Blessed are the peacemakers" (Matthew 5:9).

A realistic assessment of Middle East affairs, however, lends credence to the biblical prophecies that reveal that such peace will ultimately be found only at the return of Jesus Christ. We look forward to the day prophesied in Scripture when we will experience universal peace (Isaiah 2:4; see also Isaiah 11:1-9; Hosea 2:18; Zechariah 9:9-10). Meanwhile, the apostle Paul encourages Christians to pray "for kings and all those in authority, that we may live peaceful and quiet lives in all godliness and holiness" (1 Timothy 2:2 NIV). We should pray specifically for God to give our leaders supernatural wisdom in making correct foreign-policy decisions.

Even though true and lasting peace will not come until Christ's second coming, biblical prophecy also reveals that the deceptive, Satan-driven leader who emerges in the end-times as the head of a revived Roman Empire—the Antichrist—will bring about a three-and-a-half year period of *false* peace for Israel. This period of false peace will immediately follow this leader's signing of a covenant with Israel (Daniel 9:27). Right in the middle of the tribulation (after three-and-a-half years), however, the Antichrist will double-cross Israel, and the peace will end.

It seems clear from prophetic Scripture that Satan-inspired anti-Semitism will escalate in the end-times, especially during the tribulation. Revelation 12:13 tells us, "When the dragon saw that he was thrown down to the earth, he persecuted the woman who gave birth to the male child." When Satan is definitively cast out of heaven during the tribulation, he will engage in great persecution against the woman (Israel) who gave birth to the male child (Jesus Christ). This verse may indicate not only direct attacks by Satan against the Jews, but Satan may also inspire persecution against the Jews through others.

Much of Satan's persecution against Israel will take place through the Antichrist. This European leader at the beginning of the tribulation seems to be the friend of Israel, but it becomes clear by the middle of the tribulation, when he breaks his peace treaty with Israel, that he is her worst enemy. Following the double-cross, the Antichrist will slaughter the Jews mercilessly (see Daniel 7:25; 8:24; 11:44). He will attempt to bring to full fruition the genocide Hitler started. Zechariah 13:8 reveals that while two-thirds of the people of Israel will die, one-third will be left in the land. This persecution of Israel will be inspired by the devil himself.

Iran and Black Gold: Fast Track to End-times Power

Iran is a particularly venomous threat to Israel today, and this threat will escalate as we progress in the end-times. Of particular relevance to end-times geopolitics, Israel-hating Iran has become a major player in the global oil market, with some 100 billion barrels of proven oil reserves, and claims that it has 30 billion more.[8] The majority of Iran's crude-oil reserves are located in the southwestern Khuzestan region near the Iraqi border and the Persian Gulf. Iran at present has 32 producing oil fields—25 onshore, 7 offshore.[9]

With the world's steadily increasing demand for oil, Iran is making a fortune with its oil income. Ali Ansari tells us that Iran's position in the oil market will strengthen over time, given the present and ever-growing importance of the Persian Gulf in the world oil market.[10]

Jerome Corsi documents that Iran's gross revenue from oil is somewhere in the range of $150 million per day.[11] He tells us that oil-export revenues constitute some 80 percent of Iran's total export earnings, 40 to 50 percent of its government budget, and 10 to 20 percent of its gross domestic product.[12]

Iran has understandably been called a regional energy superpower. One analyst writes: "Home to 10 percent or more of the world's oil, it is the second largest exporter in the Organization of Petroleum Exporting Countries (OPEC), producing an average of 3.9 million barrels of oil per day."[13] While, for the most part, there have been no significant new discoveries of oil around the world, a few new discoveries of oil reservoirs in Southern Iran have significantly boosted the country's projected oil reserves. Some analysts suggest that "these discoveries, coupled with the rising price of crude oil, have done more than simply give Tehran a growing foothold in the world energy market; they have positioned the Iranian regime as a major strategic asset for energy-hungry states."[14]

In addition to oil reserves, experts tell us that Iran is in major possession of gas reserves. Indeed, "more important than oil is Iran's position as the country with the second largest natural gas reserves in the world"[15]—estimated at some 940 trillion cubic feet, second only to Russia.[16] Approximately 62 percent of Iran's natural gas reserves have yet to be developed.[17] This means that Iran is economically secure well into the future, well able to continue financing terrorism against Israel.

From an economic and geopolitical perspective, Iran's importance cannot be overstated:

> Iran is likely to be a nexus of struggle in the near future. The U.S. and Europe wish to deter Iran from developing nuclear weapons—which the Iranians see as essential to deterring American imperialist aggression. Meanwhile, both China and Russia are cooperating with Iran increasingly in the areas of energy and mutual defense. From a geopolitical perspective, Iran bridges the oil-rich regions of Middle East and Central Asia, lying adjacent to Iraq on the west and Afghanistan on the east. Iran is also a major oil and gas producer, and is thus crucial to the futures of importing nations. Moreover, the Iranian government has

voiced interest in selling its energy resources in currencies other than the U.S. dollar.[18]

It is easy to see how all this spells trouble for the United States. After all, Iran has buddied up not only with Russia and China, but also with Venezuela—a country that presently exports oil to the United States but is increasingly anti-U.S. and pro-Iran. While the United States and the rest of the world are using more oil than ever, and while the available oil is getting harder and more expensive to find due to peak oil, Iran has turned out to be a major oil player with enormous resources and influence in the Middle East. As we ponder the oil-strength of Iran, the comment of Ayatollah Ahmed Jannati, the secretary of the Iranian Guardian Council, rings in our ears: "In the final analysis, we are a nation against America. America is our enemy and we are America's enemy."[19]

This is not a healthy political state of affairs for the United States or for Israel. As noted previously, not only is Iran intent on pushing Israel into the sea, it also provides massive financial and military support to a number of terrorist organizations currently attacking Israel. Sad to say, things will get worse when Iran joins with other Muslim nations and Russia in a massive invasion into Israel.

Russia in Alliance with Muslim Nations

Some twenty-six hundred years ago, Ezekiel prophesied that the Jews would be regathered from "many nations" to the land of Israel in the endtimes (Ezekiel 36–37). He then prophesied that, sometime later, there would be an all-out invasion into Israel by a massive northern assault force whose goal will be to utterly obliterate the Jews. And with the sheer size of this assault force, Israel will have virtually no chance of defending itself. God, however, will intervene and supernaturally destroy the invaders (38:19–39:6). We read of this invading force in Ezekiel 38:1-6:

> And the word of the LORD came to me saying, "Son of man, set your face toward Gog of the land of Magog, the prince of Rosh, Meshech and Tubal, and prophesy against him and say, 'Thus says the Lord GOD, "Behold, I am against you, O Gog, prince of Rosh, Meshech and Tubal. I will turn you about and put hooks into your jaws, and I will bring you out, and all your army, horses and horsemen, all of them splendidly attired, a

> great company with buckler and shield, all of them wielding
> swords; Persia, Ethiopia and Put with them, all of them with
> shield and helmet; Gomer with all its troops; Beth-togarmah
> from the remote parts of the north with all its troops—many
> peoples with you.'"

What do all these strange words mean? A study of ancient biblical history, ancient secular history, and archeology helps us immensely in properly interpreting the passage.

Gog. Gog refers to the powerful leader of the end-times northern military coalition that will launch an invasion against Israel (Ezekiel 38). This term apparently refers to a king-like role—such as pharaoh, caesar, czar, or president. The term literally means "high," "supreme," "a height," or "a high mountain." Apparently, then, this czar-like military leader will be a man of great stature who commands tremendous respect. Note that he is *not* the Antichrist. You will end up in prophetic chaos if you try to make this identification. The Antichrist heads up a revived Roman empire (Daniel 2, 7), while Gog heads up an invasion force made up, as I will argue in a moment, of Russia and a number of Muslim nations. Moreover, Gog's invasion into Israel apparently constitutes a direct challenge to the Antichrist's covenant with Israel (Daniel 9:27). Further, Gog's moment in the limelight is short-lived (it is all over when God destroys the invading force—Ezekiel 38:18–39:6), whereas the Antichrist is in power a significant part of the tribulation period.

Magog. Magog, mentioned in the Table of Nations in Genesis 10:2, probably refers to the mountainous area near the Black and Caspian Seas, the former domain of the Scythians. More specifically, it likely refers to the area occupied today by the former southern Soviet republics of Kazakhstan, Kyrgyzstan, Uzbekistan, Turkmenistan, Tajikistan, and possibly even northern parts of modern Afghanistan. Significantly, this entire area is Muslim-dominated, with more than enough religious motivation to move against Israel.

Rosh. There has been significant debate regarding the meaning of the term *Rosh* in Ezekiel 38:2 and 39:1. Though the Hebrew term literally means "head," "top," or "chief," the debate erupts over whether the term should be taken as a proper noun or an adjective in the Ezekiel verses. Many of today's

English translations take the term as an adjective and translate the word as "chief." An example is the NIV, which reads: "Son of man, set your face against Gog, of the land of Magog, the *chief prince* of Meshech and Tubal" (emphasis added).

I believe Hebrew scholars C.F. Keil and Wilhelm Gesenius are correct in taking the term as a proper noun in Ezekiel, referring to a geographical place. The NASB, taking the term as a proper noun, reads: "Son of man, set your face toward Gog of the land of Magog, the *prince of Rosh*, Meshech and Tubal."

In recent years, evidence has surfaced that the translation of *Rosh* as an adjective ("chief prince") can be traced directly to the Latin Vulgate, translated by Jerome (AD 347–420), which in turn had been influenced by an earlier Jewish translator, Aquila. Scholar Clyde Billington informs us that "Jerome's incorrect translation of Rosh as an adjective has been followed by many of today's popular translations of the Bible. It is clear that this translation originated with the Jewish translator Aquila" and "was adopted by Jerome in the Vulgate."[20] Billington explains Jerome's faulty reasoning in translating the way he did:

> Jerome himself admits that he did not base his decision on grammatical considerations! Jerome seems to have realized that Hebrew grammar supported the translation of "prince of Rosh, Meshech, and Tubal" and that it did not support his own translation of "chief prince of Moshoch and Thubal." However, Jerome rejected translating Rosh as a proper noun because, "we could not find the name of this race [i.e. the Rosh people] mentioned either in Genesis or any other place in the Scriptures, or in Josephus." It was this non-grammatical argument that convinced Jerome to adopt Aquila's rendering of Rosh as an adjective ["chief"] in Ezekiel 38–39.[21]

Exegetically, the evidence supports taking Rosh as a proper noun (that is, as a geographical area). Hebrew scholar G.A. Cook affirms that this is "the most natural way of rendering the Hebrew."[22] Thomas Ice informs us that "normal Hebrew and Arabic grammar supports *Rosh* as a noun...Actually, Hebrew grammar demands that *Rosh* be taken as a noun. No example of Hebrew grammar has ever been cited that would support taking *Rosh* as an adjective."[23] Likewise, Randall Price concludes that "on linguistic and historical grounds, the case for taking Rosh as a proper noun rather than a noun-adjective is substantial and persuasive."[24] I agree with Billington's conclusion that the features of Hebrew grammar "dictate that Rosh be translated as a proper noun and not as an adjective...the grammatical arguments for the translation of 'Rosh' as a proper noun in Ezekiel 38–39 are conclusive and not really open for serious debate."[25]

If I am correct in taking the term as a geographical place, in company with the above scholars, then the question becomes: *Where is* this geographical place? For a number of reasons, I believe that Rosh likely refers to modern Russia. Not only have many highly respected Hebrew scholars come to this conclusion, but there is considerable historical evidence that a place known as Rosh—sometimes using alternate spellings such as Rus, Ros, and Rox—was familiar in the ancient world and was located in the territory now occupied by modern Russia. There is evidence of a people named Rosh/Rashu in the ninth through seventh centuries BC in Assyrian sources that predate the book of Ezekiel. Hence, quite early, we find evidence of a "Ros" people geographically located in today's Russia. Rosh also appears as a place name in Egyptian inscriptions as Rash, dating as early as 2600 BC. One inscription that dates to 1500 BC refers to a land called Reshu that was located to the north of Egypt (as is the case with modern Russia). Finally, in Ezekiel 39:2, Rosh is said to be "from the remotest parts of the north." The term *north* is to be understood in relation to Israel. If you draw a line straight north from Israel, you end up in Russia.

Russia, of course, has a long history of aggressions against Israel. During the 1967 Six-Day War, the Russians were poised to attack Israel, but backed down after President Lyndon Johnson ordered the U.S. 6th Fleet to steam toward Israel. When Egypt, Syria, and some other Arab/Islamic countries launched an attack against Israel in 1973, it soon became clear that Russia was providing the military muscle behind the attack, including weaponry, ammunition, intelligence, and military training. In 1982, then-Israeli Prime Minister Menachem Begin revealed that a secret but massive cache of Russian weaponry had been discovered in deep underground cellars in Lebanon, apparently pre-positioned for later use in a future invasion into Israel. The growing Russian alliance with Iran is therefore of great concern to Israel.

Meshech and Tubal. Meshech and Tubal—often mentioned together in Scripture—refer to the geographical territory to the south of the Black and Caspian Seas, which is today modern Turkey, though there may be some overlap with some neighboring countries. Meshech and Tubal are apparently the same as the *Mushki and Tabal* of the Assyrians, and the *Moschi and Tibareni* of the Greeks, who inhabited the territory that constitutes modern Turkey. This is confirmed by the ancient historian Herodotus.

Persia. Persia occupies the exact same territory presently occupied by Iran. In fact, in 1935 Persia became Iran. During the Iranian Revolution in 1979, the name changed to the Islamic Republic of Iran.

In view of what biblical prophecy reveals about the alliance between Rosh and Persia as well as other Muslim nations, it is highly revealing that Iran has now become the third largest recipient of Russian arms, with an estimated annual trade of $500 million. The Iranian government is involved in a massive, twenty-five-year national military modernization program—one entailing upgrades to its air defense, naval warfare, and land combat capabilities—built almost entirely around Russian technology and weaponry. Russia has also been assisting Iran in its nuclear program. Through Russia's assistance, Iran seems destined to become a dominant nation in the Middle East—far more dominant than Westerners (and Israelis) are comfortable with.

Ethiopia. Ethiopia is the geographical territory just south of Egypt on the Nile River—what is today known as Sudan. Sudan is a hard-line Islamic nation that is a kindred spirit with Iran in its venomous hatred of Israel. These nations are already such close allies that a mutual stand against Israel would not in the least be unexpected. This nation is infamous for its ties to terrorism and its harboring of Osama bin Laden from 1991 to 1996.

Put. Put, a land to the west of Egypt, is modern-day Libya. However, ancient Libya is larger than the Libya that exists today, and hence the boundaries of Put referred to in Ezekiel 38–39 may extend beyond modern Libya, perhaps including portions of Algeria and Tunisia.

Gomer. Gomer is likely modern-day Turkey. In support of this view, the historian Josephus said Gomer founded those whom the Greeks called the

Galatians. The Galatians of New Testament times lived in central Turkey. Hence, there is a direct connection of ancient Gomer to modern Turkey.

Moreover, many claim Gomer may be a reference to the ancient Cimmerians or Kimmerioi. History reveals that from around 700 BC, the Cimmerians occupied the geographical territory that is modern Turkey.

Beth-togarmah. Beth-togarmah is a Hebrew term that literally means "the House of Togarmah." Ezekiel 38:6 refers to Beth-togarmah as being from the remote parts of the north. Some expositors believe Beth-togarmah is another reference to modern-day Turkey, which is to the far north of Israel. (Keep in mind that Turkey used to be broken into several smaller territories.) This view is in keeping with the geography of Ezekiel's time, for in that day there was a city in Cappodocia (modern Turkey) known as Tegarma, Tagarma, Til-garimmu, and Takarama. If this identification is correct, this means that Turkey will be one of the nations in the northern military coalition that will invade Israel in the end-times.

Alliance Now Emerging. More than a few students of the Bible recognize that the very nations prophesied to join this alliance in the end-times are already coming together in our day. That this alliance is beginning to emerge after Israel became a nation again in 1948—with Jews continuing to stream into their homeland ever since, so that today more Jews are in Israel than anywhere else on earth—is considered highly significant by many. It appears that the stage may be being set for this future invasion into Israel.

A Future Invasion. Some interpreters deny that these chapters refer to a future invasion into Israel, holding instead that they refer to an invasion in the past. The evidence, however, is in favor of a future invasion:

1. There has never been an invasion into Israel on the scale of what is described in Ezekiel 38–39. Nor has there ever been an invasion into Israel involving the specific nations mentioned in the passage. Since it has not been fulfilled yet, its fulfillment must yet be future.

2. Ezekiel was clear that the things of which he spoke would be fulfilled "in the latter years" (Ezekiel 38:8) and "in the last

days" (38:16) from the standpoint of his day. Such phrases point to the end-times.

3. The unique alignment of nations as described in Ezekiel 38–39 has never occurred before, but is occurring in modern days.

4. An alliance between many of the nations mentioned in Ezekiel 38–39 may not have made good sense in Ezekiel's day (since some are not located near each other, and Islam did not yet exist), but it makes great sense today because the nations that make up the coalition are predominantly Muslim. That in itself is more than enough reason for them to unify to attack Israel, especially given current Islamic hatred for Israel.

5. Ezekiel affirmed that the invasion would occur after Israel had been regathered from all around the earth—"gathered from many nations" (Ezekiel 38:8,12)—to a land that had been a wasteland. Certainly there were occasions in Israel's history when the Jews were held in bondage. They were held in bondage in Egypt, and they went into captivity in Assyria as well as in Babylon. But in each of these cases, their deliverance involved being set free from a single nation, not *many* nations around the world. The only regathering of Jews from "many nations" around the world is the one that began in 1948 and is continuing today.

6. Since Ezekiel 36–37 is apparently being literally fulfilled (a regathering from "many nations"), it is reasonable and consistent to assume that chapters 38–39 will likewise be literally fulfilled. This is in keeping with the well-established literal fulfillment of biblical prophecies throughout the Old Testament.

7. Without a literal approach, we are left in a sea of relativism regarding what prophetic passages teach. Unless prophetic statements are taken in their normal sense, it is almost impossible to determine their meaning with any consistency. As the well-known dictum puts it, when the plain sense makes good sense, seek no other sense, lest one end up in nonsense.

I believe these various Muslim nations, along with Russia (in which

Islam is presently growing at a phenomenal pace), will invade Israel, and oil money will be the financial backbone of the invasion. Oil money is presently purchasing the weaponry and military equipment that will one day be used against Israel.

What Motivates This Invasion?

Not only do Muslims hate the Jews because they believe the land of Israel belongs to them by divine right (Allah allegedly gave it to them), Ezekiel states that the invaders want to plunder Israel's "silver and gold" and "cattle and goods" and "great spoil" (Ezekiel 38:11-13).

Arnold Fruchtenbaum notes that these are general Old Testament terms often used in reference to the spoils of war.[26] This "great spoil" might actually take a number of enticing forms. To begin, there are a number of wealthy people who live in Israel—over sixty-six hundred millionaires with total assets exceeding $24 billion.[27] The mineral resources of the Dead Sea—including forty-five billion tons of sodium, chlorine, sulfur, potassium, calcium, magnesium, and bromide[28]—are of inestimable worth. All in all, whoever controls the land of Israel can look forward to an incalculably large economic boost.

There have also been recent discoveries of gas and oil reserves in Israel. The three to five trillion cubic feet of proven gas reserves beneath Israel's soil could be worth up to $6 billion. Moreover, an Israeli oil company—Givot Olam Oil, headed by geophysicist Tovia Luskin—recently made the largest oil find in the history of the country. One news agency in Israel reports: "Israel may have struck gold—black gold, that is. A deposit close to a billion barrels may have been discovered at a site east of Kfar Saba, according to the fuel exploration company Givot Olam. The company announced…that latest estimates of the Meged-4 oil well have exceeded original predictions, and that it contains an extremely valuable deposit of oil."[29] It is reported that "the value of the oil at today's prices is approximately $46 billion."[30] The gas and oil beneath Israel's soil will surely be part of the enticement for Russia and her Muslim allies to move against Israel in the end-times. Especially with the oil fields of the Arabs presently peaking (or having *already* peaked), a large oil find in Israel would be incredibly enticing to Muslim neighbors.

Luskin, an Orthodox Jew, has been drilling for oil based on biblical guidance. *Givot Olam* means "everlasting hills" and comes from the passage in Deuteronomy where Moses blesses Ephraim and Manasseh, the descendants of Joseph, informing them that their land would yield "precious fruits" of the "deep lying beneath" of the "ancient mountains" and of the "everlasting hills" (Deuteronomy 33:13-17). Some have interpreted this as a reference to oil.[31]

Other Bible verses have led not only Luskin but others to conclude that there is oil beneath the ground in Israel. These include[32] (emphasis added):

- Genesis 49:25—"From the God of your father who helps you, and by the Almighty who blesses you with blessings of heaven above, *blessings of the deep that lies beneath,* blessings of the breasts and of the womb."

- Deuteronomy 33:13—"Of Joseph he said, 'Blessed of the LORD *be his land,* with the choice things of heaven, with the dew, and *from the deep lying beneath.*'"

- Deuteronomy 33:19—"They will call peoples to the mountain; there they will offer righteous sacrifices; for they will draw out the abundance of the seas, and *the hidden treasures of the sand.*"

- Deuteronomy 33:24—"Of Asher he said, 'More blessed than sons is Asher; may he be favored by his brothers, and *may he dip his foot in oil.*'"

- Deuteronomy 32:12-13—"The LORD alone guided him, and there was no foreign god with him. He made him ride on the high places of the earth, and he ate the produce of the field; and He made him suck honey from the rock, and *oil from the flinty rock.*"

- Isaiah 45:3—"I will give you the treasures of darkness and *hidden wealth of secret places,* so that you may know that it is I, the LORD, the God of Israel, who calls you by your name."

While many Bible scholars would probably say that seeing oil in these verses involves more eisegesis (reading a meaning into the text) than exegesis (drawing the meaning out of the text), Luskin believes such verses indicate that God has promised to bless Israel with the world's largest oil and gas fields. He believes these fields were providentially intended to be discovered in the end-times as the coming of the divine Messiah draws near. It is more likely, however, that those oil fields are the "hook in the jaw" that will draw the Muslim nations against Israel in the end-times (see Ezekiel 38:2-4).

God the Spoiler

Regardless of the massive Muslim coalition that will move against Israel in the end-times, Scripture reveals that God Himself will be the deliverer of Israel. As we discussed previously, because of its weakened condition, the United States apparently will not come to Israel's rescue.

Earthquake (Ezekiel 38:19-20)

God will first execute enemy forces by a massive earthquake. Elsewhere in prophetic Scripture, we are told that during the tribulation period there will be an increase in the number and intensity of earthquakes, just as birth pangs increase in number and intensity (see Matthew 24:7-8). The devastating earthquake described by Ezekiel—in which "the mountains... will be thrown down, the steep pathways will collapse and every wall will fall to the ground"—will cause many troops to die, transportation will be utterly disrupted, and the armies of the multinational forces will be thrown into utter chaos. So intense will this earthquake be that all the creatures on the earth feel its effect: "The fish of the sea, the birds of the heavens, the beasts of the field, all the creeping things that creep on the earth, and all the men who are on the face of the earth will shake at My presence" (Ezekiel 38:20).

Infighting Among Invaders (Ezekiel 38:21)

God will then induce the armies of the invading force to turn on each other and kill each other. There will seemingly be massive outbreaks of "friendly fire." This may be at least partially due to the confusion and chaos following the massive earthquake. As John F. Walvoord puts it, "In the pandemonium, communication between the invading armies will break down and they will begin attacking each other. Every man's sword will be against his brother (Ezek. 38:21). Fear and panic will sweep through the forces so each army will shoot indiscriminately at the others."[33] Adding to the confusion is the fact that the armies of the various nations speak different languages, and communication will be difficult at best.[34]

It may be that the Russians and Muslim nations turn on each other. Perhaps in the midst of the chaos, they suspect that the other is double-crossing them, and they respond by opening fire on each other. In any event, there will be countless casualties.

Disease (Ezekiel 38:22a)

God will then cause many troops to die due to the outbreak of disease. It's not hard to imagine how it all happens. Following the earthquake, countless dead bodies will be lying everywhere. Transportation will be disrupted so it will be difficult to transfer the wounded or bring in food and medicine. Even more dead bodies will be lying around after massive "friendly fire" breaks out. Meanwhile, myriad birds and other predatory animals will have a feast on this unburied flesh. All this is a recipe for the outbreak of pandemic disease, which, according to Ezekiel, will take many, many lives.

Rain, Hailstones, Fire, and Burning Sulfur (Ezekiel 38:22b)

Finally, God will inflict torrential rain, hailstones, fire, and burning sulfur upon the invading troops. Perhaps the powerful earthquake will set off volcanic eruptions in the region, thrusting into the atmosphere a hail of molten rock and burning sulfur (volcanic ash), which then falls upon the enemy troops and utterly destroys them. One only need recall the ultimate end of Sodom and Gomorrah to know how destructive all this will be on the northern coalition. By the time God's judgments are complete, virtually no one will be left standing.[35]

God will turn the tables on these invaders. They come to kill but are themselves killed. The invading troops believe their power to be overwhelming, but they end up being overwhelmed by the greater power of God. The invading troops come to take over a new land, but instead end up being buried in the land.

Magog Burns

Following all this, God then promises: "I will rain down fire on Magog and on all your allies who live safely on the coasts" (Ezekiel 39:6). Destruction of this area of the world (see the discussion earlier in this chapter) may include not only military targets such as missile silos, military bases, radar installations, and the like, but also religious centers, mosques, madrassas, Islamic schools and universities, and other facilities that preach hatred against Jews.[36]

This judgment will serve to nullify any possible reprisal or future attempts at invasion. No further attack against Israel by these evil forces will be possible.

Why God Destroys the Coalition

As the Protector of Israel, God's primary purpose in destroying the coalition will be to deliver Israel from harm. Ultimately, this is an outworking of the ancient covenant God made with His friend, Abraham. In Genesis 12:3, God promised Abraham: "I will bless those who bless you, and the one who curses you I will curse." Surely the Muslims—those who comprise this vast invading force—curse Israel and seek Israel's destruction, and hence God's curse falls upon the invaders in the form of an annihilating judgment.

Ponder the following scenario: This massive invading force is moving across the land like a cloud, and the Muslim invaders are shouting over and over, *Allahu Akbar*—meaning "Allah is the greatest." Following Yahweh's mighty judgment against the invaders, no one will be found anywhere shouting *Allahu Akbar*. What an awesome and glorious testimony this will be to the one true God!

The Current Threat Against Israel

Mahmoud Ahmadinejad, Iran's president, promises that Israel will soon be annihilated and will be "eliminated by one storm." This ominous threat is eye-opening when one considers that thousands of years ago, the prophet Ezekiel gave us history in advance by revealing that the future invaders will "come like a storm" and "will be like a cloud covering the land" (Ezekiel 38:9,16).

I do not believe in date-setting (Acts 1:7). Nor do I believe in sensationalism (Mark 13:32-37). I do believe, however, that we are called upon by Jesus to be accurate observers of the times (Matthew 16:1-3; Luke 21:29-33). A study of the world scene today seems to indicate that things are shaping up for the eventual military invasion envisioned by Ezekiel so long ago. One day, it will come to pass. God Himself assures everyone: "Behold, it is coming and it shall be done...That is the day of which I have spoken" (Ezekiel 39:8).

The Folly of Not Supporting Israel

Prophecy expert Charles Dyer warns that "the minute the United States turns its back on the State of Israel, we have made ourselves the enemy of God."[37] I think Dyer is correct. In Genesis 12:3 God promised Abraham and his descendants: "I will bless those who bless you, and the one who curses you I will curse." This ancient promise has never been revoked or repealed. Should the day ever come when the United States turns against Israel and (for example) joins in league with the Antichrist who heads the United States of Europe, *woe to this country*! Remember that God is a promise-keeper, and He will bless those who bless Israel and stand against those who stand against Israel.

Those who doubt this ought to consider the book of Esther, which is distinguished from other Bible books in that God is never mentioned. Yet God is at work behind the scenes all throughout the book. This short book describes how Haman launched an insidious plot to destroy the Jews. God not only thwarted the plot, but He brought the plotter's evil back upon himself (Haman was executed instead of the Jews). In order to bring about this end, God had earlier providentially placed the beautiful Esther, a Jewish woman, as the queen of the Persian king, Xerxes I, who ruled from 486 to 465 BC. I believe God elevated Esther to this position of authority specifically to save the Jews from destruction (see Esther 4:14), illustrating His providential control of human history.

God's commitment to bless those who bless Israel and to curse those who curse Israel is also illustrated for us in the Exodus. The Egyptian pharaoh cursed Israel by enslaving them. God therefore sent Moses to deliver Israel by inflicting ten plagues upon the Egyptians and their gods (Exodus 12:12).

In view of all this, were the United States to turn against Israel, it would place itself in the company of Pharaoh and Haman. After all, the Lord of Hosts affirms of Israel, "he who touches you, touches the apple of His eye" (Zechariah 2:8).

I am concerned about what stance the United States might take toward Israel following the rapture of the church. Once all Christians are removed from the United States (and from around the world), there will be far fewer pro-Israeli citizens seeking to bless Israel. Today, evangelical Christians constitute the vanguard of support for Jewish people, for they are the ones who take God's promises to Israel seriously. Following the rapture, I can envision anti-Semitism rising to ever new heights in America. If this happens, God's blessing will be removed all the more, thus further weakening America.

Mideast War Imminent?

Aside from the oil dilemma, the possibility of Iran attaining nuclear weaponry could ignite things in a big way in the Middle East. The Israeli government, under Prime Minister Benjamin Netanyahu, has repeatedly declared that a primary foreign policy objective is to prevent Iran from obtaining nuclear weapons. The reason for this is that Israel is a "one bomb state"—a single nuclear weapon would destroy it. Political analysts now say that Iran has the capability of producing a nuclear weapon—or will soon! At the time of this writing, world leaders are in talks with the Iranian government to curtail this, but most in the international community express doubts that the Iranian government will make any serious concessions on its nuclear program.

As reported in *WorldNetDaily*, "An Israeli first-strike on Iran's nuclear facilities becomes increasingly likely to the extent Israel feels isolated from the world community and concludes there is no chance the Obama administration will ever be able to induce Iran to stop enriching uranium, regardless of how seriously the president intends to push direct negotiations as a strategy."[38] Jerome Corsi, coauthor of *Showdown with Nuclear Iran*, says, "We have already seen two wars launched by Israel against terrorist surrogates financed and supported by Iran: the 2006 war against Hezbollah in Lebanon and the 2008 war against Hamas in the Gaza Strip...Now, a war between Israel and Iran is on the near horizon."[39] It is sobering to ponder that if Israel launches a first strike against Iran, a coalition of Muslim nations may retaliate with overwhelming force—and Russia may join them.

Pray for the peace of Jerusalem (Psalm 122:6).

Political Realignments in the End-Times: Other Nations

In chapter 8, I noted that biblical prophecy informs us what the political landscape will look like in the years prior to the second coming of Jesus Christ. I focused primary attention on the "super-sign" of Israel becoming a nation again after a long and worldwide dispersion. The initial fulfillment of this came in 1948, and since that year many Jews have been streaming back to Israel for repatriation. Then, in chapter 9, I focused on Israel's endangerment, as prophesied in Scripture, particularly from the end-times military coalition that will one day invade Israel. God Himself will destroy this coalition.

In this chapter, I will narrow my focus to the revived Roman Empire, a post-rapture United States, Iraq and its capital city Babylon, and China. In the process, I will reveal how the oil dilemma relates to the end-times political structure of the world.

A Shift in the Balance of Power to Europe

The Bible is clear that in the end-times, a revived Roman Empire—what we might call the United States of Europe—will become a political and economic powerhouse. God's Word addresses this in the book of Daniel. Daniel 7:3-8 refers to four beasts, representing four successive kingdoms in the unfolding of human history: "Four great beasts came up out of the sea, different from one another" (v. 3).

The first, Daniel says, was "like a lion and had eagles' wings," but "its wings were plucked off" (v. 4). This imagery represents Babylon, its lion-like quality indicating power and strength. The wings indicate rapid mobility, while the plucking of the wings indicate a removal of mobility—perhaps a reference to Nebuchadnezzar's insanity or to Babylon's deterioration following his death.

In verse 5 Daniel refers to "another beast, a second one, like a bear, an animal of great strength. It was raised up on one side. It had three ribs in its mouth between its teeth; and it was told, 'Arise, devour much flesh.'" This kingdom is Medo-Persia, and the ribs are vanquished nations—perhaps Lydia, Babylon, and Egypt. Medo-Persia was well-known for its strength and fierceness in battle (see Isaiah 13:17-18).

Daniel then describes a third beast, "like a leopard, with four wings of a bird on its back. And the beast had four heads, and dominion was given to it" (7:6). The leopard was known for its swiftness, cunning, and agility. This imagery represents Greece under Alexander the Great. The reference to the "four heads" are the four generals who divided the kingdom following Alexander's death, ruling Macedonia, Asia Minor, Syria, and Egypt.

Finally, in verses 7 and 8, Daniel describes the fourth beast—a mongrel beast composed of parts of a lion, bear, and leopard that was more terrifying and powerful than the three preceding beasts:

> Behold, a fourth beast, terrifying and dreadful and exceedingly strong. It had great iron teeth; it devoured and broke in pieces and stamped what was left with its feet. It was different from all the beasts that were before it, and it had ten horns. I considered the horns, and behold, there came up among them another horn, a little one, before which three of the first horns were plucked up by the roots. And behold, in this horn were eyes like the eyes of a man, and a mouth speaking great things.

This wild imagery refers to the Roman Empire, which fell apart in the fifth century AD. It will be revived, however, in the end-times, apparently comprised of ten nations ruled by ten kings (ten horns). An animal uses its horns as a weapon (see Psalm 69:31; 92:10). For this reason, the horn eventually came to be seen as a symbol of power and might. As an extension of this symbol, horns in biblical times were sometimes used as emblems of dominion, representing kingdoms and kings, as is the case in the books of Daniel and Revelation (see Daniel 7–8; Revelation 12:3;

13:1,11; 17:3-16). So, the ten horns in Daniel 7 refer to ten kings who rule ten nations.

An eleventh horn—a little horn (the Antichrist)—starts out in an insignificant way, but grows powerful enough (a "strong man," so to speak) to uproot three of the existing horns (kings). He eventually comes into absolute power and dominance over this revived Roman Empire (see 2 Thessalonians 2:3-10; Revelation 13:1-10).

Rome has never consisted of a ten-nation confederacy with ten co-rulers. If it has not happened in the past, this prophecy must be about the future. Note that the prophecies regarding the first three world empires have been literally fulfilled, but the last has not yet been fulfilled. Those prophecies that have not yet been fulfilled will be fulfilled just as literally as those that have already been fulfilled. This final form of the Roman Empire will be prominent during the tribulation.

Related to all this, in Daniel 2 we read of a prophetic dream that Nebuchadnezzar had. In this dream, this end-times Roman Empire was pictured as a mixture of iron and clay (see verses 41-43). Daniel, the great dream-interpreter, understood this to mean that just as iron is strong, so this latter-day Roman Empire would be strong. But just as iron and clay do not naturally mix with each other, so this latter-day Roman Empire would have some divisions. The components of this empire would not be completely integrated with each other.

Many modern biblical interpreters see the European Union as a primary prospect for the ultimate fulfillment of this prophecy. Thomas Ice notes that "the goal of the European Union is to unite all of Europe into one union that will also promote peace, harmony, and prosperity and prevent future world conflicts. This 'European Dream,' as it is often labeled, proposes a single government that will eliminate national rivalries and conflicts within Europe."[1]

In Daniel 2, it may be that the clay mixed with iron points to the diversity (race, religion, and politics) of the peoples in the ten nations that make up the empire. The clay and iron indicate weakness and strength at the same time, something that is true of the European Union today. The European Union possesses great economic and political strength, but it is also clear that the nations that comprise this union are diverse in culture, language, and politics, and are not *perfectly* united. At present, the European Union has its own parliament, a rotating presidency, a supreme court, a common currency used in many member nations, unrestricted travel of citizens among member nations, and it is working toward a unified military.[2] What is taking place in Europe today may be a prelude to the eventual revived Roman Empire of Daniel's prophecy!

It is entirely possible that a shift in the balance of power could occur as a direct result of the impending peak oil crisis. The scenario might look something like the following.

First, the United States—the world's heaviest consumer of oil—diminishes in power as a result of the oil crisis and perhaps other factors discussed previously in this book. The balance of power eventually shifts to Europe as well as to the Middle East. From that point forward, the United States may assume a posture of isolationism, or perhaps it will become an ally with the emerging European superpower (more on this shortly).

Meanwhile, European leaders recognize that their respective nations must have an uninterrupted flow of oil or they will not only suffer economically but also succumb to utter social disruption. They also recognize their need for some kind of protective guarantee that will thwart extremist Islamic terror from being imported from the Middle East. Hence, it would make sense for these European nations—ten in number—to consolidate so they can flex their collective muscle to accomplish their goals. It also makes sense that a single powerful and charismatic leader will emerge to rule this ten-nation confederacy.

On a broader level, in the coming years more and more people may decide that it is a survival necessity for a world leader to emerge who will solve the Middle East and other global problems. Perhaps things will get so bad that the only hope for survival will be a world leader who will take control. Prophecy experts John F. Walvoord and Mark Hitchcock put it this way:

> How long can the world tolerate this explosive situation with hostages, terrorist attacks, the escalating Middle East crisis, the proliferation of nuclear weapons, disrupted oil supplies, and the daily threat of war?
>
> The only real solution is a peace treaty that settles disputes, disarms the antagonists, and provides absolute guarantees. In short, a peace treaty backed up by force. A powerful leader will seize world attention by such an offer when the world is on the brink of chaos. He will give the world what it wants. He will bring

terror under control, guarantee the flow of oil, and temporarily diffuse the time bomb in the Middle East.[3]

Today we live in perpetual uncertainty and unrest. People all around the world seek peace. They yearn for safety and security. It is not just the oil crisis, but also the threat of nuclear attack, bioterrorism, chemical warfare, suicide bombers, and the like that is causing global stress as never before. People feel as if they are under constant threat. In view of this, it is understandable why many would yearn for a leader to emerge who can bring sanity to a world gone mad.

As global stresses increase over peak oil and other issues in the coming years, the stage is increasingly being set for the emergence of this powerful world leader in Europe. He is the one who will bring peace, it is believed.

When will such a peace settlement come? It is impossible and unwise (and *anti-scriptural*) to set a date. However, Scripture reveals that a covenant will be made between this European leader and Israel that will guarantee Israel the freedom and security to rebuild a Jewish temple and reactivate the Jewish sacrifices (Daniel 9:26-27). It will be a covenant backed by force.

This leader, of course, is the Antichrist. The apostle Paul warned of him, calling him a "man of lawlessness" (2 Thessalonians 2:3,8,9). This man will perform counterfeit signs and wonders and deceive many people during the tribulation (2 Thessalonians 2:9-10). The apostle John describes this anti-God person in the book of Revelation as "the beast" (Revelation 13:1-10).

After he makes his peace treaty with Israel, he will then seek to dominate the world, double-cross and destroy the Jews, persecute believers, and set up his own kingdom (Revelation 13). He will speak arrogant and boastful words in glorifying himself (2 Thessalonians 2:4). His assistant, the False Prophet who is called "the beast from the earth," will seek to make the world worship him (Revelation 13:11-12). People around the world will be forced to receive his mark, without which they cannot buy or sell, thereby controlling the global economy *and* global energy resources (Revelation 13:16-17). However, to receive this mark ensures one of being the recipient of God's wrath. The Antichrist will eventually rule the whole world (Revelation 13:7-8).

Earlier in the book, I noted that even some secular analysts now suggest that our only hope for dealing with peak oil is some kind of global control. For example, Kenneth Deffeyes warns that "if the world oil shortage becomes sufficiently painful, there could be a temptation for a military seizure of the oil fields [in the Middle East] and the establishment of a 'world protectorate.'"[4] Matthew Simmons likewise says that "a global solution is needed to address how we can use oil far more efficiently than in our present system. A global solution is the only real option for addressing the energy gap."[5]

Prophecy experts have noted that already we see the "urge for globalism in at least the following areas: government, economics, religion, the environment, military, commerce and trade, manufacturing, banking, business, population control, education, management, publishing, entertainment, personal health and well-being, wealth redistribution, agriculture, law, science, medicine, sports, travel, music, electronics, the Internet and information availability, and so many more areas."[6] The book of Revelation tells us that the Antichrist will ultimately lead a global union—an *anti-God* union (see Revelation 13:3-18).

When one considers the multiple cascading problems facing humanity—including peak oil, the Middle East conflict, terrorism, overpopulation, starvation, pollution, and economic instability—it is entirely feasible that increasing numbers of people will come to believe that such problems can be solved only on a global level. They may think that the only hope for human survival is a strong and effective world government. As these sentiments grow, the stage becomes progressively set for the emergence of the Antichrist.

The technology that makes possible a world government—including instant global media via television and radio, the Internet, and supercomputers—is now in place. To illustrate, we know from the book of Revelation that no one will be able to buy or sell who is unwilling to worship the Antichrist. Keeping track of all people and all selling establishments is possible today through advanced computer technology. It is probable that every business and every person around the globe will have a unique account number that will enable instant tracking and processing of all financial transactions. Further, high-tech weaponry—computer-guided missiles, nuclear submarines, fighter jets, and the like—presently exists to enforce obedience to such a world government.

United States: A European Ally in the End-times?

While the United States is not mentioned in biblical prophecy, it is possible that a weakened United States—no longer a superpower—will initially become an ally with the United States of Europe, the revived Roman Empire, early in the tribulation. After all, most citizens of the United States have roots in Europe and would likely be more open to become a European ally than with any other geopolitical entity.

The United States will then be subsumed in the globalism that will emerge and prevail during the tribulation. Even in our day, the Obama administration seems to be moving us away from American national sovereignty and is open to handling more and more problems globally. Mark Hitchcock says that "the United States is slowly, subtly, yet relentlessly being drawn away from national sovereignty into a globalist order. NATO, the UN, GATT, NAFTA, the WTO, and many other acronyms signal the startling trend away from U.S. sovereignty and toward our submission to multinational treaties, organizations, and courts of law."[7]

According to one report, "Dick Morris notes that Obama at the meeting of the G-20 in London has agreed to enter the United States into an economical arrangement that will regulate our economy in terms of the international interests of this European dominated oligarchy at the expense of American interests." Morris comments that "now we may no longer look to presidential appointees, confirmed by the Senate, to make policy for our economy. These decisions will be made internationally." Morris told Greta Van Susteren of *Fox News*, "It's a whole new world of financial regulation in which, essentially, all of the U.S. regulatory bodies and all U.S. companies are put under international regulation, international supervision. It really amounts to a global economic government." He concludes, "This truly creates a global economic system. From now on, don't look to Washington for the rule making, look to Brussels."[8]

We can also surmise that if the Ezekiel invasion—the invasion into Israel by Russia, Iran, Sudan, Turkey, Libya, and other Muslim nations (Ezekiel 38–39)—takes place either prior to the beginning of the tribulation or in the early part of the tribulation, with God's subsequent destruction of the invaders, this might open the door not only for the revived Roman Empire to slide into first position as the "superpower of the day," but also for the Antichrist to quickly emerge as leader of the world.

It is also relevant—and highly disturbing—that when Armageddon breaks out at the end of the tribulation, troops from the United States may be there. Zechariah 12:3 is clear: "It will come about in that day that I will make Jerusalem a heavy stone for *all the peoples*; all who lift it will be severely injured. And *all the nations of the earth* will be gathered against it" (emphasis added). The phrase, "all the nations of the earth," certainly includes the United States, assuming the country still exists at that time. Likewise, in Zechariah 14:2 we read: "For I will gather *all the nations* against Jerusalem to battle, and the city will be captured, the houses plundered, the women ravished and half of the city exiled, but the rest of the people will not be cut off from the city" (emphasis added). Again, "all the nations" includes the United States. Likewise, we read in Revelation 16:14 that "the kings of the whole world" will be gathered together "for the war of the great day of God, the Almighty." The "kings of the whole world" would include the president of the United States.

It is helpful to keep in mind that following the rapture of the church, there will not be any Christians on the earth.[9] Many of the people in the United States who had long supported Israel will have just vanished to be with the Lord in heaven. It is easy to see how a Christian-less United States could ally with the revived Roman Empire and then find itself in league with the Antichrist.

What About Iraq?

In the previous chapter, I addressed how Ezekiel 38:1-6 depicts a northern coalition of nations that will one day invade Israel. I believe this coalition will include Russia, Iran, Sudan, Turkey, Libya, Kazakhstan, Kyrgyzstan, Uzbekistan, Turkmenistan, Tajikistan, Armenia, and possibly northern Afghanistan. One is naturally curious as to why Iraq is not mentioned as a part of the invading coalition. Certainly today's Iraq would dearly love to see Israel annihilated. So why no mention?

There are several possible answers. First, Iraq may indeed be a part of this coalition. In addition to the specific nations mentioned in Ezekiel 38, we find the phrase "and many peoples with you" (verses 6,9,15,22). It may be that Iraq is a part of the "many peoples."

Another possible scenario—perhaps the better option—is that Iraq will not be a part of this Islamic invading coalition because a rebuilt Babylon (capital of Iraq) will eventually become the headquarters of the Antichrist during the tribulation (Revelation 17–18). Scripture reveals that the Antichrist will emerge as a leader in the United States of Europe and will sign a seven-year peace pact with Israel (Daniel 9:27). This will constitute the beginning of the tribulation. He apparently eventually relocates to Babylon. If the Ezekiel invasion takes place in the first half of the tribulation, Iraq could not possibly be a part of the invading force simply because Iraq, with its capital in Babylon, will be controlled by the Antichrist, who signed the peace pact with Israel. It may be that the nations of Ezekiel 38:1-6 launch an invasion into Israel in defiance of the Antichrist. In any event, God utterly destroys the invaders (Ezekiel 38:19–39:6).

When the late Saddam Hussein was in power, he spent over one billion dollars in oil money to enhance the city—essentially as a monument to himself. Apparently, however, even more oil money will be spent to rebuild Babylon as a suitable habitation for the world leader, the Antichrist. The staggering oil wealth of Iraq means that it is just a matter of time before it becomes a city of splendor.

When you think about it, it seems logical that Babylon would be involved in end-times prophecy. As Thomas Ice put it, "Just as Babylon has played an important role in past history, so she is scheduled by God—as revealed in prophecy—to play a central role in the future. Babylon will likely become the capital for the Antichrist during the coming seven-year tribulation." Indeed, based on Isaiah 13:19, Ice states that "end-times prophecy demands that Babylon be rebuilt and become an important city in the world affairs during the tribulation."[10]

It is fascinating to ponder that God Himself providentially placed that oil beneath the ground in Iraq. Indeed, an oil-rich Iraq is part of God's blueprint for the end-times. As one commentator put it, "It's no accident that Babylon is in Iraq, a nation with such staggering oil reserves. God said that Babylon will be rebuilt as a great commercial center in the end-times."[11] The oil in Iraq, then, is making possible the rebuilding of Babylon, in fulfillment of biblical prophecy. No one would have thought this possible eighty years ago. But with the discovery of an abundance of oil there in 1927, it now becomes clear why the Antichrist would one day set up headquarters there. It will be a veritable throne of wealth.[12]

Babylon's appeal to the Antichrist may also relate to how nicely positioned the city is, strategically located in close proximity to other oil-rich nations, such as Iran, Kuwait, and Saudi Arabia. As Nathan Jones put it, the Antichrist's residence in Babylon would be logical "because if he has a peace treaty with Israel and it is all about the resources of the Middle East, it would be very smart to have a capital in the oil fields where you can defend it well."[13] One cannot help but ponder: *What if the Antichrist succeeds where Saddam Hussein failed and is able to bring these nations under his wings?* He would control immense wealth and power—up to two-thirds of the remaining oil on the planet. It is hard to think of a better economic and commercial center in the world. Other countries, such as China, may find it difficult to control their lust for the oil treasures associated with this global center.

China, Oil, and the Middle East

In Revelation 9:16 we read of a large army in which "the number of mounted troops was twice ten thousand times ten thousand"—which is 200 million. These 200 million are said to be led by four fallen angels (Revelation 9:14-15). Some expositors believe the 200 million might be demonic spirits, given the description of these "mounted troops" in verse 17. Others, however, believe this may be a metaphorical reference to the army of China, which even now has a standing army of 200 million.

China, of course, is now the world's second largest guzzler of oil, and its oil consumption is annually increasing seven times faster than that of the United States. At current rates, China will one day surpass the United States in the volume of oil it requires. This is significant for end-times geopolitics.

Like the United States, China has to make any deals it can to find enough oil to feed the ever-increasing demand. China recently has been cultivating a relationship with Saudi Arabia, and it is noteworthy that "Saudi Arabia's exports to the U.S. have been declining, while its exports to China have been increasing."[14] China has also entered into oil agreements with Venezuela, one of the oil suppliers for the United States. China is also seeking to make oil deals with Canada, another of the U.S.'s suppliers. Still further, China is seeking Iran's favor, and is even selling some of its sophisticated missiles to Iran.

China to Iran: "We like your oil."

Iran to China: "We like your missiles."

One to another: "Let's do business."

Meanwhile, as an intelligence report reveals, "there is no doubt that

Iran's nuclear program is a potential source of an imminent showdown with the West. Therefore, China's support for Iran becomes critical—the kind of support that can turn a regional conflict into a global one."[15]

Presently, about 58 percent of China's oil comes from the Middle East, but that figure will rise to about 70 percent in the next five years. This means several things. China, from here on out, will be competing directly with the United States and other nations for that precious remaining oil in the Middle East. This, in turn, makes the Middle East all the richer and all the more strategically important to protect. All eyes are now on the Middle East. All eyes are on the shrinking (oil) pie in the Middle East.

Fears about peak oil could increasingly "exacerbate tensions among great powers. For example, note China's obsessive concern about energy and Washington's growing concern about China's rising power. Imagine how tense Sino-U.S. relations could become against the backdrop of dwindling oil supplies or even the rising perception of such dwindling supplies."[16]

Biblical prophecies indicate that there will one day be an invasion from the east against the Antichrist and his forces. It will apparently take place at the very end of the tribulation period. Speaking of the Antichrist, Daniel 11:44 tells us, "But rumors from the East and from the North will disturb him, and he will go forth with great wrath to destroy and annihilate many." Apparently, China will seek to challenge the authority of the Antichrist, and it infuriates him. With a standing army of some 200 million, the challenge will be substantial. In fact, one-third of the global population will be slaughtered during this invasion (see Revelation 9:15,18).

Revelation 16:12 tells us that "the sixth angel poured out his bowl on the great river, the Euphrates; and its water was dried up, so that the way would be prepared for the kings from the east." This movement of troops is apparently part of a worldwide gathering of nations that will participate in "the battle on the great day of God Almighty." Verse 16 indicates that the geographical epicenter of the battle is Mount Megiddo to the north of Jerusalem, also called Armageddon.

Why does China launch this invasion in the end-times as the tribulation comes to a climax? It is entirely possible that it will be a desperate act of survival. China's military action will be a direct challenge to the authority of the Antichrist, who—headquartered in Babylon at this time—will be in control of the world's oil supply in the Middle East. This control of the world's oil makes it easy for him to choke off any nation he chooses. It may be that China gets desperate for fuel and has no other choice but to move against the Satan-inspired oil czar who rules Babylon. Biblical prophecy reveals that the Chinese army is able to destroy this city of the Antichrist, and with Babylon in ruins, the Antichrist retreats to Israel. Walvoord and Hitchcock explain it this way:

> By this time the Antichrist will have retreated to Israel, so the great eastern army will advance to Israel for the final show-down of *east versus west*. The horrific clash of armies comes at Armageddon in northern Israel. The word Armageddon literally means "Mount of Megiddo," and refers to a location about 60 miles north of Jerusalem. This is the location of Barak's battle with the Canaanites (Judges 4) and Gideon's battle with the Midianites (Judges 7). This will be the site for the final horrific battles of humankind just prior to the second coming (Revelation 16:16).[17]

Napoleon is reported to have once commented that this site is the greatest battlefield he had ever witnessed. Of course, the battles Napoleon fought will dim in comparison to Armageddon. So horrible will Armageddon be that no one would survive if it were not for Christ coming again (Matthew 24:22). Scripture reveals that God Himself will destroy the armies of the Antichrist and False Prophet, and all other armies that participate in the "battle on the great day of God the Almighty" (Revelation 16:14). This will occur when He shall gather them "to the place that in Hebrew is called Armageddon" (Revelation 16:16 NIV).

Oil Crisis and Global Apocalypse

A good case can be made that oil has an awful lot to do with the geo-political structure of the world in the end-times, as well as the conflicts that will erupt. Here are the main facts to keep in mind:

■ The precedent has already been set for nations going to war over oil. The Gulf War is a prime example.

■ Just as nations have gone to war over oil in the past, they will likely do so in the future. The stage is even now being set for global conflict.

- Peak oil and its aftermath will likely be a strong contributing factor to the ultimate demise of the United States. Other contributing factors might include implosion due to moral degeneracy, the possibility of a nuclear attack, the possibility of an EMP attack, and perhaps the rapture. Following this demise, it seems viable that the United States will become an ally with the United States of Europe—the revived Roman Empire—which will be a future economic and political powerhouse in the end-times.

- China is a huge consumer of oil and may one day surpass the United States in its thirst for oil. It is therefore making deals with Saudi Arabia, Iran, Venezuela, and other oil-rich countries.

- The world is engulfed in such unrest, insecurity, and turmoil that people yearn for a solution that will restore sanity to the world. Many believe that only a global leader will be able to bring about security and peace. The Antichrist will fill this need and will—at least temporarily—bring sanity, having solved the Middle East crisis.

- The Antichrist, who first comes into power as the head of the revived Roman Empire, will bring about peace by signing a covenant with Israel.

- With Iraq's oil wealth, Babylon will also rise to become a powerful economic center in the end-times.

- The Antichrist will, at some point, transfer his headquarters to Babylon, strategically located near Iran, Kuwait, and Saudi Arabia, with a view to control all the oil wealth in the Middle East.

- One day, the Ezekiel invasion will take place. This will involve Russia, Iran, Sudan, Turkey, Libya, and other Muslim nations launching a massive invasion into Israel. This will be done in staunch defiance of the Antichrist. The entire campaign will apparently be financed by oil money.

- God will destroy the invaders, and this may create a shift in the balance of power that enables the Antichrist to come into global dominion, headquartered in Babylon.

- Toward the end of the tribulation, China—perhaps in an act of desperation to obtain the oil it needs to survive—will defy the Antichrist and move against him. China and the various other nations gather at the Mount of Megiddo for a horrible campaign known as Armageddon.

- Christ Himself returns at the height of this campaign, destroying all the anti-God armies of the world.

- Christ then sets up His millennial kingdom, over which He will rule for a thousand years.

Maranatha!

11

The Convergence Factor:
Concurrent Signs of the Times

I n this book, we have traversed some rather startling territory. To review:

- The United States is now using more oil than ever. China and India are close behind. In reality, all 192 nations of the world are oil addicts.

- At present, the margin between the supply of oil and demand for oil is razor thin.

- We are facing an imminent and severe oil crisis—*peak oil*— that could serve not only to weaken the United States and damage the world economy, but also generate increasing world tensions as nations seek to protect their portion of the remaining oil reserves.

- In the coming years, the supply of oil will increasingly be exceeded by the demand for oil.

- The infrastructure of American society is heavily dependent on oil (transportation, manufacturing, farming, and the like). The infrastructure cannot shift to alternative energies overnight. Such a shift could take a decade or more.

- Iran, who hates the United States, has become a major player in the global oil market and exercises immense influence in the Middle East.

- Other Middle Eastern nations also dislike the United States.

- Some of these Middle Eastern nations are using some of their immense oil profits to fund terrorist organizations.

- The United States now finds itself in the untenable position of spending great amounts of money to fight terrorism while at the same time spending great amounts of money to purchase oil from Middle Eastern countries that ends up funding terrorism.

- In terrorist efforts to bring ruin to the United States, various "choke points" related to major oil fields may be attacked.

- Middle Eastern dollars are also being spent to alter the way Americans think about Islam by financially underwriting pro-Islamic courses at American universities.

- Every U.S. president has been ineffective in achieving energy independence for our country.

- Meanwhile, Iran continues its hot pursuit of nuclear weapons, with Russia's assistance.

- Concurrently, Israel continues to be a sore spot in the world, as prophesied in Scripture (Zechariah 12:2-3).

- Alliances are currently emerging (or have already emerged) between Russia, Iran, and other Muslim nations—the *precise* nations Ezekiel identifies as part of the northern military coalition that will one day invade Israel (Ezekiel 38:1-6).

- Many of these Muslim nations—especially Iran—are spewing forth increasingly vitriolic threats against Israel. They seek to literally wipe Israel off the map. Mahmoud Ahmadinejad, the president of Iran, promises that this will happen in the near future.

- Nations have gone to war over oil in the past. They will likely do so again—including possibly during the future tribulation period.

■ Most Americans today are living in denial, with nary a worry (much like the days of Noah). This means that the years following peak oil—because of American indifference and unpreparedness—will be especially painful for many in this country.

■ Humanity is clearly on a collision course with geology.

Throughout this book (especially in the latter half), I have sought to demonstrate how the impending global oil dilemma relates to biblical prophecy. Among other things, we have seen that this dilemma greatly affects the geopolitical structure of the world in the end-times, and relates directly to the continued escalation of Middle East tensions. We have also seen that, one day, the Antichrist will set up headquarters in Babylon, in the vicinity of all the Middle Eastern oil fields, thereby gaining and maintaining control of immense oil wealth. Oil may play a role in the events directly leading up to Armageddon.

If the impending oil dilemma does relate to biblical prophecy and the end-times, as I have argued, then one would naturally expect to find other prophecies in the Bible that verify that we are indeed living in the end-times. I believe that the "signs of the times" recorded for us in the pages of Scripture point to the reality that we are living in the end-times. In a number of cases, the stage is apparently being set for signs that will find ultimate fulfillment in the tribulation.

God Predicts the Future

God has the ability to foretell the future. His ability to foretell future events separates Him from all the false gods of paganism. Addressing the polytheism of Isaiah's time, God Himself said:

> "Who then is like me? Let him proclaim it.
>   Let him declare and lay out before me
> what has happened since I established my ancient people,
>   and what is yet to come—
>   yes, let him foretell what will come.
> Do not tremble, do not be afraid.
>   Did I not proclaim this and foretell it long ago?
> You are my witnesses. Is there any God besides me?
>   No, there is no other Rock; I know not one."
>   (Isaiah 44:7-8 NIV)

> "Who foretold this long ago,
>   who declared it from the distant past?
> Was it not I, the LORD?
>   And there is no God apart from me."
>   (Isaiah 45:21 NIV)

> "I foretold the former things long ago,
>   my mouth announced them and I made them known;
>   then suddenly I acted, and they came to pass...
> Therefore I told you these things long ago;
>   before they happened I announced them to you
> so that you could not say,
>   'My idols did them;
>   my wooden image and metal god ordained them.'"
>   (Isaiah 48:3,5 NIV)

Of course, anyone can make predictions—that is easy. Having them fulfilled is another story altogether. The more statements you make about the future and the greater the detail, the better the chances are that you will be proven wrong. But *God has never been wrong.* There are well over one hundred prophecies in the Old Testament that refer to the coming Messiah, and all of them were literally fulfilled.

For example, Scripture prophesies that the Messiah would be: 1) from the seed of a woman (Genesis 3:15); 2) the offspring of Abraham (Genesis 12:3); 3) from the tribe of Judah (Genesis 49:10); 4) the son of David (Jeremiah 23:5-6); 5) conceived of a virgin (Isaiah 7:14); 6) born in Bethlehem (Micah 5:2); 7) the heralded Messiah (Isaiah 40:3); 8) the coming King (Zechariah 9:9); 9) the One suffering for our sins (Isaiah 53); 10) the One pierced in His side (Zechariah 12:10); 11) the One dying about AD 33 (Daniel 9:24-25); and 12) the One rising from the dead (Psalm 2; 16).

A Literal Method

Because prophecies about the first coming of Christ were literally fulfilled, the precedent has been set, and we may expect that all the prophecies about the second coming and the events that lead up to it (the "signs of the times") will be fulfilled literally as well. This is very important, for one out of every twenty-five verses in the New Testament refers to the second coming!

There are other reasons for interpreting Scripture (and prophecy) literally. For example, 1) a literal approach is the normal approach in all languages; 2) the greater part of the Bible makes sense when taken literally; 3) the "literal method" will take the secondary (or metaphorical) meaning whenever it is demanded (such as when Jesus said He was the "door"—John 10:7); 4) it is the only safe check on the subjectively prone imagination of man; and 5) it is the only approach in line with the nature of inspiration (every word of Scripture is "God-breathed"—2 Timothy 3:16).

As we examine the Scriptures, we find confirmation for a literal method of interpretation within its very pages. For example:

1. Later biblical texts take earlier ones as literal. To illustrate, the creation events in Genesis 1–2 are taken literally by later books (see, for example, Exodus 20:10-11). This is likewise the case regarding the creation of Adam and Eve (Matthew 19:4-6; 1 Timothy 2:13), the Fall of Adam and his resulting death (Romans 5:12-14), Noah's flood (Matthew 24:38-39), and the accounts of Jonah (Matthew 12:39-42), Moses (1 Corinthians 10:1-5), and numerous other historical figures.

2. By specifically indicating within the text the presence of "parables" (see Matthew 13:3) or an "allegory" (Galatians 4:24), the Bible thereby indicates that the usual meaning is a literal one.

3. By giving the interpretation of a parable, Jesus revealed that there is a literal meaning behind them (Matthew 13:18-23).

4. By rebuking those who did not interpret the resurrection literally, Jesus indicated the literal interpretation of the Old Testament was the correct one (Matthew 22:29-32; see also Psalm 2; 16).

5. By interpreting prophecy literally (Luke 4:16-21), Jesus indicated His acceptance of the literal interpretation of the Old Testament.

God Is All-Knowing

Christians have often referred to prophecy as history written in advance. I think it is more accurate to say that prophecy is *God's revelation* of history in advance. We cannot leave God out of the equation, for only God in His omniscience knows the future.

In some Christian circles today it is fashionable to deny that God is all-knowing or knows the future (as is the case with "open theists"). Such a view is contrary to the Bible. Because God transcends time—because He is *above* time—He can see the past, present, and future as a single act. "God's knowledge of all things is from the vantage point of eternity, so that the past, present, and future are all encompassed in one ever-present 'now' to Him."[1]

God knows all things, both actual and possible (Matthew 11:21-23). He knows all things past (Isaiah 41:22), present (Hebrews 4:13), and future (Isaiah 46:10). Because He knows all things, there can be no increase or decrease in His knowledge. Psalm 147:5 affirms that God's understanding "is infinite." His knowledge has no limit (Psalm 33:13-15; 139:11-12; 147:5; Proverbs 15:3; Isaiah 40:14; 46:10; 1 John 3:20; Hebrews 4:13).

You and I can trust Bible prophecy for it comes from the God who knows the end from the beginning. As God Himself affirms,

> "I am God, and there is no other;
>   I am God, and there is none like me,
> declaring the end from the beginning
>   and from ancient times things not yet done,
> saying, My counsel shall stand,
>   and I will accomplish all my purpose...
> I have spoken, and I will bring it to pass;
>   I have purposed, and I will do it."
>   (Isaiah 46:9-11 ESV)

What Are "Signs of the Times"?

A "sign of the times" is an event of prophetic significance that points to the end-times. Today, powerful nations have intelligence agencies—the United States has the Central Intelligence Agency (CIA), Israel has the Mossad, and Russia has the KGB. Based on the "intel" that these respective agencies gather, their nations make key policy decisions. We might say that the "signs of the times" found in Scripture constitute God's "intel in advance" about what the world will look like as we enter into the end-times.

Be Thoughtful Observers of the Signs

In the New Testament Jesus urged His followers to be thoughtful observers of the times. One day when He was speaking to the Sadducees and Pharisees, who rejected Him as the Messiah, He said: "When it is evening, you say, 'It will be fair weather, for the sky is red.' And in the morning, 'It will be stormy today, for the sky is red and threatening.' You know how to interpret the appearance of the sky, but you cannot interpret the signs of the times" (Matthew 16:1-3 ESV).

These Jewish leaders were supposed to be experts in interpreting the Old Testament Scriptures. In messianic passages such as Isaiah 11 and Isaiah 35, we are told that when the Messiah came, the lame would walk, the deaf would hear, and the blind would see. When Jesus came on the scene, this is precisely what happened. Hence, these Jewish leaders should have been able to read the "signs of the times" and recognize that Jesus indeed was the promised Messiah. But they were blind to this reality. You and I are called by Jesus to be thoughtful observers of the times. We are to be aware of what biblical prophecy teaches, and then keep a close eye on unfolding events so that we become aware of possible correlations between world events and biblical prophecy.

Current events must never be the means of interpreting the prophetic Scriptures; rather the prophetic Scriptures must interpret current events. When events transpiring in our world today—such as the political alliances emerging between Russia, Iran, and other Muslim nations—seem to be setting the stage for the fulfillment of the end-time prophecies described in Ezekiel 38–39, it is not because newspaper headlines have been found and then forced as the definitive fulfillment of these prophecies. Rather, because these Scriptures reveal specific details about this end-times invasion into Israel, we can accurately "discern the times," something Christ clearly desires of us (see Matthew 16:1-3; Luke 21:29-33).

If we conclude there is a legitimate correlation between current events and what the Bible reveals, we can rejoice in God's sovereign control of human history while at the same time resist the temptation to set dates, recognizing that this is something God forbids (Acts 1:7). All the while, we avoid sensationalism, recognizing that Christ calls His followers to live soberly and alertly as they await His coming (Mark 13:32-37).

Now, while we are not to set dates, and we do not know the specific day or hour of Jesus' coming, we can know the *general season* of the Lord's return by virtue of the signs of the times. Jesus once urged: "Now learn the parable from the fig tree: when its branch has already become tender and puts forth its leaves, you know that summer is near; so, you too, when you see all these things, recognize that He is near, right at the door" (Matthew 24:32-33). Jesus indicates that there are certain things God has revealed (particularly related to the future tribulation) that ought to cause people who know the Bible to understand that a fulfillment of prophecy is taking place—or the stage is being set for a prophecy to eventually be fulfilled. Jesus informs His followers to seek to be accurate observers of the times so that when biblical prophecies are fulfilled, or the stage is being set, they will recognize it (see also Luke 21:25-28).

Categories of Signs

To make it easier for you to grasp, I have organized the "signs of the times" into six primary categories: earth and sky signs, moral signs, religious signs, the realignment-of-nations signs, technological signs, and the rebirth-of-Israel sign. Let's give brief consideration to each of these.

Earth and Sky Signs

Scripture reveals that in the end-times there will be a great increase in frequency and intensity of earthquakes, famines, pestilences, and signs in the heavens. In Luke 21:11 (NIV) we read: "There will be great earthquakes, famines and pestilences in various places, and fearful events and great signs from heaven." Such things are said to be the beginning of "birth pangs" (Matthew 24:8). Just as birth pangs increase in frequency and intensity, so these signs will do the same. They have particular relevance to the future seven-year tribulation, but I believe that just as tremors (or foreshocks) often occur before major earthquakes, so preliminary manifestations of some of these signs may emerge prior to the tribulation.

What are the "fearful events" mentioned in this passage? Scripture does not specify this for us, but the Greek phrase literally means "terror," "sights of terror," or "terrifying things." We live in a day when global terrorism has never been more prominent. And it would seem that the rise of terrorism is going to get worse as we go into the future.

Signs in the heavens could include any number of things, including strange weather patterns, falling stars, a darkening of the moon and other celestial bodies (during the tribulation), and large bodies striking the earth. For example, in the context of the future tribulation, we find reference to "wormwood" in Revelation 8:10-12 (NIV):

> The third angel sounded, and a great star fell from heaven, burning like a torch, and it fell on a third of the rivers and on the springs of waters. The name of the star is called Wormwood; and a third of the waters became wormwood, and many men died from the waters, because they were made bitter.
>
> The fourth angel sounded, and a third of the sun and a third of the moon and a third of the stars were struck, so that a third of them would be darkened and the day would not shine for a third of it, and the night in the same way.

Many believe this "star" will, in fact, be a case of near-extinction-level "deep impact" of a large meteor or an asteroid striking planet earth. It has the appearance of a star because it literally bursts into flames—burning like a torch—as it plummets through earth's atmosphere. It turns a third of the waters bitter so that people who drink it die. It may contaminate this large volume of water by the residue from the meteor disintegrating as it blasts through earth's atmosphere. Or it may be that the meteor plummets into the headwaters from which some of the world's major rivers and underground water sources flow, thereby spreading the poisonous water to many people on earth.

Some scholars have speculated that it may be this "deep impact" that ultimately causes a reduction in sunlight and other celestial bodies. Following this impact, a catastrophic level of dust will be kicked up into the atmosphere, thereby blocking light.

What is both fascinating and sobering is that today's top scientists are saying that it is not a matter of *if* such a celestial body will strike earth, it is a matter of *when* it will happen. The mathematical probabilities render this a certainty at some point in the future. And when it happens, it will likely involve a significant celestial body striking the earth with a minimum velocity of 130,000 miles per hour. The sad reality is that this event will, in fact, happen during the tribulation, and the result will be truly catastrophic. Many will die.[2]

Some have also speculated that the signs in the heavens may include some unidentified flying object (UFO) phenomena. Not only are there countless sightings of UFOs around the world, but many today believe that "space brothers" are contacting us via psychics and mediums. I find it highly revealing that these "aliens" are not contacting us via physical means, such as radios, but by using occultism. I also find it highly revealing that many of the "revelations" coming from the "space brothers" deny essential doctrines of Christianity, including humanity's sin problem, the reality of hell, and the need to trust in Jesus Christ for salvation. Moreover, one must wonder why these "aliens" have come millions (billions?) of miles only to tell us the same things that New Agers have been telling us for decades. Almost without exception, those claiming to have been abducted by aliens have a prior involvement in some form of the occult. The typical abduction experience has notable similarities to occultic Shamanistic initiation ceremonies.

I see Satan's fingerprints all over current UFO phenomena. Please do not get me wrong. I am not saying that every time somebody sees a UFO that it is the devil. As I document in one of my previous books, *Alien Obsession: What Lies Behind Abductions, Sightings, and the Attraction to the Paranormal*, many times people are seeing natural phenomena, such as space junk (there are over seven thousand pieces of space junk floating around the earth), planet Venus, ball lightning (a form of lightning that takes an oval shape, sizzles, and can move around the sky at great speeds), a high-flying weather balloon, a jet, or something else. At the same time, however, a great deal of occultism and psychic phenomena accompanies UFO phenomena. These have given rise to many "doctrines of demons," which Scripture reveals will characterize the end-times (see 1 Timothy 4:1-2; see also 2 Timothy 4:3-4).

Moral Signs

In 2 Timothy 3:1-5 we read:

> But realize this, that in the last days difficult times will come. For men will be lovers of self, lovers of money, boastful, arrogant, revilers, disobedient to parents, ungrateful, unholy, unloving, irreconcilable, malicious gossips, without self-control, brutal, haters of good, treacherous, reckless, conceited, lovers of pleasure rather than lovers of God, holding to a form of godliness, although they have denied its power. Avoid such men as these.

Notice that in the last days there will be a lovers of self (*humanism*), lovers of money (*materialism*), and lovers of pleasure (*hedonism*). It is significant that humanism, materialism, and hedonism are three of the most prominent philosophies in our world today, and they often go together in a complementary fashion.

Related to this, Jesus Himself warned: "Because lawlessness is increased, most people's love will grow cold...For the coming of the Son of Man will be just like the days of Noah. For as in those days before the flood they were eating and drinking, marrying and giving in marriage, until the day that Noah entered the ark, and they did not understand until the flood came and took them all away; so will the coming of the Son of Man be" (Matthew 24:12,37-39). While this passage has specific reference to the future tribulation, we see the attitude Jesus described even in our own day. People are merrily going about their way, seemingly with no concern for the things of God.

America is engulfed in a moral crisis. The moral fiber of this country is eroding before our very eyes, and if the trend continues, it is only a matter of time before the country capitulates. The signs of decline I identified earlier bear repeating. Today there is widespread acceptance of homosexuality. Abortion continues to be widely practiced, with some fifty million unborn babies murdered since the enactment of *Roe v. Wade* in 1973. Pornography is pervasive and freely available on the Internet, enslaving millions as sex addicts. Drug abuse and alcoholism are pervasive as well, among both teenagers and adults. Promiscuity, fornication, and adultery continue to escalate to ever new heights, bringing about the carnage of sexually transmitted diseases. Meanwhile, the family unit is disintegrating. The divorce rate is around 50 percent, and many today live together outside of marriage. Out-of-wedlock births have escalated to new highs, with 40 percent of women not being married when they gave birth. As well, gay couples are adopting children, raising them in a homosexual atmosphere. People are far more interested in happiness than in holiness. They yearn more for pleasure than for praising God. All of these are compatible with humanism, materialism, and hedonism.

Religious Signs

False Christs. In Matthew 24:24 (NIV) Jesus Himself warned about the end-times: "For false Christs and false prophets will appear and perform great signs and miracles to deceive even the elect—if that were possible" (see also Mark 13:22). The apostle Paul also warned of a different Jesus (2 Corinthians 11:4). The danger, of course, is that a counterfeit Jesus who preaches a counterfeit gospel yields a counterfeit salvation (Galatians 1:8). There are no exceptions to this maxim.

Even in our day, we witness an unprecedented rise in false Christs and self-constituted messiahs affiliated with the kingdom of the cults and the occult. This will no doubt continue as we move further into the end-times. (For more on this, you may wish to consult some of my books on the cults and occultism.[3])

False Prophets and Teachers. Scripture contains many warnings against false prophets and false teachers for the simple reason that it is well possible for God's own people to be deceived. Ezekiel 34:1-7, for example, indicates that God's sheep can be abused and led astray by wicked shepherds. Jesus warned His followers: "Watch out for false prophets. They come to you in sheep's clothing, but inwardly they are ferocious wolves" (Matthew 7:15-16 NIV). Why would Jesus warn His followers to "watch out" if there were no possibility that they could be deceived? The apostle Paul likewise warned his Christian readers about the possibility of deception (2 Corinthians 11:2-4; see also Acts 20:28-30). It is in view of this that the Bible exhorts believers to "test" those who claim to be prophets (1 John 4:1f.).

How can believers recognize a false prophet? Deuteronomy 18:21-22 indicates that false prophets are those who give false prophecies that do not come true. Other verses in the Bible indicate that false prophets sometimes cause people to follow false gods or idols (Exodus 20:3-4; Deuteronomy 13:1-3); they often deny the deity of Jesus Christ (Colossians 2:8-9); they sometimes deny the humanity of Jesus Christ (1 John 4:1-2); they sometimes advocate abstaining from certain foods or meats for spiritual reasons (1 Timothy 4:3-4); they sometimes deprecate or deny the need for marriage (1 Timothy 4:3); they often promote immorality (Jude 4-7); and they often encourage legalistic self-denial (Colossians 2:16-23). A basic rule of thumb is that if a so-called prophet says *anything* that clearly contradicts any part of God's Word, his teachings should be rejected (Acts 17:11; 1 Thessalonians 5:19-22).

False Apostles. The apostle Paul warned of false apostles who are "deceitful workmen, masquerading as apostles of Christ" (2 Corinthians 11:13 NIV). The two key characteristics we see here are that these individuals

1) deceive people doctrinally, and 2) they pretend to be true apostles of Jesus Christ.

Christ commends those who take a stand against false apostles. In Revelation 2:2 (NIV), we read Christ's commendation to the church of Ephesus: "I know your deeds, your hard work and your perseverance. I know that you cannot tolerate wicked men, that you have tested those who *claim to be apostles but are not*, and have found them false."

How can the claims of apostles be "tested." Like the ancient Bereans, all Christians should make a regular habit of testing all things against Scripture (Acts 17:11), for Scripture is our only infallible barometer of truth. No true apostle will ever say anything that will contradict the Word of God (see Galatians 1:8).

Apostasy. The word *apostasy* comes from the Greek word *apostasia* and means "falling away." The word refers to a determined, willful "defection from the faith" or "abandonment of the faith."

In the New Testament, Judas Iscariot and his betrayal of Jesus for thirty pieces of silver is a classic example of apostasy and its effects (see Matthew 26:14-25,47-57; 27:3-10). Other examples include Hymenaeus and Alexander, who experienced a "shipwreck" of their faith (1 Timothy 1:19-20), and Demas, who turned away from the apostle Paul because of his love for the present world (2 Timothy 4:10).

Apostasy is often encouraged by false teachers (Matthew 24:11; Galatians 2:4), and escalates during times of trial (Matthew 24:9-10; Luke 8:13). The apostles often warned of the danger of apostasy (Hebrews 6:4-8; 10:26). Apostasy also occurred in Old Testament times among the Israelites (2 Chronicles 33:18-20; Jeremiah 2:19; 5:6). Scripture specifically prophesies a great end-times apostasy involving a massive defection from the truth (2 Thessalonians 2:3-4; see also Matthew 24:10-12).

In keeping with this, 1 Timothy 4:1-2 (ESV) warns: "The Spirit expressly says that in later times some will depart from the faith by devoting themselves to deceitful spirits and teachings of demons, through the insincerity of liars whose consciences are seared." Likewise, 2 Timothy 4:3-4 (ESV) warns: "The time is coming when people will not endure sound teaching, but having itching ears they will accumulate for themselves teachers to suit their own passions, and will turn away from listening to the truth and wander off into myths." Can any doubt that we are witnessing such things in our own day?

Specific ways that many apostatize are a denial of God (2 Timothy 3:4-5), a denial of Christ (1 John 2:18), a denial of Christ's return (2 Peter 3:3-4), a denial of the faith (1 Timothy 4:1-2), a denial of sound doctrine (2 Timothy 4:3-4), a denial of morals (2 Timothy 3:1-8), and a denial of authority (2 Timothy 3:2-4). We are living in days of deception!

The Realignment-of-Nations Sign

I have dedicated three chapters in this book to the realignment of nations in the end-times (see chapters 8, 9, and 10). In sum, Scripture reveals that in the end-times there will be the emergence of a United States of Europe—a ten-nation confederacy that constitutes a revival of the Roman Empire (see Daniel 2:40-44; 7:7,23-24; Revelation 17:12-13). There will also be an end-times military coalition that arises against Israel that includes Russia, Iran, Sudan, Turkey, Libya, and other Muslim nations (Ezekiel 38–39). It may be that Iraq does not participate in this invasion because a rebuilt Babylon (capital of Iraq) will be the headquarters of the Antichrist in the end-times (Revelation 17–18). America will likely weaken due to any number of factors, including the peak oil crisis, the possibility of a nuclear attack, the possibility of an EMP attack, implosion due to moral degeneracy, or perhaps the rapture. In the end-times America may become an ally with the revived Roman Empire. In any event, we seem to be witnessing the setting of the stage for such alignments. For example, the military coalition of Ezekiel 38–39 seems to be forming before our very eyes, and the present European Union (EU) may be the forerunner of a revived Roman Empire.

Technological Signs

Certain technological advances must be made to make possible some of the things prophesied of the end-times. Many prophecy scholars believe that the technology is now in place for these things to occur.

For example, Matthew 24:14 tells us that prior to the second coming of Christ, the gospel must be preached to every nation. With today's technology—satellites, the Internet, global media, translation technologies, publishing technologies, rapid transportation, and the like—this has never been more possible.

We do not know specifically what form the mark of the beast will take, but we do know that the False Prophet will control who will be able to buy and sell, depending on whether they submit to the Antichrist (Revelation 13:16-17). With today's satellites, the Internet, and super-computers, every selling establishment and every buyer could have a separate account number that would enable such control by the False Prophet. This technology exists today.

Prophetic Scripture may indicate that nuclear detonations will occur in the end-times. For example, Revelation 8:7 tells us that "a third of the earth was burned up, and a third of the trees were burned up, and all the green grass was burned up." Revelation 16:2 tells us that people around the world will break out with loathsome and malignant sores. Could this be a result of radiation poisoning following the detonation of nuclear weapons? Some believe Jesus may have been alluding to nuclear weaponry when He spoke of "men fainting from fear and the expectation of the things which are coming upon the world; for the powers of the heavens will be shaken" (Luke 21:26). Whether this is so, it is clear that the technology now exists for a third of the earth to be burned up and for mass casualties.

The Rebirth-of-Israel Sign

I addressed the rebirth of Israel previously (see chapter 8). Here I only summarize that Scripture reveals that the Jews would be regathered from the "four corners of the earth" in the end-times (Isaiah 11:10-12), and their state would be reestablished (Isaiah 66:7-8). God promised: "I will take you out of the nations; I will gather you from all the countries and bring you back into your own land" (Ezekiel 36:24 NIV). Notice that these verses do not say the Jews would be regathered from a single nation, as was the case in the Babylonian Captivity and the Assyrian Captivity. Rather, the Jews would be regathered from "the nations" and "all the countries" and be brought back to their own land.

This is what makes the year 1948 so significant, for it was this year that Israel achieved statehood. Then, in 1967, Israel captured Jerusalem and the West Bank during the Six-Day War. Jews have been returning to their homeland ever since. While we might call the present regather-ing a "regathering in unbelief," a day is coming—I believe at the second coming—when the Jews will finally recognize Jesus as the Messiah and call upon Him for deliverance from the anti-God armies gathered for Armageddon (Zechariah 12:10; Matthew 23:37-39; see also Isaiah 53:1-9), at which point their deliverance will surely come (see Romans 9–11).

Significance

These various categories of signs point to the reality that we are living in the end-times. When these are understood in conjunction with how oil relates to the current Middle East crisis, radical Muslim theology and their use of oil as a weapon, the realignment of nations in the end-times (including the emergence of the northern military coalition that will attack Israel), oil-rich Babylon as the eventual headquarters of the Antichrist, and the like, everything appears to be converging at a point in the not-too-distant future. The stage is being set for events that will transpire in the tribulation—a period that will climax with the second coming of the divine Messiah, Jesus Christ.

How, Then, Shall We Live?

I n this book I have focused detailed attention on oil, the Middle East, global tensions, and biblical prophecy. The question I wish to address in closing is this: *How, then, shall we live?* More specifically:

- Should we change the way we live our lives?

- Should we be worried about the future?

- Should we be discouraged about world events?

- What should be our attitude as we live in the end-times?

In this chapter, I am writing both as a concerned citizen and as a Bible-believing Christian. As a concerned citizen of the United States, my goal is to communicate a few tips regarding how we can live responsibly in view of impending peak oil. As a Bible-believing Christian, my goal is to communicate what the Bible says our attitude ought to be as we progress toward the last days. Both are vitally important.

Living as a Responsible Citizen

I sometimes hear people say, "Why polish the brass on a sinking ship?" The idea is, Why should we make sustained efforts to turn things around in society if the biblical prophets indicated that things would get worse and worse? The answer is that you and I, as Christians, are not to contribute to things getting worse and worse, but should always seek the betterment of our fellow human beings. One cannot read Jesus' Sermon on the Mount for long before seeing that He taught that we, as salt and light, ought to positively influence society around us (see Matthew 5–7).

In view of this, what steps can we take to live as responsible citizens? Below are a few suggestions:

1. Stay Informed

Most news magazines and newspapers feature articles on energy, oil, how all this relates to the national and global economies, global tensions, and other relevant subjects. Let's choose to stay informed about what is going on in our world.

2. Let's Not Ignore the Coming Crisis

For whatever reason, people in the United States seem reluctant to face up to the reality of impending peak oil. As one article put it, "public understanding about the ecological and socioeconomic consequences of an oil peak is alarmingly low. We are preceded by four generations of blind faith in unlimited economic growth fuelled on cheap, abundant oil, which makes it difficult for anyone today to witness and understand the current reversal."[1] A widely known expert, Robert Hirsch, laments that "no one has really started to work on the problem anywhere in the world...In most places, the problem is still unthinkable and not politically correct."[2]

Some have noted that since 1973, when the Middle Eastern nations imposed an oil embargo on us, we have had over thirty years to get used to the idea that a lack of oil could endanger us. Yet today, many take such endangerment less seriously than then.

The danger of indifference, of course, is that if people ignore the crisis now, they will not be prepared to act later. It is sheer folly to wait until things reach a crisis and become urgent. It is better to take steps now to avoid what former British Energy Minister Michael Meacher forecasts could be "the sharpest and perhaps the most violent dislocation (of society) in recent history."[3]

3. Let's Recognize that the Future May Involve Some Sacrifice

It is entirely feasible that at some point fuel rationing will be implemented. One reporter noted that "oil has made us fat and lazy." Indeed, "it was a 150-year addiction to an energy source we didn't appreciate or use particularly wisely. It distorted our economy. Now it's going. And we can't go back to business as usual."[4] So, in the not-too-distant future, we may need to get into a frame of mind of adjustment.

Both people *and* nations can get nasty when it comes to protecting their interests. One researcher has warned that "if sacrifice is not shared equitably, it can lead to a breakdown in civil government and society."[5] This is one reason many leaders are saying we need a global solution, and this issue may contribute to the eventual emergence of a globalized government, as prophesied in Scripture.

In any event, we need a better energy plan to be put in place now so that we will be better prepared to meet the crisis when it emerges. Such a plan needs to target such issues as transportation, manufacturing, petrochemicals, farming, and all other aspects of society that would be affected by an oil shortage.

4. It is Wise to Reduce Consumption, Reduce Dependence, and Conserve

There really is no other choice but to reduce our consumption of oil, reduce our dependence on foreign nations (especially Middle Eastern nations), and make efforts to conserve fuel in any way we can. As one reporter put it, "Our best chance to minimize the early effects of peak oil is conservation."[6] Conservation especially needs to take place in the United States. Accounting for only 5 percent of the world population, America currently uses a quarter of the world's oil, according to the Energy Information Administration.[7] If the United States does not take steps to conserve, then our economy will pay for it later.

There are many options one might consider that can make a real difference. For example, one might carpool to work with a friend or choose to make more frequent use of public transportation. If distance permits, one could ride a bike to work. With today's technology, many companies could make heavier use of telecommuting. In a day in which many people commute to work for up to an hour, many might consider relocating closer to their place of employment or finding a job nearby. One might also choose to walk a lot more. (What a novel idea! Maybe that's why the Creator gave us legs.) All this would greatly reduce the amount of oil we consume.

Concurrently, government leaders must continue to explore the use of alternative energies, including both wind and solar power for generating electricity. Natural gas is also worth pursuing for transportation needs.

5. Work Toward Overhauling the Infrastructure

Our oil-based infrastructure needs to be overhauled. Fatih Birol, the chief economist at the International Energy Agency, said that "one day we will run out of oil and we have to leave oil before oil leaves us, and we have to prepare ourselves for that day...The earlier we start, the better, because all of our economic and social system is based on oil, so to change from that will take a lot of time and a lot of money and we should take this issue very seriously."[8]

Delay is not an option. A British expert said that "the world had to move quickly towards the massive deployment of renewable energy and to a dramatic increase in energy efficiency, both as a way to combat climate change and to ensure that the lights stay on."[9] As citizens, you and I can vote for government officials who are committed to making a difference on energy issues. Americans have a powerful collective voice in this regard.

Living as Biblical Christians

We all know that many extremists in the past have taken unhealthy paths as a result of their understanding of Bible prophecy. To avoid such extremes, I always advise people to *live* their lives as if the rapture could happen today but to *plan* their lives as if they will be here their entire lifetime expectancy. That way they are prepared for time *and* eternity.

Additionally, Scripture gives us a number of helpful exhortations that clarify what our attitude ought to be as we live in the end-times. I urge you to meditate on these truths so that when things seem to be going haywire in our world, you will have an anchor to keep your life on track.

1. Let's Be Sober-minded, Maintain Sound Judgment, Pray, and Be Loving

We find much wisdom in 1 Peter 4:7-10 regarding how we ought to live in view of biblical prophecy:

> The end of all things is near; therefore, be of sound judgment and sober spirit for the purpose of prayer. Above all, keep fervent in your love for one another, because love covers a multitude of sins. Be hospitable to one another without complaint. As each one has received a special gift, employ it in serving one another as good stewards of the manifold grace of God.

It is unfortunate that many people become sensationalistic and alarmist about end-time prophecies. God tells us to be *sober-minded*. God instructs us to maintain *sound judgment*. The best way to be sober-minded and maintain sound judgment is to regularly feed our minds upon the Word of God. Keeping our minds focused upon the Scriptures will keep us on track in our thinking and in our life choices.

2. Let's Not Be Troubled But Trust in God and Jesus Christ

Jesus speaks words of great comfort to His disciples in John 14:1-3:

> Do not let your heart be troubled; believe in God, believe also in Me. In My Father's house are many dwelling places; if it were not so, I would have told you; for I go to prepare a place for you. If I go and prepare a place for you, I will come again and receive you to Myself, that where I am, there you may be also.

My professor John F. Walvoord has a great insight on this passage:

> These verses are the Bible's first revelation of the rapture, in which Christ will come back to take His own to heaven. He exhorted the disciples not to be troubled. Since they trusted the Father, they also should trust Christ, whose power was demonstrated in His many miracles. Having referred to Himself as the Source of peace, Jesus spoke of His coming to take them to heaven. They need not be anxious about His leaving because later He would return for them.[10]

Jesus' words mean that no matter what happens in this world, we need not be troubled. Why not? Because we know and trust in the Prince of Peace, Jesus Christ. He is the source of peace, and the peace He gives is not dependent on circumstances (John 14:27). We trust in Him, and He gives us peace. We need not worry! We need not fear! Besides, as Jesus said, He's now preparing our eternal homes (14:1-3). That future reality is enough to strengthen us through any present difficulties.

Here are some more great verses on trusting God that you can meditate on:

- Trust in Christ, your high priest—Hebrews 4:15.

- Trust God for all things; He will help you—Psalm 37:5.

- Trust God in times of trouble—Psalm 50:15.

- Trust in God at all times—Psalm 62:8.

- Trust in the Lord, not man—Psalm 118:8.

- Trust in the Lord with your whole heart—Proverbs 3:5-6.

3. Let's Seek to Live Righteously

God does not give us prophecy to teach us mere facts about eschatology. It is highly revealing that exhortations to personal purity follow many prophetic verses in the Bible. As we study Bible prophecy, it ought to change the way we live. It ought to have an effect on our behavior.

Consider the apostle Paul's exhortation in Romans 13:11-14, which is in a context of biblical prophecy:

> Do this, knowing the time, that it is already the hour for you to awaken from sleep; for now salvation is nearer to us than when we believed. The night is almost gone, and the day is near. Therefore let us lay aside the deeds of darkness and put on the armor of light. Let us behave properly as in the day, not in carousing and drunkenness, not in sexual promiscuity and sensuality, not in strife and jealousy. But put on the Lord Jesus Christ, and make no provision for the flesh in regard to its lusts.

We also see the connection between biblical prophecy and purity in 2 Peter 3:10-14:

> The day of the Lord will come like a thief, in which the heavens will pass away with a roar and the elements will be destroyed with intense heat, and the earth and its works will be burned up.

> Since all these things are to be destroyed in this way, what sort of people ought you to be in holy conduct and godliness, looking for and hastening the coming of the day of God, because of which the heavens will be destroyed by burning, and the elements will melt with intense heat! But according to His promise we are looking for new heavens and a new earth, in which righteousness dwells.

> Therefore, beloved, since you look for these things, be diligent to be found by Him in peace, spotless and blameless.

First John 3:2-3 likewise instructs:

> Beloved, now we are children of God, and it has not appeared as yet what we will be. We know that when He appears, we will be like Him, because we will see Him just as He is. And everyone who has this hope fixed on Him purifies himself, just as He is pure.

John is here referring to the rapture. And what a glorious day that will be. One scholar put it this way: "The hope of the rapture, when we will meet the Savior, should be a sanctifying force in our lives. We will be made completely like Him then; so we should endeavor with His help to serve Him faithfully now and to lead lives of purity."[11]

We find an analogy in ancient Jewish marriage customs. In biblical times, following the marriage betrothal, the groom would go to his father's house to prepare a place for the couple to stay. Meanwhile, the betrothed woman would eagerly await the coming of her groom to take her away to his father's house in marriage celebration. During this time of anticipation, the bride's loyalty to her groom was tested. Likewise, as the Bride of Christ (the church) awaits the messianic Groom, the church is motivated to live in purity and godliness until He comes for us (see John 14:1-3). Let us daily choose purity.

4. Let Us Be People of Prayer

First Peter 4:7 (NIV) instructs us, "The end of all things is near. Therefore be clear minded and self-controlled so that you can pray." The shortness of time that remains should motivate us to pray. As pilgrims on our way to heaven, where our true citizenship lies, prayer needs to be a high priority, for nothing strengthens us more than regular communication with God, who Himself awaits us in heaven.

Prayer is so critically important that I want to go into a bit of detail. Let us first recognize that prayer is not just asking for things from God. Prayer also involves thanksgiving, praise, worship, and confession.

Thanksgiving. In prayer we ought always to give thanks to God for everything we have (Ephesians 5:20; Colossians 3:15). We should "enter his gates with thanksgiving" (Psalm 100:4; see also Psalm 95:2).

Praise. Like David, praise for God should always be on our lips (Psalm 34:1). We should praise God in the depths of our heart (Psalm 103:1-5,20-22), and continually "offer to God a sacrifice of praise" (Hebrews 13:15 NIV). One means of praising God is through spiritual songs (Psalm

69:30). How comforting it is to be able to take time to praise the Lord, even while things on earth are troublesome.

Worship. Like the psalmist of old, we should bow down in worship before the Lord our Maker (Psalm 95:6). We are to worship Him "who made the heavens, the earth, the sea and the springs of water" (Revelation 14:7 NIV). We should worship Him with "reverence and awe" (Hebrews 12:28) and worship Him alone (Exodus 20:3-5; Deuteronomy 5:7).

Confession. Confession in prayer is wise, for "he who conceals his sins does not prosper, but whoever confesses and renounces them finds mercy" (Proverbs 28:13 NIV). We are promised that "if we confess our sins, he is faithful and just and will forgive us our sins and purify us from all unrighteousness" (1 John 1:9 NIV).

Requests. We can also go to God for specific requests. In the Lord's Prayer, we are exhorted to pray for our daily bread (Matthew 6:11). The apostle Paul wrote: "Do not be anxious about anything, but in everything, by prayer and petition, with thanksgiving, *present your requests to God.* And the peace of God, which transcends all understanding, will guard your hearts and your minds in Christ Jesus" (Philippians 4:6-7 NIV, emphasis added).

Scripture provides a number of principles for effective praying:

1. We must remember that all our prayers are subject to the sovereign will of God. If we ask for something God does not want us to have, He will sovereignly deny that request. First John 5:14 (NIV) instructs us, "This is the confidence we have in approaching God: that if we ask anything according to his will, he hears us."

2. Prayer should not be an occasional practice but a continual practice. We are instructed in 1 Thessalonians 5:17 (NIV) to "pray continually."

3. Recognize that sin is a hindrance to prayer being answered. Psalm 66:18 (NIV) says, "If I had cherished sin in my heart, the Lord would not have listened."

4. Living righteously, on the other hand, is a great benefit to prayer being answered. Proverbs 15:29 (NIV) says, "The LORD is far from the wicked but he hears the prayer of the righteous."

5. A good model prayer is the Lord's Prayer found in Matthew 6:9-13. In this one prayer we find praise (v. 9), personal requests (vv. 11-13), and an affirmation of God's will (v. 10).

6. Be persistent. In Matthew 7:7-8 (NIV), Jesus said, "Ask and it will be given to you; seek and you will find; knock and the door will be opened to you. For everyone who asks receives; he who seeks finds; and to him who knocks, the door will be opened." The verb tenses in the Greek carry the idea, "*Keep on asking* and it will be given; *keep on seeking* and you will find; *keep on knocking* and the door will be opened."

7. Pray in faith. As Mark 11:22-24 puts it, we need to place our faith in God and believe that we have received what we have asked for. If what we have asked for is within God's will, we will receive it.

8. Pray in Jesus' name (John 14:13-14). Jesus is the "bridge" between humanity and God the Father. We have the wonderful privilege of going to the Father and praying in the name of His dear Son.

9. If your prayer seems unanswered, keep trusting God no matter what. He has a reason for the delay. You can count on it.

Effectiveness of prayer. God promises that He answers the prayers of His people. Below are just a few of the benefits of prayer:

■ Prayer can bring enlightenment regarding God's purposes for us (Ephesians 1:18-19).

■ Prayer can help us understand God's will (Colossians 1:9-12).

■ Prayer can increase our love for other people (1 Thessalonians 3:10-13).

■ Prayer can bring about encouragement and strength (2 Thessalonians 2:16-17).

■ Prayer can keep us from harm and pain (1 Chronicles 4:10).

■ Prayer can deliver people from their troubles (Psalm 34:15-22).

- Prayer can keep us from succumbing to lies and falsehood (Proverbs 30:7-9).

- Prayer can bring about our daily food (Matthew 6:11).

- Prayer can help us to live righteously (1 Thessalonians 5:23).

- Prayer can bring about healing (James 5:14-15).

5. Never Set Dates

God Himself controls the timing of end-time events, and He has not provided us the specific details. Jesus told His apostles before He ascended into heaven: "It is not for you to know times or epochs which the Father has fixed by His own authority" (Acts 1:7). We can be accurate observers of the times, as Jesus instructed (Matthew 24:32-33; Luke 21:25-28), but we do not have precise details on the timing. We must simply resolve to trust God with those details.

Christians who get caught up in date-setting (such as setting a date for the rapture) do damage to the cause of Christ. Humanists enjoy scorning Christians who put stock in end-times predictions—especially when specific dates have been attached to specific events. Why give ammo to the enemies of Christ? We can be excited about events that appear to be setting the stage for the fulfillment of prophecy without engaging in such sensationalism. Remember, Christ calls His followers to live soberly and alertly as they await His coming (Mark 13:32-37).

6. Always Remember that Bible Prophecy Points to the Awesome Greatness of God

I never tire of reminding Bible students that prophecy constantly and relentlessly points to the awesome greatness of God. For example, in Isaiah 44:6-8 we read:

Thus says the LORD, the King of Israel and his Redeemer, the LORD of hosts:

> "I am the first and I am the last,
> And there is no God besides Me.
> Who is like Me? Let him proclaim and declare it;
> Yes, let him recount it to Me in order,
> From the time that I established the ancient nation.
> And let them declare to them the things that are coming

And the events that are going to take place.
Do not tremble and do not be afraid;
Have I not long since announced it to you and declared it?
And you are My witnesses.
Is there any God besides Me,
Or is there any other Rock?
I know of none.'"

In the book of Daniel, we read:

"Let the name of God be blessed forever and ever,
For wisdom and power belong to Him.
It is He who changes the times and the epochs;
He removes kings and establishes kings;
He gives wisdom to wise men
And knowledge to men of understanding.
It is He who reveals the profound and hidden things;
He knows what is in the darkness,
And the light dwells with Him."
(Daniel 2:20-22)

Can there be any doubt that our God is an awesome God? The Bible reveals some phenomenal facts about this awesome God. Let us meditate on these truths as they relate to the unfolding of God's prophetic plan on earth.

God Is Eternal. One theologian describes God as "the eternal without beginning, He who is above the whole course of time, He who in harmony beyond explanation possesses unity and life, the Father, the Son, and the Holy Spirit, the basis of eternity, the Living One, the only God."[12] God transcends time altogether. He is above the space-time universe. As an eternal being, He has always existed. He is the King eternal (1 Timothy 1:17), who alone is immortal (6:16). He is the "Alpha and Omega" (Revelation 1:8) and is the "first and the last" (Isaiah 44:6; 48:12). He exists "from eternity" (Isaiah 43:13) and "from everlasting to everlasting" (Psalm 90:2). He lives forever from eternal ages past (Psalm 41:13; 102:12,27; Isaiah 57:15). So, while events transpire daily here on planet earth, and while prophecies are fulfilled temporally, God Himself is beyond time altogether.

We can have absolute confidence that God will never cease to exist.

He will always be there for us. His continued providential control of our lives is assured. Human leaders come and go. Countries come and go. But God is eternal and is always there!

God Is Everywhere-Present. This does not mean that God is diffused throughout space as if part of Him is here and part of Him is there. Rather, God in His whole being is in every place. There is nowhere one can go where God is not (Psalm 139:7-8; Jeremiah 23:23-24; Acts 17:27-28). Whether one is in the United States or Iran or Russia or Sudan or Libya or anywhere in the entire universe, *God is there.*

While things in this world so often seem to be spinning out of control, how comforting to know that no matter where we go, we will never escape the presence of our beloved God. Because He is everywhere-present, we can be confident of His real presence at all times. We will always know the blessing of walking with Him in every trial and circumstance.

God Is All-Knowing. Because God transcends time—because He is above time—He can see the past, present, and future as a single act. God's knowledge of all things is from the vantage point of eternity, so that the past (Isaiah 41:22), present (Hebrews 4:13), and future (Isaiah 46:10) are all encompassed in one ever-present "now" to Him. God knows all things, both actual and possible (Matthew 11:21-23). Because He knows all things, there can be no increase or decrease in His knowledge. Psalm 147:5 affirms that God's understanding "has no limit." His knowledge is infinite (Psalm 33:13-15; 139:11-12; 147:5; Proverbs 15:3; Isaiah 40:14; 46:10; Hebrews 4:13; 1 John 3:20). This is why we can trust God when He communicates to us prophecies about the future. God knows all!

God Is All-Powerful. Scripture portrays God as being all-powerful (Jeremiah 32:17). He has the power to do all that He desires and wills. Some fifty-six times Scripture declares that God is almighty. God is abundant in strength (Psalm 147:5) and has incomparably great power (2 Chronicles 20:6; Ephesians 1:19-21). No one can hold back His hand (Daniel 4:35). No one can reverse Him (Isaiah 43:13) and no one can thwart Him (Isaiah 14:27). Nothing is impossible with Him (Matthew 19:26; Mark 10:27; Luke 1:37) and nothing is too difficult for Him (Genesis 18:14; Jeremiah 32:17,27). The Almighty reigns (Revelation 19:6). This means that none of the nations of the world are beyond God's control. No matter what threat one nation might make against another—such as Iran threatening Israel—we must remember that our God, who is all-powerful, is in control. No one can thwart His plans.

God Is Sovereign. Scripture portrays God as being absolutely sovereign. He rules the universe, controls all things, and is Lord over all (see Ephesians 1). There is nothing that can happen in this universe that is beyond His control. All forms of existence are within the scope of His absolute dominion. Psalm 50:1 (NIV) refers to God as the Mighty One who "speaks and summons the earth from the rising of the sun to the place where it sets." Psalm 66:7 (NIV) affirms that "He rules forever by his power." We are assured in Psalm 93:1 (NIV) that "the LORD reigns" and "is armed with strength." God asserts, "My purpose will stand, and I will do all that I please" (Isaiah 46:10 NIV). God assures us, "Surely, as I have planned, so it will be, and as I have purposed, so it will stand" (Isaiah 14:24 NIV). Proverbs 16:9 (NIV) tells us, "In his heart a man plans his course, but the LORD determines his steps." Proverbs 19:21 (NIV) says, "Many are the plans in a man's heart, but it is the LORD's purpose that prevails."

Supreme peace in the heart is the natural result of trusting that God sovereignly oversees all that comes into our lives. No matter what we may encounter—no matter how much we may fail to understand why certain things happen, and no matter how horrible the headlines in newspapers may often be—the knowledge that our sovereign God is in control is a firm anchor in the midst of life's storms.

God Is Holy. God's holiness means not just that He is entirely separate from all evil but also that He is absolutely righteous (Leviticus 19:2). He is pure in every way. The Scriptures lay great stress upon this attribute of God (the following verses are all from the NIV):

- "Who is like you—majestic in holiness…?" (Exodus 15:11).

- "There is no one holy like the LORD" (1 Samuel 2:2).

- "The LORD our God is holy" (Psalm 99:9).

- "Holy and awesome is his name" (Psalm 111:9).

- "Holy, holy, holy is the LORD Almighty" (Isaiah 6:3).

- "You alone are holy" (Revelation 15:4).

One important ramification of God's holiness is that He will not allow persons or nations to get away with sinful actions. So, for example, when the northern military coalition launches a massive invasion into Israel, God responds to this defiant sinful act by utterly destroying them. As well, I noted previously the possibility that the United States will weaken and fall due to an implosion from moral degeneracy.

God Is Just. That God is just means that He carries out His righteous standards justly and with equity. There is never any partiality or unfairness in God's dealings with people (Genesis 18:25; Psalm 11:7; Zephaniah 3:5; John 17:25; Romans 3:26; Hebrews 6:10). The fact that God is just is both a comfort and a warning. It is a comfort for those who have been wronged in life. They can rest assured that God will right all wrongs in the end. It is a warning for those who think they have been getting away with evil. Justice will prevail in the end!

7. Let's Maintain an Eternal Perspective

Does it not create an excitement in each of our hearts that we, as Christians, will live for all eternity on the heavenly new earth with our wondrous God (Revelation 21–22)? No matter what takes place on this earth, even if we do run out of oil and the nations vie against each other for remaining reserves, we each have a splendorous destiny ahead. I never tire of saying that a daily pondering of the incredible glory of the afterlife is one of the surest ways to stay motivated to live faithfully during our relatively short time on earth. We are but pilgrims on our way to another land—where God Himself dwells with His people (Revelation 21:3).

J.I. Packer says that the "lack of long, strong thinking about our promised hope of glory is a major cause of our plodding, lackluster lifestyle." He points to the Puritans as a much-needed example for us, for they believed that "it is the heavenly Christian that is the lively Christian." The Puritans understood that we "run so slowly, and strive so lazily, because we so little mind the prize...So let Christians animate themselves daily to run the race set before them by practicing heavenly meditation."[13]

Puritan Richard Baxter's daily habit was to "dwell on the glory of the heavenly life to which one was going." Baxter daily practiced "holding heaven at the forefront of his thoughts and desires." The hope of heaven brought him joy, and joy brought him strength. Baxter once said, "A heavenly mind is a joyful mind; this is the nearest and truest way to live a life of comfort...A heart in heaven will be a most excellent preservative against temptations, a powerful means to kill thy corruptions."[14]

Such comments reflect the exhortation of the apostle Paul in Colossians 3:1-2 (NIV): "Since, then, you have been raised with Christ, set your hearts on things above, where Christ is seated at the right hand of God. Set your minds on things above, not on earthly things." The original Greek of this verse is intense, communicating the idea, "diligently, actively, single-mindedly pursue the things above." Moreover, the Greek present tense communicates the idea, "perpetually keep on seeking the things above...make it an ongoing process." This ought to be our attitude every single day.

It is also wise to keep in mind the temporal nature of this life. We ought to pray with the psalmist: "Teach us to number our days aright, that we may gain a heart of wisdom" (Psalm 90:12 NIV). And: "Show me, O LORD, my life's end and the number of my days; let me know how fleeting is my life" (Psalm 39:4 NIV). Those Christians who wisely ponder their mortality are most committed to an eternal perspective.

■ ■ ■

Though I assume most of my readers are Christians, there is a possibility that you are not. Perhaps you picked up this book because the title intrigued you, or because you are interested in peak oil or Middle East tensions. If you are not a Christian, and you would like to come into a personal relationship with the God I have described above, I urge you to read appendix A. I wrote it specifically for you.

If You Are Not a Christian...

I was first exposed to biblical prophecy back in the 1970s. At that time, I was not a Christian. However, I quickly became one once I understood what the Bible teaches about the end-times, especially the second coming of Jesus Christ, the Messiah. It may be that you too—having now been exposed to biblical prophecy—have a desire to become a Christian.

A personal relationship with Jesus is the most important decision and commitment you could ever make. It is unlike any other relationship. If you go into eternity without *this* relationship, you will spend eternity apart from Him.

Here's how you can come into a personal relationship with Jesus.

First you need to recognize that...

God Desires a Personal Relationship with You

God created you (Genesis 1:27). And He did not create you to exist all alone and apart from Him. He created you to come into a personal relationship with Him.

God had face-to-face encounters and fellowship with Adam and Eve, the first couple (Genesis 3:8-20). Just as God fellowshipped with them, so He desires to fellowship with you (1 John 1:3-7). God loves you (John 3:16). Never forget that.

The problem is...

Humanity Has a Sin Problem that Blocks a Relationship with God

When Adam and Eve chose to sin against God in the Garden of Eden, they catapulted the entire human race—to which they gave birth—into sin. Since that time, every human being has been born into the world with a propensity to sin.

The apostle Paul affirmed that "sin entered the world through one man [Adam], and death through sin" (Romans 5:12).[1] We are told that "through the disobedience of the one man the many were made sinners" (Romans 5:19). Ultimately this means that "death came through a man... in Adam all die" (1 Corinthians 15:21-22).

Jesus often spoke of sin in metaphors that illustrate the havoc sin can wreak in one's life. He described sin as blindness (Matthew 23:16-26), sickness (Matthew 9:12), being enslaved in bondage (John 8:34), and living in darkness (John 8:12; 12:35-46). Moreover, Jesus taught that this is a universal condition and that all people are guilty before God (Luke 7:37-48).

Jesus also taught that both inner thoughts and external acts render a person guilty (Matthew 5:28). He taught that from within the human heart come "evil thoughts, sexual immorality, theft, murder, adultery, greed, malice, deceit, lewdness, envy, slander, arrogance, and folly" (Mark 7:21-22). He affirmed that God is fully aware of every person's sins, both external acts and inner thoughts; nothing escapes His notice (Matthew 22:18; Luke 6:8; John 4:17-19).

·   Some people are more morally upright than others. However, we all fall short of God's perfect standards (Romans 3:23). In a contest to see who can throw a rock to the moon, I am sure a muscular athlete would be able to throw the rock much farther than I could. But all human beings ultimately fall short of the task. Similarly, all of us fall short of measuring up to God's perfect holy standards.

Though the sin problem is a serious one, God has graciously provided a solution.

Jesus Died for Our Sins and Made Salvation Possible

God's absolute holiness demands that sin be punished. The good news of the gospel, however, is that Jesus has taken this punishment on Himself. God loves us so much that He sent Jesus to bear the penalty for our sins.

Jesus affirmed that it was for the very purpose of dying that He came into the world (John 12:27). Moreover, He understood His death to be a sacrificial offering for the sins of humanity (Matthew 26:26-28). Jesus took His sacrificial mission with utmost seriousness, for He knew that without Him, humanity would perish (Matthew 16:25-26; John 3:16) and spend eternity apart from God in a place of great suffering (Matthew 10:28; 11:23; 23:33; 25:41; Luke 16:22-28).

Jesus therefore described His mission this way: "The Son of Man did not come to be served, but to serve, and to give his life as a ransom for many" (Matthew 20:28). "The Son of Man came to seek and to save what was lost" (Luke 19:10). "God did not send his Son into the world to condemn the world, but to save the world through him" (John 3:17).

However, the benefits of Christ's death on the cross are not automatically applied to your life. To receive the gift of salvation, you must...

Believe in Jesus Christ the Savior

By His sacrificial death on the cross, Jesus took the sins of the entire world on Himself and made salvation available for everyone (1 John 2:2). But this salvation is not automatic. Only those who choose to believe in Christ are saved. This is the consistent testimony of the biblical Jesus. Listen to His words:

- "For God so loved the world that he gave his one and only Son, that whoever believes in him shall not perish but have eternal life" (John 3:16).

- "For my Father's will is that everyone who looks to the Son and believes in him shall have eternal life, and I will raise him up at the last day" (John 6:40).

- "I am the resurrection and the life. He who believes in me will live, even though he dies" (John 11:25).

Choosing *not* to believe in Jesus, by contrast, leads to eternal condemnation: "Whoever believes in him is not condemned, but whoever does not believe stands condemned already because he has not believed in the name of God's one and only Son" (John 3:18).

Free at Last: Forgiven of All Sins

When you believe in Christ the Savior, a wonderful thing happens. God forgives you of all your sins. *All of them!* He puts them completely out of His sight. Ponder for a few minutes the following verses, which speak of the forgiveness of those who have believed in Christ:

- "In him we have redemption through his blood, the forgiveness of sins, in accordance with the riches of God's grace" (Ephesians 1:7).

- God said, "Their sins and lawless acts I will remember no more" (Hebrews 10:17).

- "Blessed is he whose transgressions are forgiven, whose sins are covered. Blessed is the man whose sin the LORD does not count against him and in whose spirit is no deceit" (Psalm 32:1-2).

- "For as high as the heavens are above the earth, so great is his love for those who fear him; as far as the east is from the west, so far has he removed our transgressions from us" (Psalm 103:11-12).

Such forgiveness is wonderful indeed, for none of us can possibly work our way into heaven or be good enough to warrant God's good favor. Because of what Jesus has done for us, we can freely receive the gift of salvation. It is a gift provided solely through the grace of God (Ephesians 2:8-9). It becomes ours by placing our faith in Jesus.

Don't Put It Off

It is highly dangerous to put off turning to Christ for salvation, for you do not know the day of your death. What if it happens this evening? "Death is the destiny of every man; the living should take this to heart" (Ecclesiastes 7:2).

If God is speaking to your heart now, then now is your door of opportunity to believe. "Seek the LORD while he may be found; call on him while he is near" (Isaiah 55:6).

Follow Me in Prayer

Would you like to place your faith in Jesus for the forgiveness of sins, thereby guaranteeing your eternal place in His presence? If so, pray the following prayer with me. Keep in mind that the prayer itself does not saves you. The faith in your heart saves you. So let the following prayer be a simple expression of the faith that is in your heart:

Dear Jesus:
I want to have a relationship with You. I know I cannot save myself because I am a sinner. Thank You for dying on the cross on my behalf. I believe You died for me, in my place, and I accept Your free gift of salvation. Thank You, Jesus. Amen.

Welcome to God's Forever Family

On the authority of the Word of God, I can assure you that you are now a part of God's forever family. If you prayed the above prayer with a heart of faith, you will spend all eternity with Jesus. Welcome to God's family!

What to Do Next

First, purchase a contemporary translation of the Bible, such as the New International Version or the New Living Translation, and read from it daily. Read at least one chapter a day, followed by a time of prayer. I recommend you start with the Gospel of John.

Second, join a Bible-believing church immediately. Get involved in it. Join a Bible study group at the church so you will have regular fellowship with other Christians.

Third, *please write to me:* Ron Rhodes, P.O. Box 2526, Frisco, TX 75034. I would love to hear from you if you made a decision for Christ.

Prophetic Bible Verses on Persons and Events Mentioned in This Book

Antichrist

Beast, the—Revelation 13:1-10.

Commercial genius—Daniel 11:43; Revelation 13:16-17.

Counterfeit signs and wonders—2 Thessalonians 2:9-10.

Dominion of, during tribulation—Revelation 13.

Emerges from reunited Roman empire—Daniel 7:8; 9:26.

Energized by Satan—2 Thessalonians 2:9.

False Prophet will seek to make world worship him—Revelation 13:11-12.

Headquarters in Rome—Revelation 17:8-9.

Heads up revived Roman empire—Daniel 2, 7.

Inhabitants of earth will worship—Revelation 13:8.

Makes covenant with Israel—Daniel 9:27.

Man of lawlessness—2 Thessalonians 2:1-10.

Military genius—Revelation 6:2; 13:2-4.

Oratorical genius—Daniel 11:36.

Political genius—Revelation 17:11-13.

Speaks arrogant, boastful words—2 Thessalonians 2:4.

Will be defeated by Jesus at second coming—2 Thessalonians 2:8; Revelation 19:11-20.

Will deceive many—Revelation 19:20.

Will eventually rule whole world—Revelation 13:7.

Will persecute Christians—Revelation 13:7.

World will follow—Revelation 13:3.

Armageddon

Prior to second coming—Revelation 16:16.

Catastrophic series of battles—Daniel 11:40-45; Joel 3:9-17; Zechariah 14:1-3; Revelation 16:14-16.

Devastating to humanity—Matthew 24:22.

Place of final battle—Revelation 16:14,16.

Antichrist's allies assembled—Psalm 2:1-3; Joel 3:9-11; Revelation 16:12-16.

Antichrist's armies at Bozrah—Jeremiah 49:13-14.

Horrific battle from Bozrah to Valley of Jehoshaphat—Jeremiah 49:20-22; Joel 3:12-13; Zechariah 14:12-15.

Antichrist's campaign into Egypt—Daniel 11:40-45.

Babylon destroyed—Isaiah 13–14; Jeremiah 50–51; Zechariah 5:5-11; Revelation 17–18.

Ascent on Mount of Olives—Joel 3:14-17; Zechariah 14:3-5; Matthew 24:29-31; Revelation 16:17-21; 19:11-21.

Jerusalem falls—Micah 4:11–5:3; Zechariah 12–14.

Siege of Jerusalem—Zechariah 14:2.

War on great day of God—Revelation 16:14.

No one would survive if not for Christ coming—Matthew 24:22.

Babylon (Political and Religious)

Center of false religion—Revelation 17:4-5; 18:1-2.

Center of world commerce—Revelation 18:9-19.

Global importance—Revelation 17:15,18.

Literal city in end-times—Revelation 17:18.

Persecutes God's people—Revelation 17:6; 18:20,24.

Revived, rebuilt by Antichrist—Revelation 18.

Conversion of Israel, End-times

Israel now in state of judicial blindness—Romans 9:31-32.

Gospel now preached to Gentiles, causing Jewish jealousy—Romans 11:11.

Israel will repent, turn to Messiah in end-times—Zechariah 12:10; Matthew 23:37-39; Isaiah 53:1-9.

Ezekiel Invasion, End-Times Invasion into Israel

Beth-togarmah (modern Turkey)—Ezekiel 38:6.

Ethiopia (modern Sudan)—Ezekiel 38:5.

Gomer (modern Turkey)—Ezekiel 38:6.
Magog (modern southern portion of former Soviet Union)—Ezekiel 38:2.
Meshech and Tubal (modern Turkey)—Ezekiel 38:2-3.
Persia (modern Iran)—Ezekiel 38:5.
Put (modern Libya)—Ezekiel 38:5.
Rosh (modern Russia)—Ezekiel 38:3.

God, Protector of Israel

God battles Israel's enemies—Exodus 15:3-4; Psalm 24:8; 25:19-22.
God is "Lord of Hosts"—2 Samuel 6:2,18.
"He who keeps Israel will neither slumber nor sleep"—Psalm 121:4.
No weapon formed against Israel will prosper—Isaiah 54:17.

Iraq

Babylon (in Iraq), headquarters of Antichrist during tribulation—
Revelation 17–18.
May be among "many peoples with you" that invade Israel in end-
times—Ezekiel 38:6,9,15,22.
Not specifically mentioned among nations that invade Israel in end-
times—Ezekiel 38:1-6.

Israel's Gatherings

First worldwide gathering in unbelief (1948 and following)—Isaiah 11:11-
12; Ezekiel 20:33-38; 22:17-22; 36:22-24; 38–39; Zephaniah 2:1-2.
Second worldwide gathering in belief (related to millennial kingdom)—
Deuteronomy 4:29-31; 30:1-10; Isaiah 27:12-13; 43:5-7; Jeremiah
16:14-15; 31:7-10; Ezekiel 11:14-18; Amos 9:14-15; Zechariah 10:8-12;
Matthew 24:31.

Israel in Tribulation

Tribulation is "time of Jacob's trouble"—Jeremiah 30:7 niv.
Israel to experience purging judgments—Zechariah 13:8-9.
Israel partially delivered from Satan in tribulation—Revelation 12:14-17.
Portion of Israel delivered, others martyred in tribulation—Revelation
7:4-17.

Israel, Rebirth of

Gathered from many nations—Ezekiel 36:24.

Converts at Armageddon—Zechariah 12:2–13:1.

Will "mourn" for Messiah—Zechariah 12:10; see also Matthew 23:37-39; Isaiah 53:1-9.

Israel's national sin will be confessed—Leviticus 26:40-42; Deuteronomy 4:29-31; 30:6-8; Jeremiah 3:11-18; Hosea 5:15.

Spiritual awakening—Joel 2:28-29.

Towns will be inhabited, ruins rebuilt—Ezekiel 36:10.

Vision of dry bones—Ezekiel 37.

Will again be prosperous—Ezekiel 36:30,34-35.

Jerusalem, Pray for

In end-times, Jerusalem sore spot in world—Zechariah 12:2-3.

Pray for peace of Jerusalem—Psalm 122:6.

Prayers answered, for Israel will finally recognize Messiah—Joel 2:28-29; Zechariah 12:2–13:1; Romans 9:3-4; 10:13-14; 11:1,4.

Land Promises to Israel

Abraham's descendants, numerous as stars—Genesis 12:1-3; 13:14-17.

God promised land to Abraham and descendants—Genesis 12:1-7.

Parameters of land promises—Genesis 15:18-21.

Promises passed to Isaac's line—Genesis 26:2-4.

Promises passed to Jacob's line—Genesis 28:13-14.

Promises reaffirmed later—Psalm 105:8-11.

Land permanently restored to Israel—Deuteronomy 30:5; Isaiah 11:11-12; Jeremiah 23:3-8; Ezekiel 37:21-25.

Rapture

All believers will be changed—1 Corinthians 15:50-52.

Awaiting Christ's return—1 Thessalonians 1:10.

Christ will bring raptured church to place He prepared—John 14:1-3.

Church delivered from time of trouble—Revelation 3:10.

Church not appointed to wrath— Romans 5:9; 1 Thessalonians 1:10; 5:9.

Church will be raptured—1 Thessalonians 4:13-17.

Jesus promised to come and take followers to heaven—John 14:3; see also Philippians 3:20-21; 1 Thessalonians 1:9-10; 3:13; 4:13-17; 5:1-11; 2 Thessalonians 2:1.

Purified by blessed hope—Titus 2:11-14.

Rapture is a mystery—1 Corinthians 15:51-55.

Watch for Lord to come—Luke 12:35-40.

When trumpet sounds, rapture occurs—1 Corinthians 15:51-52;
1 Thessalonians 4:16-17.

Rebuilding of the Temple

Antichrist will exalt himself as God in temple—2 Thessalonians 2:4.

Temple must be rebuilt for abomination of desolation to occur—
Matthew 24:15-16; see also Daniel 9:27; 12:11.

Roman Empire, Future

Antichrist heads revived Roman empire—Daniel 2, 7.

Ten horns: Revived empire, ten nations—Daniel 7–8.

Little horn: Antichrist, gains control over empire—Daniel 7:8–8:26.

More terrifying/powerful than three preceding beasts—Daniel 7:7.

Second Coming of Christ

Christ will come like thief—1 Thessalonians 5:1-3; Revelation 16:15.

Christ will come visibly—Acts 1:9-11.

Coming from heaven—1 Thessalonians 1:10.

Coming same way as He left (physically and visibly)—Acts 1:11.

Coming soon—Philippians 4:5; Revelation 22:12,20.

Coming with clouds (of glory)—Revelation 1:7.

Every eye will see Him—Zechariah 12:10; Revelation 1:7.

No one knows hour—Matthew 24:42,44,46-50.

Return of Lord Jesus—1 Corinthians 1:7-8; Hebrews 9:28.

Scoffers in last days—2 Peter 3:4.

Son of Man coming in His kingdom—Matthew 16:28.

Son of Man is coming in Father's glory with angels—Matthew 16:27;
see also 25:31.

We eagerly wait—Philippians 3:20; Titus 2:13.

Will come in glory—Matthew 16:27; 25:31; Mark 8:38; Luke 9:26.

Second Coming, Readiness for

Await Master—Luke 12:35-36.

Be on alert; don't know when Master is coming—Mark 13:35.

Be ready for bridegroom—Matthew 25:1-13.

Bride made ready—Revelation 19:7.

Readiness—Luke 12:35.

Soberness or self-controlled—1 Thessalonians 5:6; 1 Timothy 3:2,11;
1 Peter 1:13; 4:7.

Will come when we don't think He will—Matthew 24:44.

Signs of the Times

Apostasy—Matthew 24:3-11; 2 Timothy 4:3-4.

Appearance of false teachers and Antichrist—Matthew 24:5,23-24,26;
Luke 21:8; 2 Thessalonians 2:1-10; 1 John 2:18-23; 4:3; 2 John 7;
Revelation 13:1-8; 19:20.

Betrayal—Mark 13:3-4,12; Luke 21:16.

Depart from the faith—1 Timothy 4:1.

Earthquakes—Matthew 24:7; Mark 13:8.

False Christs—Matthew 24:24-25; Mark 13:5,21-23; Luke 21:8; John
5:41-44.

False prophets—Matthew 24:11; Mark 13:6,21-23.

Famines—Matthew 24:7; Mark 13:8; Revelation 6:5-6.

General time (parable of fig tree)—Matthew 24:36-44; Mark 13.

Increase of evil—Matthew 24:12; 2 Timothy 3:1-5; 2 Peter 3:3-4.

Innumerable vices—2 Timothy 3:1-5.

International strife—Matthew 24:7; Mark 13:8; Luke 21:10; Revelation
6:3-4.

Lawlessness—Matthew 24:12; 2 Thessalonians 2:3,7-12.

Many fall away—Matthew 24:10.

Persecution of believers—Matthew 24:9; Mark 13:9-11,13; Luke 21:12-17;
2 Timothy 3:1-5,10-13; Revelation 6:9-11; 12:17; 20:4.

Pestilence and plagues—Luke 21:11; Revelation 6:7-8.

Tribulation, death, hatred of believers—Matthew 24:9.

Unparalleled distress—Matthew 24:21; Mark 13:17-19; Luke 21:23.

Wars, rumors of wars—Matthew 24:6; Mark 13:7; Luke 21:9.

Worldwide proclamation of gospel—Matthew 24:14; Mark 13:10;
Revelation 14:6-7.

Super-Sign

The reconstitution of Israel as a nation is a "super-sign" for the end-times.

Israel will be regathered to land—Ezekiel 36:24.

Jews will be regathered—Jeremiah 16:15.

Valley of dry bones prophecy—Ezekiel 37.

Many verses in Old Testament speak of land promises—Isaiah 60:18,21;
Jeremiah 23:8; 24:5-6; 30:18; 32:37-40; 33:6-9; Ezekiel 28:25-26;
34:11-12; 36:24-26; 37; 39:28; Hosea 3:4-5; Joel 2:18-29; Amos 9:14-
15; Micah 2:12; 4:6-7; Zephaniah 3:19-20; Zechariah 8:7-8.

Temple, Rebuilding of

Antichrist will exalt himself as God in temple—2 Thessalonians 2:4.

Temple must be rebuilt for abomination of desolation to occur—
Matthew 24:15-16; see also Daniel 9:27; 12:11.

Tribulation Period

Babylon (in Iraq), headquarters of Antichrist during tribulation—
Revelation 17–18.

Day of the Lord will be darkness—Amos 5:18.

Day of alarm—Zephaniah 1:15-16.

Day of calamity—Deuteronomy 32:35; Obadiah 12-14.

Day of gloom—Joel 2:2; Amos 5:18,20; Zephaniah 1:15.

Day of Lord's anger—Zephaniah 2:2-3.

Day of ruin—Joel 1:15.

Day of thick darkness—Joel 2:2; Zephaniah 1:15.

Day of vengeance—Isaiah 34:8; 35:4; 61:2; 63:4.

Day of wrath—Zephaniah 1:15.

Demons torment those on earth—Revelation 9:2-4.

Desolation—Daniel 9:27.

Destruction—Joel 1:15.

Dominion of Antichrist—Revelation 13.

Earth made a wasteland—Isaiah 24:1-4.

Events of tribulation—Revelation 4–18.

Final "week" of seven years, Antichrist signs covenant—Daniel 9:27.

Great and terrible day—Malachi 4:5.

Great tribulation—Matthew 24:21.

Hour of judgment—Revelation 14:7.

Hour of trial—Revelation 3:10.

Indignation—Isaiah 26:20-21.

Israel, conversion at end of tribulation—Romans 9–11.

Judgments of tribulation—Isaiah 24; Revelation 14:7.

Light of sun, moon, stars darkened during tribulation—Revelation 8:12.

No New Testament passage on tribulation mentions church—
    Matthew 13:30,39-42,48-50; 24:15-31; 1 Thessalonians 1:9-10; 5:4-9;
    2 Thessalonians 2:1-11; Revelation 4–18.
No Old Testament passage on tribulation mentions church—
    Deuteronomy 4:29-30; Jeremiah 30:4-11; Daniel 8:24-27; 12:1-2.
People will faint with fear—Luke 21:25-26.
People will long for death—Revelation 9:6.
Punishment—Isaiah 24:20-21.
Scourge—Isaiah 28:15,18.
Seven years long—Daniel 9:27.
Sun becomes black, full moon like blood—Revelation 6:12.
Time of distress—Daniel 12:1.
Time of Jacob's distress—Jeremiah 30:7.
Trial—Revelation 3:10.
Trouble—Jeremiah 30:7.
Worldwide—Revelation 3:10.
Wrath—Zephaniah 1:15,18.
Wrath of God—Revelation 14:10,19; 15:1,7; 16:1.
Wrath of Lamb—Revelation 6:16-17.
Wrath to come—1 Thessalonians 1:10.

Bibliography

Ankerberg, John, and Dillon Burroughs. *Middle East Meltdown*. Eugene, OR: Harvest House Publishers, 2007.

Ansari, Ali. *Confronting Iran: The Failure of American Foreign Policy and the Next Great Conflict in the Middle East*. New York: Basic Books, 2006.

Berman, Ilan. *Tehran Rising: Iran's Challenge to the United States*. New York: Rowman and Littlefield, 2005.

Black, Edwin. *The Plan: How to Rescue Society When the Oil Stops—Or the Day Before*. Washington: Dialog Press, 2008.

Corsi, Jerome. *Atomic Iran: How the Terrorist Regime Bought the Bomb and American Politicians*. Nashville, TN: WND Books, 2005.

Deffeyes, Kenneth. *Beyond Oil: The View from Hubbert's Peak*. New York: Hill and Wang, 2005.

———. *Hubbert's Peak: The Impending World Oil Shortage*. Princeton, NJ: Princeton University Press, 2009.

Ehrenfeld, Rachel. *Funding Evil: How Terrorism is Financed—and How to Stop It*. Chicago: Bonus Books, 2005.

Gabriel, Mark. *Islam and the Jews: The Unfinished Battle*. Lake Mary, FL: Charisma House, 2003.

———. *Journey into the Mind of an Islamic Terrorist*. Lake Mary, FL: Front Line, 2006.

Gaffney, Frank. *War Footing: Ten Steps America Must Take to Prevail in the War for the Free World*. Annapolis, MD: Naval Institute Press, 2006.

Gold, Dore. *The Fight for Jerusalem: Radical Islam, the West, and the Future of the Holy City*. Washington: Regnery, 2007.

Heinberg, Richard. *The Party's Over: Oil, War, and the Fate of Industrial Nations*. Gabriola Island, BC: New Society Publishers, 2008.

Hitchcock, Mark. *Bible Prophecy*. Wheaton, IL: Tyndale House Publishers, 1999.

———. *Iran: The Coming Crisis*. Sisters, OR: Multnomah Publishers, 2006.

———. *Is America in Bible Prophecy?* Sisters, OR: Multnomah Publishers, 2002.

———. *The Coming Islamic Invasion of Israel*. Sisters, OR: Multnomah Publishers, 2002.

———. *The Late Great United States*. Colorado Springs: Multnomah Books, 2009.

———. *The Second Coming of Babylon*. Sisters, OR: Multnomah Publishers, 2003.

Klein, Aaron. *The Late Great State of Israel: How Enemies Within and Without Threaten the Jewish Nation's Survival*. New York: WND Books, 2009.

Leeb, Stephen. *The Coming Economic Collapse*. New York: Warner Business Books, 2006.

Phares, Walid. *Future Jihad: Terrorist Strategies Against the West*. New York: Palgrave MacMillan, 2005.

Pollack, Kenneth. *The Persian Puzzle: The Conflict Between Iran and America*. New York: Random House, 2005.

Price, Randall. *Fast Facts on the Middle East Conflict*. Eugene, OR: Harvest House Publishers, 2003.

———. *Unholy War*. Eugene, OR: Harvest House Publishers, 2001.

Reid, T.R. *The United States of Europe: The New Superpower and the End of American Supremacy*. New York: Penguin Books, 2004.

Rhodes, Ron. *Northern Storm Rising: Russia, Iran, and the Emerging End-Times Military Coalition Against Israel*. Eugene, OR: Harvest House Publishers, 2008.

Roberts, Paul. *The End of Oil: On the Edge of a Perilous New World*. New York: Houghton Mifflin, 2004.

Rosenberg, Joel. *Epicenter: Why Current Rumblings in the Middle East Will Change Your Future.* Carol Stream, IL: Tyndale House Publishers, 2006.

Simmons, Matthew. *Twilight in the Desert: The Coming Saudi Oil Shock and the World Economy.* Hoboken, NJ: Wiley, 2005.

Tertzakian, Peter. *A Thousand Barrels a Second.* New York: McGraw-Hill, 2007.

Timmerman, Kenneth. *Countdown to Crisis: The Coming Nuclear Showdown with Iran.* New York: Three Rivers Press, 2006.

Venter, Al. *Iran's Nuclear Option: Tehran's Quest for the Atomic Bomb.* Philadelphia: Casemate, 2005.

Walvoord, John F., and John E. Walvoord. *Armageddon, Oil, and the Middle East Crisis.* Grand Rapids, MI: Zondervan, 1975.

Walvoord, John F., with Mark Hitchcock. *Armageddon, Oil, and Terror.* Carol Stream, IL: Tyndale House Publishers, 2007.

Yergin, Daniel. *The Price: The Epic Quest for Oil, Money, & Power.* New York: Free Press, 2009.

Notes

Introduction—"Oil Storm"

1. Edwin Black, *The Plan: How to Rescue Society When the Oil Stops—Or the Day Before* (Washington: Dialog Press, 2008), 7.

2. Katie Benner, "Oil: Is the End at Hand?" CNN/Money, November 3, 2004, Internet edition.

3. Warren Brown, "We're Running Out of Oil," *The Washington Post*, May 28, 2006, Internet edition.

4. "Escape from Suburbia: Beyond the American Dream," directed by Gregory Greene, produced by Dara Rowland, viewed on Sundance, November 10, 2009.

5. Ibid.

6. Joel Bainerman, "Is the World Running Out of Oil?" *The Middle East*, April 1, 2004, Internet edition.

7. Mark Hitchcock, *Iran: The Coming Crisis* (Sisters, OR: Multnomah Publishers, 2006), 98.

8. Richard Vodra, "The Next Energy Crisis," *Financial Planning*, October 1, 2005, Internet edition.

9. Estimates vary regarding how much oil is recoverable through proven oil reserves. Oil industry journal *World Oil* puts it at 1.1 trillion barrels. The oil company BP estimates it at 1.2 trillion barrels. The *Oil and Gas Journal* estimates 1.3 trillion barrels. IHS Energy estimates it between 1.3 trillion and 2.4 trillion barrels. See Ronald Bailey, "Peak Oil Panic: Is the Planet Running Out of Gas?" *Reason*, May 1, 2006, Internet edition.

10. George Jahn, "The End of Oil: Experts Say the World is Running Out—But How Soon?" *The Cincinnati Post*, September 17, 2005, Internet edition.

11. *National Geographic*, cited in Hitchcock, *Iran*, 100-101.

12. Vodra, "The Next Energy Crisis."

13. Bainerman, "Is the World Running Out of Oil?"

14. Gal Luft and Anne Korin, "Provide for U.S. Energy Security," in Frank Gaffney, *War Footing* (Annapolis, MD: Naval Institute Press, 2006), 46.

15. David O'Reilly, cited in Gaffney, *War Footing*, 46.

16. Mike Bowlin, cited in Bainerman, "Is the World Running Out of Oil?"

17. Colin Campbell, cited in Bainerman, "Is the World Running Out of Oil?"

18. Stephen Leeb, *The Coming Economic Collapse* (New York: Warner Business Books, 2006), 19.

19. Adam Porter, "Running on Empty: Oil is Disappearing Fast," *New Internationalist*, October 1, 2003, Internet edition.

20. Leeb, *Coming Economic Collapse*, 131.

21. Paul Roberts, *The End of Oil* (New York: Houghton Mifflin, 2004), 7.

22. Kenneth Deffeyes, *Beyond Oil: The View from Hubbert's Peak* (New York: Hill and Wang, 2005), 179.

23. Peter Tertzakian, *A Thousand Barrels a Second* (New York: McGraw-Hill, 2007), 93.

24. Deffeyes, *Beyond Oil*, 179.

25. Ibid., xiii.

26. See Roberts, *End of Oil*, 3.

27. Some of the data regarding Abu Yahya al-Libi, Zakir Naik, Omar Bakri Mohammed, Imam Johari Abdul Malik, and Abdul Alim Musa is documented in "The Third Jihad: Radical Islam's Vision for America," Wayne Kopping, director; copyright 2008, Publicscope Films.

28. "The Third Jihad."

29. Arnold Fruchtenbaum, *The Footsteps of the Messiah* (San Antonio, TX: Ariel Publishers, 2004), 108.

Chapter 1—The Global Addiction to Oil

1. Katie Benner, "Oil: Is the End at Hand?" CNN/Money, November 3, 2004, Internet edition.

2. Jasmin Melvin and Missy Ryan, "World Crude Production Has Peaked," Reuters, July 17, 2008, Internet edition.

3. Peter Tertzakian, *A Thousand Barrels a Second* (New York: McGraw-Hill, 2007), 59.

4. Paul Roberts, *The End of Oil* (New York: Houghton Mifflin, 2004), 41-42.

5. See Tertzakian, *A Thousand Barrels*.

6. Mark Hitchcock, *Iran: The Coming Crisis* (Sisters, OR: Multnomah Publishers, 2006), 98.

7. Edwin Black, *The Plan: How to Rescue Society When the Oil Stops—Or the Day Before* (Washington: Dialog Press, 2008), 6.

8. Ibid., 7.

9. *USA Today*, cited in Mark Hitchcock, *The Late Great United States* (Colorado Springs: Multnomah Books, 2009), 50.

10. Roberts, *End of Oil*, 334.

11. Chris Skrebowski, cited in ibid.

12. Cited in Benner, "Oil: Is the End at Hand?"

13. "Strategic Significance of America's Shale Oil Resource," vol. 1, "Assessment of Strategic Issues," Office of Deputy Assistant Secretary for Petroleum Reserves, Office of Naval Petroleum and Oil Shale Reserves, U.S. Department of Energy, March 2004; cited in Richard Heinberg, *The Party's Over: Oil, War, and the Fate of Industrial Societies* (Gabriola Island: British Columbia: New Society Publishers, 2008), 113.

14. Benner, "Oil: Is the End at Hand?"

15. Black, *The Plan*, 8.

16. Tertzakian, *A Thousand Barrels*, 4.

17. Hon Edward Schreyer, cited in "Escape from Suburbia: Beyond the American Dream," directed by Gregory Greene, produced by Dara Rowland, viewed on Sundance, November 10, 2009.

18. Tertzakian, *A Thousand Barrels*, ix.

19. Hitchcock, *Late Great United States*, 45.

20. Melvin and Ryan, "World Crude Production Has Peaked."

21. "World Oil Demand 'To Rise by 37%,'" BBC, June 20, 2006.

22. Roberts, *End of Oil*, 41-42.

23. Frank Gaffney, *War Footing: 10 Steps America Must Take to Prevail in the War for the Free World* (Annapolis, MD: Naval Institute Press, 2006), 45.

24. Colin J. Campbell and Jean H. Laherrère, "The End of Cheap Oil," *Scientific American*, March 1998, Internet edition.

25. Chuck Taylor, "Peak Oil: Now What?" *Light & Medium Truck*, September 1, 2008, Internet edition.

26. Ronald G. Nelson, "Worldwide Peak Oil May Already Be Here—Now What?" *Pipeline & Gas Journal*, January 1, 2008, Internet edition.

27. See http://www.whitehouse.gov/stateoftheunion/2006/.

28. Richard Nixon, cited in Thomas D. Kraemer, "Addicted to Oil: Strategic Implications of American Oil Policy," May 2006, http://www.StrategicStudiesInstitute.army.mil/.

29. Jimmy Carter, cited in Kraemer, "Addicted to Oil."

30. Stephen Leeb, *The Coming Economic Collapse* (New York: Warner Business Books, 2006), 2.

31. Campbell and Laherrère, "The End of Cheap Oil."

32. Roberts, *End of Oil*, 94-95.

Chapter 2—Understanding Peak Oil

1. See Paul Roberts, *The End of Oil* (New York: Houghton Mifflin, 2004), 47.

2. Katie Benner, "Oil: Is the End at Hand?" CNN/Money, November 3, 2004, Internet edition.

3. Stephen Leeb, *The Coming Economic Collapse* (New York: Warner Business Books, 2006), 19.

4. Jonathan Eley, "Do You Believe in 'Peak Oil'?" *Investors Chronicle*, June 23, 2009, Internet edition.

5. Kenneth Deffeyes, *Beyond Oil: The View from Hubbert's Peak* (New York: Hill and Wang, 2005), 177.

6. Chuck Taylor, "Peak Oil: Now What?" *Light and Medium Truck*, September 1, 2008, Internet edition.

7. Ronald G. Nelson, "Worldwide Peak Oil May Already Be Here—Now What?" *Pipeline and Gas Journal*, January 1, 2008, Internet edition.

8. Roberts, *End of Oil*, 47-48.

9. Nelson, "Worldwide Peak Oil May Already Be Here."

10. David Goodstein, *Out of Gas* (New York: Norton, 2004), 16-17.

11. Estimates vary as to how much oil is recoverable through proven oil reserves. Oil industry journal *World Oil* puts it at 1.1 trillion barrels. The oil company BP estimates it at 1.2 trillion barrels. The *Oil and Gas Journal* estimates 1.3 trillion barrels. IHS Energy estimates between 1.3 trillion and 2.4 trillion barrels. See Ronald Bailey, "Peak Oil Panic: Is the Planet Running Out of Gas?" *Reason*, May 1, 2006, Internet edition.

12. George Jahn, "The End of Oil: Experts Say the World Is Running Out—But How Soon?" *The Cincinnati Post*, September 17, 2005, Internet edition.

13. Colin J. Campbell and Jean H. Laherrère, "The End of Cheap Oil," *Scientific American*, March 1998, Internet edition.

14. Sivuyile Mangxamba, "'Peak Oil' Period Close—Expert; 'It Could Occur In 2011,'" *Cape Argus*, March 19, 2008, Internet edition.

15. Richard Vodra, "The Next Energy Crisis," *Financial Planning*, October 1, 2005, Internet edition.

16. Steve Connor, "Warning: Oil Supplies Are Running Out Fast," *The Independent*, August 3, 2009, Internet edition.

17. Steve Yetiv, "Calculating Peak Oil's Due Date," *The Virginian-Pilot*, June 24, 2008, Internet edition.

18. Joel Bainerman, "Is the World Running Out of Oil?" *The Middle East*, April 1, 2004, Internet edition.

19. Richard Gwyn, "Demand for Oil Outstripping Supply," *Toronto Star*, January 28, 2004, Internet edition.

20. Ibid.

21. Ashley Seager, "Steep Decline in Oil Production Brings Risk of War and Unrest, Says New Study," *The Guardian*, October 22, 2007, Internet edition.

22. Goodstein, *Out of Gas*, 16-17.

23. "Oil Company CFO's Weigh In on Peak Oil, Market for Renewable Energy," *Energy Resource*, January 12, 2009, Internet edition.

24. William Cummings, cited in John Donnelly, "Price Rise and New Deep-Water Technology Opened up Offshore Drilling," *The Boston Globe*, December 11, 2005, Internet edition.

25. Connor, "Warning."

26. Richard Heinberg, cited in "Escape from Suburbia: Beyond the American Dream," directed by Gregory Greene, produced by Dara Rowland, viewed on Sundance Channel, November 10, 2009.

27. Michael Ruppert, cited in "Escape from Suburbia."

28. Jasmin Melvin and Missy Ryan, "World Crude Production Has Peaked," Reuters, July 17, 2008, Internet edition.

29. Richard Heinberg, cited in "Escape from Suburbia."

30. See Campbell and Laherrère, "The End of Cheap Oil."

31. Ibid.

32. Cathal Kelly, "Take Peak Oil Seriously—It'll Be Here Much Sooner Than You Think," *The Toronto Star*, February 15, 2009, Internet edition.

33. Bainerman, "Is the World Running Out of Oil?"

34. Goodstein, *Out of Gas*, 35.

35. Ibid., 35-36.

36. Jane Bryant Quinn, "The Price of Our Addiction," *Newsweek*, April 24, 2006, Internet edition, emphasis added.

37. Vodra, "Next Energy Crisis."

38. Edward L. Morse and James Richard, "The Battle for Energy Dominance," *Foreign Affairs*, March/April 2002, Internet edition, bracketed inserts added.

39. Ibid.

40. Leeb, *Coming Economic Collapse*, 22.

41. Matthew Simmons, *Twilight in the Desert: The Coming Saudi Oil Shock and the World Economy* (Hoboken: Wiley, 2005), 70. See also D.T. Cochrane, "Peak Oil?: Oil Supply and Accumulation," *Cultural Shifts*, March 8, 2008, Internet edition; Tim Wood, "Oil Doomsday is Nigh, Tar Sands Not a Substitute," *Resource Investor*, May 11, 2005, Internet edition.

42. Simmons, *Twilight in the Desert*, 70.

43. Ibid., xxxiv.

44. Ibid., 244.

45. Nelson, "Worldwide Peak Oil May Already Be Here."

46. John F. Walvoord and Mark Hitchcock, *Armageddon, Oil, and Terror* (Carol Stream, IL: Tyndale House Publishers, 2007), 25-26.

47. Kenneth Deffeyes, *Hubbert's Peak: The Impending World Oil Shortage* (Princeton, NJ: Princeton University Press, 2009), 1.

48. Kelly, "Take Peak Oil Seriously."

49. Nelson, "Worldwide Peak Oil May Already Be Here."

Chapter 3—A World in Denial

1. Leonardo Maugeri, "Oil: Never Cry Wolf—Why the Petroleum Age Is Far from Over," *Science*, May 20, 2004, Internet edition.

2. Daniel Yergin, *The Price: The Epic Quest for Oil, Money, & Power* (New York: Free Press, 2009), 771.

3. Ibid.

4. See Kenneth Deffeyes, *Hubbert's Peak: The Impending World Oil Shortage* (Princeton, NJ: Princeton University Press, 2009), 3-4.

5. Peter Tertzakian, *A Thousand Barrels a Second* (New York: McGraw-Hill, 2007), 3.

6. Michael C. Lynch, "The New Pessimism about Petroleum Resources: Debunking the Hubbert Model," *Minerals and Energy—Raw Materials Report*, Volume 18, Issue 1, 2003, Internet edition.

7. Lynch, "The New Pessimism about Petroleum Resources."

8. Maugeri, "Oil: Never Cry Wolf."

9. Carl Mortished, "World Not Running Out of Oil, Say Experts," *The Times*, January 18, 2008, Internet edition.

10. "CERA Says Peak Oil Theory is Faulty," Cambridge Energy Research Associates (CERA), November 14, 2006, Internet edition.

11. Ibid.; see also Scott W. Tinker, "Of Peaks and Valleys: Doomsday Energy Scenarios Burn Away Under Scrutiny," op-ed for the *Dallas Morning News*, June 25, 2005.

12. Goodstein, pp. 31-32.

13. See Ronald G. Nelson, "Worldwide Peak Oil May Already Be Here—Now What?" *Pipeline and Gas Journal*, January 1, 2008, Internet edition.

14. David Goodstein, *Out of Gas* (New York: Norton, 2004), 31-32.

15. Richard Gwyn, "Demand for Oil Outstripping Supply," *Toronto Star*, January 28, 2004, Internet edition.

16. "Escape from Suburbia: Beyond the American Dream," directed by Gregory Greene, produced by Dara Rowland, viewed on Sundance, November 10, 2009.

17. Robert Hirsch, cited in Thilo Kunzemann, "Energy Future: A Significant Period of Discomfort," Allianz.com Press, June 20, 2008, Internet edition.

18. Colin J. Campbell and Jean H. Laherrère, "The End of Cheap Oil," *Scientific American*, March 1998, Internet edition.

19. See Tinker, "Of Peaks And Valleys."

20. For example, John Hess, CEO of the Hess Corporation; see Mark Hitchcock, *The Late Great United States* (Colorado Springs: Multnomah Publishers, 2009), 54-55.

21. Nelson, "Worldwide Peak Oil May Already Be Here."

22. Campbell and Laherrère, "The End of Cheap Oil."

23. Connor, "Warning: Oil Supplies Are Running Out Fast."

24. Ibid.

25. Hirsch, cited in Kunzemann, "Energy Future," insert added.

26. John F. Walvoord and Mark Hitchcock, *Armageddon, Oil, and Terror* (Carol Stream, IL: Tyndale House Publishers, 2007), 26-27.

27. Hitchcock, *Late Great United States*, 58-59.

28. Ibid., 54-55.

29. Kenneth Deffeyes, *Beyond Oil: The View from Hubbert's Peak* (New York: Hill and Wang, 2005), 98.

30. Stephen Leeb, *The Coming Economic Collapse* (New York: Warner Business Books, 2006), 137.

31. Jeremy Leggett, cited in Connor, "Warning: Oil Supplies Are Running Out Fast."

32. Deffeyes, *Beyond Oil*, 98.

33. Hirsch, cited in Kunzemann, "Energy Future."

34. Leeb, *Coming Economic Collapse*, 137.

35. See Roger Fillion, "Much Higher Oil Prices Seen in U.S. Future—Peak Oil Expert Says Coping Will Be Hard," *Rocky Mountain News*, November 7, 2007, Internet edition.

36. Granted, the sun shines all the time. However, its light is not accessible 24-7 in the United States.

37. Hirsch, cited in Kunzemann, "Energy Future."

38. Daniel Yergin, cited in Leeb, *Coming Economic Collapse*, 118.

39. Leeb, *Coming Economic Collapse*, 118.

40. Matthew Simmons, *Twilight in the Desert: The Coming Saudi Oil Shock and the World Economy* (Hoboken, NJ: Wiley, 2005), xxvi.

Chapter 4—The Global Consequences of Oil Depletion

1. Ken Deffeyes, cited in George Jahn, "The End of Oil: Experts Say the World is Running Out—But How Soon?" *The Cincinnati Post*, September 17, 2005, Internet edition.

2. Ronald Bailey, "Peak Oil Panic: Is the Planet Running Out of Gas?" *Reason*, May 1, 2006, Internet edition.

3. Jahn, "The End of Oil"

4. See www.dictionary.com.

5. See "Escape from Suburbia: Beyond the American Dream," directed by Gregory Greene, produced by Dara Rowland, viewed on Sundance, November 10, 2009.

6. Ibid.

7. See Mark Hitchcock, *The Late Great United States* (Colorado Springs: Multnomah Books, 2009), 52.

8. Adam Porter, "Running on Empty: Oil Is Disappearing Fast," *New Internationalist*, October 1, 2003, Internet edition.

9. Ibid.

10. David Goodstein, *Out of Gas* (New York: Norton, 2004), 30-31.

11. Richard Heinberg, *The Party's Over: Oil, War, and the Fate of Industrial Societies* (British Columbia: New Society Publishers, 2008), 191.

12. Ibid., 190.

13. Ibid.

14. Katharine Mieszkowski, "The Oil Is Going, The Oil Is Going!" *Salon*, May 15, 2005, Internet edition, insert added.

15. Ashley Seager, "Steep Decline in Oil Production Brings Risk of War and Unrest, Says New Study," *The Guardian*, October 22, 2007, Internet edition.

16. Goodstein, *Out of Gas*, 37.

17. Kenneth Deffeyes, *Beyond Oil: The View from Hubbert's Peak* (New York: Hill and Wang, 2005), 6.

18. Porter, "Running on Empty."

19. Cathal Kelly, "Take Peak Oil Seriously—It'll Be Here Much Sooner Than You Think," *The Toronto Star*, February 15, 2009, Internet edition.

20. Stephen Leeb, *The Coming Economic Collapse* (New York: Warner Business Books, 2006), 121-22.

21. Heinberg, *The Party's Over*, 193.

22. Edwin Black, *The Plan: How to Rescue Society When the Oil Stops—Or the Day Before* (Washington: Dialog Press, 2008), xv, 1.

23. See Hitchcock, *The Late Great United States*, 61.

24. John F. Walvoord and Mark Hitchcock, *Armageddon, Oil, and Terror* (Carol Stream, IL: Tyndale House Publishers, 2007), 30-31.

25. Matthew Simmons, *Twilight in the Desert: The Coming Saudi Oil Shock and the World Economy* (Hoboken, NJ: Wiley, 2005), 343.

26. Steve Yetiv, "Calculating Peak Oil's Due Date," *The Virginian-Pilot*, June 24, 2008, Internet edition.

27. Deffeyes, *Beyond Oil*, 9.

28. Simmons, *Twilight in the Desert*, 348.

29. Kenneth Deffeyes, *Hubbert's Peak: The Impending World Oil Shortage* (Princeton, NJ: Princeton University Press, 2009), 149.

30. Deffeyes, *Beyond Oil*, 8.

31. Goodstein, *Out of Gas*, 30-31.

32. Paul Roberts, *The End of Oil* (New York: Houghton Mifflin, 2004), 39.

33. Ibid., 40.

34. Hitchcock, *The Late Great United States*, 49.

35. Roberts, *The End of Oil*, 341.

36. Black, *The Plan*, 3.

37. Heinberg, *The Party's Over*, 198.

38. Black, *The Plan*, 3; see also Leeb, *The Coming Economic Collapse*, 122.

39. Walvoord and Hitchcock, *Armageddon, Oil, and Terror*, 16.

40. See Jonathan Eley, "Do You Believe in 'Peak Oil'?" *Investors Chronicle*, June 23, 2009, Internet edition.

41. Leeb, *The Coming Economic Collapse*, 73.

42. See Walvoord and Hitchcock, *Armageddon, Oil, and Terror*, 17.

43. Goodstein, *Out of Gas*, 37.

44. Heinberg, *The Party's Over*, 187.

45. Roberts, *The End of Oil*, 341.

46. Roscoe Bartlett, cited in "Escape from Suburbia."

47. Leeb, *The Coming Economic Collapse*, 27.

48. Tim Appenzeller, "End of Cheap Oil," National Geographic Society website, 2005.

49. Leeb, *The Coming Economic Collapse*, 28.

Chapter 5—Running on Fumes: Oil and Our Fragile Economy

1. Ashley Seager, "Steep Decline in Oil Production Brings Risk of War and Unrest, Says New Study," *The Guardian*, October 22, 2007, Internet edition.

2. Robert Beriault, "Peak Oil and the Fate of Humanity," *Canadian Chemical News*, September 1, 2005, Internet edition.

3. Steve Connor, "Warning: Oil Supplies Are Running Out Fast," *The Independent*, August 3, 2009, Internet edition.

4. Ibid.

5. Jasmin Melvin and Missy Ryan, "World Crude Production Has Peaked," Reuters, July 17, 2008, Internet edition.

6. Edwin Black, *The Plan: How to Rescue Society When the Oil Stops—Or the Day Before* (Washington: Dialog Press, 2008), 26-27.

7. Ibid.

8. "Bush Strategy Doctrine Calls Iran Great Challenge," Bloomberg.com, March 16, 2006, Internet edition.

9. Paul Roberts, *The End of Oil* (New York: Houghton Mifflin, 2004), 93.

10. Kenneth Deffeyes, *Hubbert's Peak: The Impending World Oil Shortage* (Princeton, NJ: Princeton University Press, 2009), 159-60.

11. Ibid., 10.

12. Seager, "Steep Decline in Oil Production Brings Risk."

13. Matt Crenson, "Is the World Running Out of Gas?" *Wisconsin State Journal*, May 29, 2005, Internet edition.

14. Connor, "Warning."

15. Chuck Taylor, "Peak Oil: Now What?" *Light and Medium Truck*, September 1, 2008, Internet edition.

16. Joel Bainerman, "Is the World Running Out of Oil?" *The Middle East*, April 1, 2004, Internet edition.

17. Jane Bryant Quinn, "The Price of Our Addiction," *Newsweek*, April 24, 2006, Internet edition.

18. Joseph Farah, "China's Drive to the Middle East," *G2 Newsletter*, March 24, 2006, Internet edition.

19. Michael Maloof, "Russian Energy Now 'Lever for Blackmail,'" *G2 Newsletter*, May 20, 2009, Internet edition.

20. Bainerman, "Is the World Running Out of Oil?"

21. Ronald Bailey, "Peak Oil Panic: Is the Planet Running Out of Gas?" *Reason*, May 1, 2006, Internet edition.

22. Quinn, "The Price of Our Addiction."

23. Robert Hirsch, cited in Thilo Kunzemann, "Energy Future: A Significant Period of Discomfort," Allianz.com Press, June 20, 2008, Internet edition.

24. Steve Yetiv, "Calculating Peak Oil's Due Date," *The Virginian-Pilot*, June 24, 2008, Internet edition.

25. George Jahn, "The End of Oil: Experts Say the World Is Running Out—But How Soon?" *The Cincinnati Post*, September 17, 2005, Internet edition.

Chapter 6—Oil and the Funding of Terrorism

1. Alex Alexiev, "Salvage Europe," in Frank Gaffney, *War Footing* (Annapolis, MD: Naval Institute Press, 2006), 222.

2. Alex Alexiev, "Know the Enemy," in Gaffney, *War Footing*, 5-6.

3. Ali Ansari, *Confronting Iran: The Failure of American Foreign Policy and the Next Great Conflict in the Middle East* (New York: Basic Books, 2006), 3.

4. Mortimer B. Zuckerman, "Moscow's Mad Gamble," *U.S. News and World Report*, January 22, 2006, Internet edition.

5. Dore Gold, *The Fight for Jerusalem: Radical Islam, the West, and the Future of the Holy City* (Washington: Regnery, 2007), 22.

6. Mahmoud Ahmadinejad, cited in ibid., 232.

7. Gold, *The Fight for Jerusalem,* 232.

8. Joshua Yasmeh, "Ahmadinejad: The Next Hitler?" *Tribe,* February 2, 2007, Internet edition.

9. "Iran's Ahmadinejad: Israel, U.S. Soon Will Die," NewsMax.com, January 24, 2007, Internet edition.

10. See Joel C. Rosenberg, "State of the Union: The President Must Lay Out a Clear and Convincing Plan to Stop Iran. Period," *Flash Traffic,* January 23, 2007, Internet edition.

11. Jack Kinsella, "A World Without Ahmadinejad," *The Omega Letter Daily Intelligence Digest,* Volume 64, Issue 18, January 20, 2007, Internet edition.

12. Kenneth Timmerman, *Countdown to Crisis* (New York: Three Rivers Press, 2006), 325.

13. Ibid.

14. Gaffney, *War Footing,* 42.

15. Thomas D. Kraemer, "Addicted to Oil: Strategic Implications of American Oil Policy," May 2006, http://www.StrategicStudiesInstitute.army.mil/.

16. Gaffney, *War Footing,* 47.

17. Kraemer, "Addicted to Oil."

18. David Goldmann, *Islam and the Bible: Why Two Faiths Collide* (Chicago: Moody Publishing, 2004), 18.

19. Jamal Elias, *Islam* (Upper Saddle River, NJ: Prentice Hall, 1999), 73.

20. Frederick Denny, *An Introduction to Islam* (New York: Macmillan, 1985), 136.

21. Ibid.

22. Elias, *Islam,* 73.

23. John Ankerberg and John Weldon, *Fast Facts on Islam* (Eugene, OR: Harvest House Publishers, 2001), 105.

24. Ergun Mehmet Caner and Emir Fethi Caner, *Unveiling Islam: An Insider's Look at Muslim Life and Beliefs* (Grand Rapids, MI: Kregel Publications, 2002), 49.

25. Goldmann, *Islam and the Bible,* 22.

26. Ankerberg and Weldon, *Fast Facts on Islam,* 19.

27. Quoted in Caner and Caner, *Unveiling Islam,* 183-84.

28. Walid Phares, *Future Jihad* (New York: Palgrave Macmillan, 2005), 93-94.

29. Ilan Berman, *Tehran Rising* (New York: Rowman and Littlefield, 2005), 115.

30. Wayne Simmons, cited in *The Third Jihad: Radical Islam's Vision for America,* Wayne Kopping, director; copyright 2008, Publicscope Films.

31. Mark Steyn, cited in *The Third Jihad.*

32. Juhdi Jasser, cited in *The Third Jihad.*

33. See Bernard Lewis, in "The Coming of Eurabia," International Analyst Network, January 2, 2008, Internet edition.

34. "Secretary Rumsfeld Interview with Larry King," CNN transcript, December 18, 2002, http://www.defenselink.mil/transcripts.

35. Rachel Ehrenfeld, *Funding Evil: How Terrorism is Financed—and How to Stop It* (Chicago: Bonus Books, 2005), 24-26.

36. F. Michael Maloof, "Saudi Extremism in U.S. Mosques," *Joseph Farah's G2 Bulletin*, October 18, 2006, Internet edition.

37. Brigitte Gabriel, cited in ibid.

38. James R. Woolsey, "World War IV," FrontPageMagazine.com, November 22, 2002, Internet edition.

39. Paul Wolfowitz, cited in Linda D. Kozaryn, "Wolfowitz: Al Qaeda Is an Infectious Disease With No One-Shot Cure," American Forces Press Service, June 26, 2002, Internet edition.

40. Ehrenfeld, *Funding Evil*, 35.

41. George Braswell, *What You Need to Know About Islam and Muslims* (Nashville: Broadman and Holman, 2000), 34.

42. Goldmann, *Islam and the Bible*, 118.

43. Caner and Caner, *Unveiling Islam*, 125.

44. Ehrenfeld, *Funding Evil*, 37

45. Ophir Falk and Henry Morgenstern, *Suicide Terror: Understanding and Confronting the Threat* (New York: Wiley, 2009), 53.

46. Yossef Bodansky, *Bin Laden: The Man Who Declared War on America* (New York: Prima Lifestyles, 2001), 364.

47. Ehrenfeld, *Funding Evil*, 125-26.

48. "Iran and Syria as Strategic Support for Palestinian Terrorism," *Israel Defense Forces/ Military Intelligence*, September 30, 2002, Internet edition, posted at http://www.mfa.gov.

49. Ehrenfeld, *Funding Evil*, 133.

50. James Woolsey, cited in *The Third Jihad*.

Chapter 7—Will the Oil Card Be Played Against the United States?

1. Chuck Taylor, "Peak Oil: Now What?" *Light and Medium Truck*, September 1, 2008, Internet edition.

2. Steve Yetiv, "Calculating Peak Oil's Due Date," *The Virginian-Pilot*, June 24, 2008, Internet edition.

3. Jerome Corsi, *Atomic Iran* (Nashville: WND Books, 2005), 179.

4. Steve Connor, "Warning: Oil Supplies Are Running Out Fast," *The Independent*, August 3, 2009, Internet edition.

5. John F. Walvoord and Mark Hitchcock, *Armageddon, Oil, and Terror* (Carol Stream, IL: Tyndale House Publishers, 2007), 72.

6. Excellent information on all this is found in Mark Hitchcock, *The Late Great United States* (Colorado Springs: Multnomah Books, 2009), 93ff.

7. Shibley Telhami, cited in Tim LaHaye and Ed Hindson, *Global Warning: Are We on the Brink of World War III?* (Eugene, OR: Harvest House Publishers, 2008), 19.

8. Frank Gaffney, *War Footing: 10 Steps America Must Take to Prevail in the War for the Free World* (Annapolis, MD: Naval Institute Press, 2006), 42.

9. Walvoord and Hitchcock, *Armageddon, Oil, and Terror*, 21.

10. Edwin Black, *The Plan: How to Rescue Society When the Oil Stops—Or the Day Before* (Washington: Dialog Press, 2008), 6.

11. John Kilduff, cited in LaHaye and Hindson, *Global Warning*, 18.

12. Walvoord and Hitchcock, *Armageddon, Oil, and Terror*, 4-5.

13. Hugo Chavez, cited in LaHaye and Hindson, *Global Warning*, 18.

14. Black, *The Plan*, 24.

15. Peter Tertzakian, *A Thousand Barrels a Second* (New York: McGraw-Hill, 2007), 134-35.

16. Black, *The Plan*, 22-23.

17. Joseph Farah, "Iran Threatens Oil Transport Route," *Joseph's Farah's G2 Bulletin*, WorldNetDaily, September 26, 2009, Internet edition.

18. Cited in Simon Henderson, "Energy Security Implications of an Iran in Transition," *Journal of Energy Security*, October 6, 2008, Internet edition.

19. Farah, "Iran Threatens Oil Transport Route."

20. Ibid.

21. "Flashpoint Hormuz: US and Allies Brace for Trouble in the Choke-Point Strait of Hormuz," *The Middle East*, August 1, 2009, Internet edition.

22. Ibid.

23. Farah, "Iran Threatens Oil Transport Route."

24. Ilan Berman, *Tehran Rising* (New York: Rowman and Littlefield, 2005), 52.

25. Yetiv, "Calculating Peak Oil's Due Date."

26. "Flashpoint Hormuz."

27. Ibid.

28. Black, *The Plan*, 23.

29. Robert Hirsch, cited in Thilo Kunzemann, "Energy Future: A Significant Period of Discomfort," Allianz.com Press, June 20, 2008, Internet edition.

30. Joshua Yasmeh, "Ahmadinejad: The Next Hitler?" *Tribe*, February 2, 2007, Internet edition.

31. "Iran's Ahmadinejad: Israel, U.S. Soon Will Die," NewsMax.com, January 24, 2007, Internet edition.

32. J.I. Packer, *Knowing God* (Downers Grove, IL: InterVarsity Press, 1983), 126.

33. Hitchcock, *The Late Great United States*, 91.

Chapter 8—Political Realignments in the End-Times: Rebirth of Israel

1. Peter Tertzakian, *A Thousand Barrels a Second* (New York: McGraw-Hill, 2007), ix.

2. "World Oil Demand 'To Rise by 37%,'" BBC, June 20, 2006, Internet report.

3. Joel Bainerman, "Is the World Running Out of Oil?" *The Middle East*, April 1, 2004, Internet edition.

4. David Goodstein, *Out of Gas* (New York: Norton, 2004), 30-31.

5. Joel Rosenberg, *Epicenter: Why Current Rumblings in the Middle East Will Change Your Future* (Carol Stream, IL: Tyndale House Publishers, 2006), 27.

6. This information about the gradual return of Jews to their homeland is based on James Combs, "Israel in Two Centuries," in *Prophecy Study Bible*, ed. Tim LaHaye (Chattanooga, TN: AMG Publishers, 2001), 970.

7. Thomas Ice, "Is It Time for the Temple?" Pre-Trib Research Center, http://www.pre-trib.org/articles/view/is-it-time-for-temple. See also Randall Price, *The Coming Last Days Temple* (Eugene, OR: Harvest House Publishers, 1999), pp. 395-416.

8. Those interested in further study of this aspect of biblical prophecy should consult Randall Price, *The Temple and Bible Prophecy: A Definitive Look at Its Past, Present, and Future* (Eugene, OR: Harvest House Publishers, 2005).

9. Mark Hitchcock, *The Late Great United States* (Colorado Springs: Multnomah Books, 2009), 129-30.

10. The entire Middle East has been an arena of conflict for the past sixty years. Wars in the region include the War of Independence (which brought Israel's statehood—1947-1948), the Suez War/Sinai Campaign (1956), the Six-Day War (1967), the War of Attrition (1968-1970), the Yom Kippur/October War (1973), the Lebanese Civil War (1975-1976), the Iran-Iraq War (1980-1988), the Lebanon War (1982-1985), the Persian Gulf War (1991), the War on Terror (2001 to present), and the War with Iraq (1991-2003).

Chapter 9—Political Realignments in the End-Times: Israel Endangered

1. Aaron Klein, *The Late Great State of Israel* (New York: WND Books, 2009), x.

2. Ibid., 139.

3. Ibid., 141.

4. Ibid., 150.

5. Ibid.

6. Ibid., 155, insert added.

7. Richard Heinberg, *The Party's Over: Oil, War, and the Fate of Industrial Societies* (Gabriola Island, BC: New Society Publishers, 2008), 211-12.

8. Al Venter, *Iran's Nuclear Option* (Philadelphia: Casemate, 2005), 326.

9. Ibid.

10. Ali Ansari, *Confronting Iran* (New York: Basic Books, 2006), 2.

11. Jerome Corsi, *Atomic Iran* (Nashville: WND Books, 2005), 180.

12. Ibid.

13. Ilan Berman, *Tehran Rising* (New York: Rowman and Littlefield, 2005), 79; see also Frank Gaffney, *War Footing: 10 Steps America Must Take to Prevail in the War for the Free World* (Annapolis, MD: Naval Institute Press, 2006), 42.

14. Berman, *Tehran Rising*, 79.

15. Ansari, *Confronting Iran*, 2.

16. Berman, *Tehran Rising*, 79; see also Gaffney, *War Footing*, 79.

17. Venter, *Iran's Nuclear Option*, 326.

18. Heinberg, *The Party's Over*, 214.

19. *The Third Jihad: Radical Islam's Vision for America*, Wayne Kopping, director; Publicscope Films, 2008.

20. Clyde Billington, "The Rosh People in History and Prophecy," Part 1, *Michigan Theological Journal*, 3:1, Spring 1992, 65.

21. Ibid., Part 1, 61-62.

22. G.A. Cook, *A Critical and Exegetical Commentary on the Book of Ezekiel* (Edinburgh: T&T Clark, 1936), 408-9.

23. Thomas Ice, "Ezekiel 38 and 39," Part 4, *Pre-Trib Perspectives*, Vol. 8, Number 44, April 2007, 6.

24. Randall Price, "Ezekiel" in *The Popular Bible Prophecy Commentary*, eds. Tim LaHaye and Ed Hindson (Eugene, OR: Harvest House Publishers, 2007), 190.

25. Billington, "The Rosh People in History and Prophecy," Part 1, 56.

26. Arnold Fruchtenbaum, *The Footsteps of the Messiah* (San Antonio, TX: Ariel Publishers, 2004), 111-12.

27. Joel Rosenberg, *Epicenter* (Carol Stream, IL: Tyndale House Publishers, 2006), 63.

28. Fruchtenbaum, *Footsteps of the Messiah*, 63.

29. "Israel Strikes Black Oil Deposit," IsraelNationalNews.com, May 6, 2004, Internet edition.

30. Ibid.

31. Rosenberg, *Epicenter*, 58.

32. See ibid., 61.

33. *The Bible Knowledge Commentary*, ed. John F. Walvoord and Roy B. Zuck (Wheaton, IL: Victor Books, 1983-1985), Logos Bible Software.

34. Mark Hitchcock, *Iran: The Coming Crisis* (Sisters, OR: Multnomah Publishers, 2006), 172-73.

35. The King James Version indicates that all will be destroyed except for one-sixth of the invaders. This is a faulty rendering. As Arnold Fruchtenbaum puts it: "The King James Version indicates that one-sixth of the invading army is left alive. This is not found in the Hebrew text and has not been translated that way by subsequent translations. It is not true that one-sixth of the invading army will be left alive. The entire invading army will be destroyed when they invade Israel and nothing will remain, not even one-sixth." See Fruchtenbaum, *Footsteps of the Messiah*, 115.

36. Rosenberg, *Epicenter*, 163-64.

37. Charles Dyer, cited in Mark Hitchcock, *The Late Great United States* (Colorado Springs: Multnomah Books, 2009), 133.

38. "Why Mideast War Imminent," *WorldNetDaily*, August 17, 2009, Internet edition.

39. Jerome Corsi, cited in ibid.

Chapter 10—Political Realignments in the End-Times: Other Nations

1. Thomas Ice, "The Emerging Global Community," posted at the Pre-Trib Research Center website: www.pre-trib.org. Ice notes, however, that "it is impossible to know if the European Union is the embryonic form of the government that will ally itself with a

final global religion as described in Revelation 17. However, at the very least, it serves as a powerful example of just how such an alliance could develop."

2. John F. Walvoord and Mark Hitchcock, *Armageddon, Oil, and Terror* (Carol Stream, IL: Tyndale House Publishers, 2007), 82-84.

3. Ibid., 76.

4. Kenneth Deffeyes, *Beyond Oil: The View from Hubbert's Peak* (New York: Hill and Wang, 2005), 9.

5. Matthew Simmons, *Twilight in the Desert: The Coming Saudi Oil Shock and the World Economy* (Hoboken, NJ: Wiley, 2005), 348.

6. Thomas Ice, "Preparation for the Antichrist," posted at the Pre-Trib Research Center website: www.pre-trib.org.

7. Mark Hitchcock, *The Late Great United States* (Colorado Springs: Multnomah Books, 2009), 122.

8. Dick Morris, cited in Thomas Ice, "The Late Great U.S.A.," posted at the Pre-Trib Research Center website: www.pre-trib.org.

9. Eventually there will be new believers on the earth during the tribulation. This will be a result of the Holy Spirit's continued ministry, the two prophetic witnesses of Revelation 11, as well as the testimonies of the 144,000 evangelistic Jews of Revelation 7 and 14.

10. Thomas Ice, "Babylon in Bible Prophecy," posted at the Pre-Trib Research Center website: www.pre-trib.org.

11. Mark Hitchcock, *The Second Coming of Babylon* (Sisters, OR: Multnomah Publishers, 2003), 147-50.

12. Ibid. Note that not all believe that "Babylon" in the book of Revelation refers to literal Babylon. Some believe it is a metaphorical reference to the revived Roman Empire.

13. Nathan Jones, "Antichrist Will Be Headquartered in Rome," Lamb and Lion Ministries website, posted June 29, 2009.

14. "China's Drive to the Middle East," *Joseph Farah's G2 Bulletin*, March 24, 2006, Internet edition.

15. Ibid.

16. Steve Yetiv, "Calculating Peak Oil's Due Date," *The Virginian-Pilot*, June 24, 2008, Internet edition.

17. Walvoord and Hitchcock, *Armageddon, Oil, and Terror*, 158.

Chapter 11—The Convergence Factor: Concurrent Signs of the Times

1. Norman Geisler, Wayne House, and Max Herrera, *The Battle for God* (Grand Rapids, MI: Kregel, 2001), 24.

2. Even in our day (before the tribulation), many scientists and observers are studying this issue, anticipating the eventuality of the day of impact. Books I have come across include *Comet and Asteroid Impact Hazards on a Populated Earth* by John S. Lewis; *Rogue Asteroids and Doomsday Comets: The Search for the Million Megaton Menace That Threatens Life on Earth* by Duncan Steel; *Impact Earth: Asteroids, Comets and Meteors: The Growing Threat* by Austen Atkinson; *Threat of Near-Earth Asteroids: The Hearing Before the Committee on Science, U.S. House of Representatives* by Dana Rohrabacher; *If an Asteroid Hit Earth* by Ray Spangenburg; and *Asteroids and Meteorites: Catastrophic Collisions with Earth (The Hazardous Earth)* by Timothy Kusky.

3. See my books *The Challenge of the Cults and New Religions* (Zondervan); *The New Age Movement* (Zondervan); *Reasoning from the Scriptures with Jehovah's Witnesses* (Harvest House Publishers); *Reasoning from the Scriptures with Mormons* (Harvest House Publishers); and *The Truth Behind Ghosts, Mediums, and Psychic Phenomena* (Harvest House Publishers).

Chapter 12—How, Then, Shall We Live?

1. Robert Beriault, "Peak Oil and the Fate of Humanity," *Canadian Chemical News*, September 1, 2005, Internet edition.

2. Robert Hirsch, cited in Thilo Kunzemann, "Energy Future: A Significant Period of Discomfort," Allianz.com Press, June 20, 2008, Internet edition.

3. Richard Gwyn, "Demand for Oil Outstripping Supply," *Toronto Star*, January 28, 2004, Internet edition.

4. Cathal Kelly, "Take Peak Oil Seriously—It'll Be Here Much Sooner Than You Think," *The Toronto Star*, February 15, 2009, Internet edition.

5. Ronald G. Nelson, "Worldwide Peak Oil May Already Be Here—Now What?" *Pipeline and Gas Journal*, January 1, 2008, Internet edition.

6. Chuck Taylor, "Peak Oil: Now What?" *Light and Medium Truck*, September 1, 2008, Internet edition.

7. Katie Benner, "Oil: Is the End at Hand?" CNN/Money, November 3, 2004, Internet edition.

8. Fatih Birol, cited in Steve Connor, "Warning: Oil Supplies Are Running Out Fast," *The Independent*, August 3, 2009, Internet edition.

9. Ashley Seager, "Steep Decline in Oil Production Brings Risk of War and Unrest, Says New Study," *The Guardian*, October 22, 2007, Internet edition.

10. John F. Walvoord, *End-times* (Nashville, TN: Word, 1998), 218.

11. Ibid., 219.

12. Erich Sauer, *From Eternity to Eternity* (Grand Rapids, MI: Wm. B. Eerdmans Publishing Co., 1979), 13.

13. J.I. Packer, ed. *Alive to God* (Downers Grove, IL: InterVarsity Press, 1992), 171.

14. Richard Baxter, cited in ibid., 167.

Appendix A: If You Are Not a Christian...

1. All Scripture quotations are from the New International Version (NIV).

If you have any questions or comments, feel free to
contact Reasoning from the Scriptures Ministries.

RON RHODES
Reasoning from the Scriptures Ministries

PHONE: 214-618-0912
EMAIL: ronrhodes@earthlink.net
WEB: www.ronrhodes.org

Free newsletter available upon request

Other Great Harvest House Reading

by Ron Rhodes

*The 10 Most Important Things
You Can Say to a Catholic*

*The 10 Most Important Things
You Can Say to a Jehovah's Witness*

*The 10 Most Important Things
You Can Say to a Mason*

*The 10 Most Important Things
You Can Say to a Mormon*

*10 Things You Need to Know
About Islam*

5-Minute Apologetics for Today

Angels Among Us

*Answering the Objections of Atheists,
Agnostics, and Skeptics*

*Archaeology and the Bible:
What You Need to Know*

The Book of Bible Promises

*Christian Views of War:
What You Need to Know*

Christianity According to the Bible

Commonly Misunderstood Bible Verses

The Complete Guide to Bible Translations

*The Complete Guide to Christian
Denominations*

Conviction Without Compromise
(with Norman Geisler)

Find It Fast in the Bible

Halloween: What You Need to Know

*Homosexuality:
What You Need to Know*

Islam: What You Need to Know

*Jehovah's Witnesses:
What You Need to Know*

*The Middle East Conflict:
What You Need to Know*

Northern Storm Rising

The Popular Dictionary of Bible Prophecy

*Reasoning from the Scriptures
with Catholics*

*Reasoning from the Scriptures
with Masons*

*Reasoning from the Scriptures
with Muslims*

*Reasoning from the Scriptures
with the Jehovah's Witnesses*

*Reasoning from the Scriptures
with the Mormons*

The Topical Handbook of Bible Prophecy

*The Truth Behind Ghosts, Mediums, and
Psychic Phenomena*

Understanding the Bible from A to Z

What Does the Bible Say About...?

*Why Do Bad Things Happen
If God Is Good?*

The Wonder of Heaven

*World Religions:
What You Need to Know*

To learn more about other Harvest House books
or to read sample chapters, log on to our website:

www.harvesthousepublishers.com

HARVEST HOUSE PUBLISHERS

EUGENE, OREGON